compiled and edited by
Jay Marshall

how to
perform
INSTANT
MAGIC

Bailey Bros. & Swinfen Ltd.
Folkestone

Cover Design: **Joe Mistak & Associates**
Cover Photograph: **Patrick K. Snook**
Book Design: **MacDonald Graphics and Ruth Guest**
Illustrations: **Richard Wahl**
Typesetting: **Hagle**
Editorial Direction: **Sandra N. Herzog**
Production Coordinator: **Ruth Guest**

HOW TO PERFORM INSTANT MAGIC
Copyright © 1980 Quality Books, Inc.

First published in Great Britain in 1980 by
Bailey Bros. & Swinfen Ltd.
Warner House
Folkestone, Kent CT19 6PH
England

1 2 3 4 5 6 7 8 9 10

Manufactured in the United States of America

ISBN 561-00308-4 (pbk.)
ISBN 561-00307-6 (cloth)

contents

chapter two

TRICKS WITH COINS AND CARDS 66

preface

How to Perform Instant Magic is a luring title; but damned few can just pick up this stuff and do it. You've got to go through the motions a couple of times just to make sure you've got things in the right order before you try a trick on your friends. The real fun comes when you *do* the trick and the MAGIC happens. You see, MAGIC is another way of saying "Surprise!" and most people like surprises.

Before you get too far along, I'm going to give you the ABC secret formula for learning MAGIC, in case you get hooked and really want to pursue this amusing art.

> A. Learn How the Trick Is Done
> B. Learn How to Do It
> C. Figure Out How to Present It

A. LEARN HOW THE TRICK IS DONE. This first part is easy. Here are several ways:

1. Read the directions in this book.
2. Watch a lousy magician and you'll see how it's done.
3. Watch a good magician several times and you'll catch on. (That's why you shouldn't repeat a trick for the same audience.)
4. Buy a trick in a magic shop and read the directions. (In a magic shop, part of the deal is that the seller shows the buyer how the trick works. If you buy magic by mail, every trick is supposed to have complete instructions. Even if you buy the trick in a shop, read the directions, because the fellow who shows you how it's done may have missed some of the fine points. There is an old magic shop adage: "When all else fails, read the instructions.")
5. Ask a magician or someone who knows. Magicians are generally helpful to brother magicians, particularly if they are explaining someone else's tricks. It is only their own tricks they get secretive about.
6. Figure it out for yourself.   There have been many cases in MAGIC of someone seeing a trick and figuring out a better, simpler method than was used by the original performer.

B. LEARN HOW TO DO IT. It really starts here, because there's a hell of a difference between knowing how a trick is done and being able to do it. The best way is to *learn by doing*. As of now you've read the directions and you know how it works, so we're going to take the doing of it step by step.

1. Visualize the effect. Don't just think of it as you will present it; but think how it will look to those who are watching it.

2. Make sure you have all the props and everything works.

3. Write down the steps in the trick.

4. Go through the whole trick slowly, with all the props. Don't be afraid to stop and think what comes next.

5. Go through the whole trick again and again, picking up speed. Keep moving now, and if something goes wrong try to keep going. Correct your mistake on the next play-though.

6. Plan what you are going to say and fit it in with what you're doing. You can use a tape recorder to hear your words and a mirror to watch your actions.

7. Go out and bore a few friends by doing the trick. By the time you've run out of friends, you should have the trick down pat.

C. LEARN HOW TO PRESENT IT. Here, now, is the tough one. You know how the trick is done and you're able to do it. So now you've got to make a gradual change to make it different. The start of being great is being different; BUT it has to be acceptable and amusing, not just different. The secret here is to *think*. Observe things about you. Study and THINK. Daydreaming is a clue. Think of ways you can change. Ask yourself questions. Can you change the size, shape, color, or material? Look at pictures, books, magazines, catalogs, or anything that will trigger your imagination. Look at TV, movies, or shows. Make notes on music, design, movement, and acting. Study salesmanship and psychology—in fact, study life and everything about you because LEARNING HOW TO PRESENT IT is an individual thing and all I can tell you is to STUDY and THINK.

Okay, now you know. GO DO IT. Just reading about it is not the way. Sometimes you have to stick a wet toe into a hot socket to find out if the juice is on!

Good Luck,

Jay Marshall

To
Martin Gardner
a genius who
enjoys this sort of
nonsense

introduction

For centuries, man has amused his fellow beings with fascinating sleight of hand, seemingly insoluble puzzles, marvels of misdirection, tests of telepathy and the creation of an enormous range of unnatural and supernatural images and effects—in a word, magic.

The spirit of magic, or a simple yearning for mystery and the inexplicable in a very pragmatic world, never seems to wane in people. Perhaps we long to have the contents of the magician's bag of tricks revealed to us because we really do want to believe in sorcery, extrasensory powers and a world in which spirits occasionally take control. Or, possibly, we simply appreciate the art, agility and showmanship that the magician puts into his act.

Regardless of how strongly we feel about magic tricks, few among us have not ached to know the mysteries behind the magician's wondrous creations after watching a well performed show. Those who follow up this desire often end with an unused repertoire of impressive magic tricks and nowhere to perform them. As in other performing arts, unfortunately, only the best and most dedicated magicians are given the stage.

But for those who like to amaze friends with an occasional feat of magic, thousands of tricks have been developed by amateur and professional conjurers alike, intended for performance at the dinner table or in the living room. These tricks use ordinary objects available in most households and call for simple steps in preparation. No gimmick props need to be purchased, and no live rabbits need to be pulled from a silk top hat.

The tricks included in this book can be called "instant magic"—those bewitching stunts you can run through spontaneously when you sense a lag in the action around you. As such, most are less elaborate in effect than those you might see performed on a large commercial stage. On the other hand, your impromptu audiences are not likely to expect the best from you; in fact, they may not suspect you have developed the few skills necessary to succeed with this type trick.

The magic unveiled in the following chapters is instant in another respect as well. For the most part, no moves described require long-nurtured skills developed by the veteran magician. Rather, basic, simple palming and passing techniques must be practiced, and the magician must learn to become an actor as well as a conjurer. This can be the final key to successful results. No matter how smooth your delivery, if you do not provide an amusing narrative to go along with your actions, the trick is likely to fall flat. This is the worst that can happen to a magician, for at all costs the conjurer must look for the extreme reaction from his spectators. No matter how simple the technique, dramatize the performance and aim for the gasp of surprise, the disbelieving double take, the delighted laughter, the raised eyebrows.

In chapter 1, you will learn a wide range of tricks specifically suited to performance at the dinner table, at home or in a restaurant. More tricks of the instant variety may fall into this category than any other. For some reason, past magicians invented long lists of routines with which to amuse your fellow diners. Many tricks in this chapter can be transferred to the living room; in general, anywhere in the house will do. All the props should be available in a standard household.

Chapter 2 introduces the novice magician to the vast world of card and coin tricks. Naturally, there is an endless index of additional tricks using cards and coins, but many are based on the same concepts, given a new twist by an inventive magician. The tricks included serve as starting points for your own creations and as a base on which to build, using tricks you learn from fellow home sorcerers.

Chapter 3 leads into the occult, describing a wealth of tricks through which you read the minds of audience members, or make a prop perform some inexplicable movement caused, you may claim, by spirits. They may be performed in various settings, some more suitable for at-home than onstage performance.

In chapter 4 are a variety of instant tricks you may put together for a cohesive stage act. If you do not plan to hit the nightclub circuit, you may want to have some of these on hand at a large party, or for entertaining children at birthday celebrations. In addition, most, while better suited to stage performance, may also be done at home.

Finally, chapter 5 includes a representative selection of miscellaneous tricks that cannot be accurately labeled magic. These conversation-starters, based on scientific principles, are gags, puzzles and mysteries with which you can amuse, shock, humiliate and confuse your friends.

Consider this your conjurer's primer. Do not hesitate to add to and vary the tricks according to your own tastes and innovations. Whatever and wherever you perform the tricks in this book, always remember that if the trick is not convincing to you—if you really do not believe it yourself—your audience will not fall for your magic either.

tricks you can do at the dinner table

Perhaps the ultimate in impromptu or "instant" magic is the trick that requires no props at all but rather focuses on parts of the magician's—or spectator's—body. Most center on the magician's hands; in many, the hands serve as not only the object but also the tools of whatever magic is to be performed. Delightfully, these feats can be performed any place, any time. An additional benefit is that your audience hardly can accuse you of rigging your own hand. Certainly, a skeptical spectator may suspect a gimmick fingertip or such prop, but if you willingly go to whatever lengths necessary to prove that "nothing is up your sleeve," doubters will be forced to admire your sleight of hand abilities.

Before you attempt any tricks in this section, note that they are impromptu in effect *only*. You will have to practice if you expect to carry them off impressively. Movements made with fingers and hands must be smooth and quick to avoid detection by a hawk-eyed spectator.

Most tricks included are appropriate for performance at the dinner table, although your intended victim should be seated across from you. (Anyone seated next to you may spot your secret maneuvers.) Several are meant for performance at close range but require the magician and sometimes the spectator to stand. These are suitable for living room performances, or for the dining room if you don't mind jumping up from the table.

For finger tricks that follow, your hands, fingers and thumbs must be fairly limber. If you'd like to focus most attention on these tricks, or if you find you're having trouble achieving the finger contortions required in others, consult and practice the following finger exercises.

LIMBERING UP

It's quite simple to get your hands into shape. With a little practice, you can usually loosen the muscles sufficiently to bend your fingers every way, opening a whole area of sleight-type skills to you, the novice magician. Merely position your fingers as indicated in the eight diagrams until you achieve them all. You can practice almost unconsciously while doing other things. When you accomplish each position with both hands, you should succeed at all the following tricks.

To learn similar tricks better adapted to stage performance, see chapter 4.

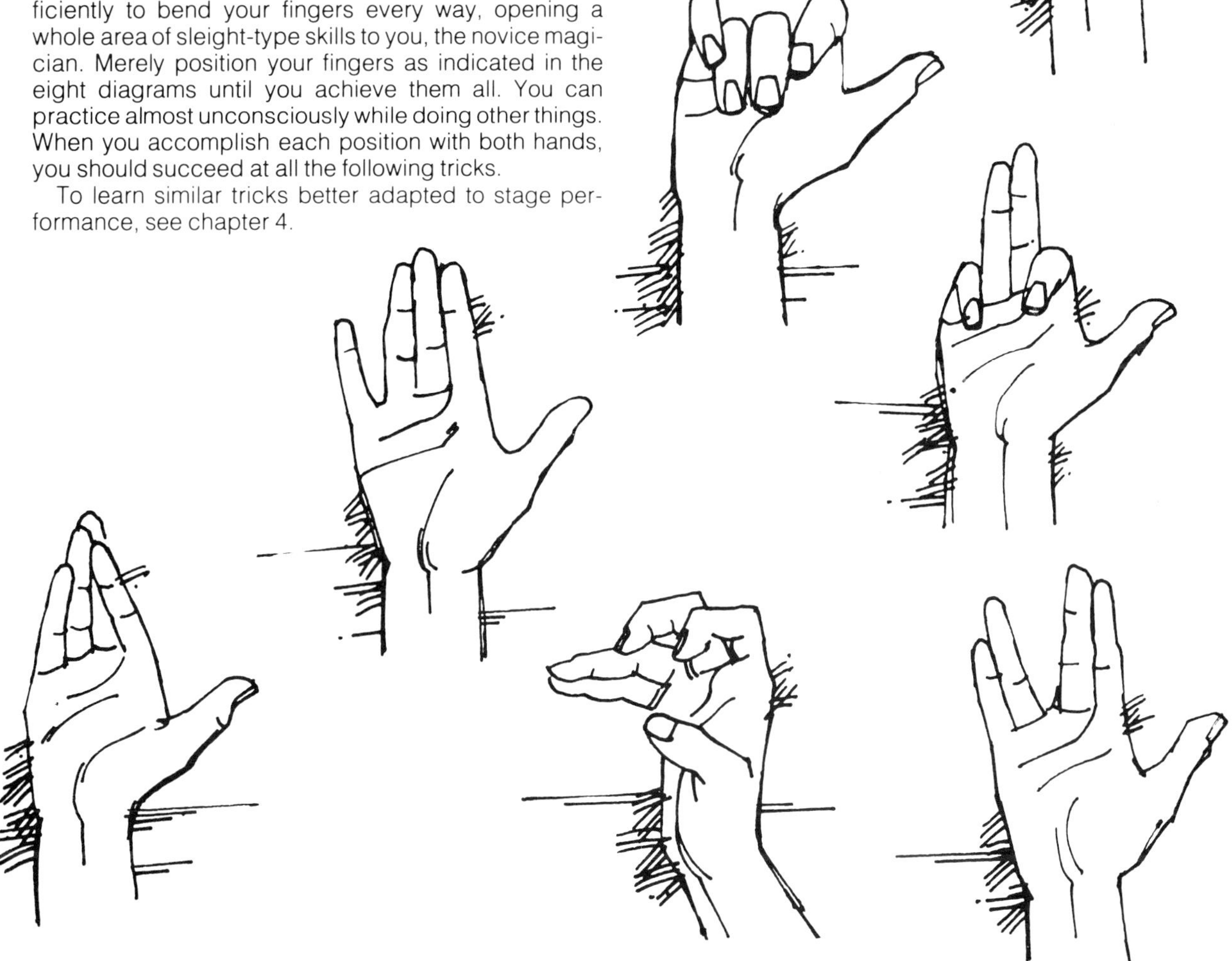

THE MAGIC MINI-SAW

This great little impromptu trick can shock some-one at table but since it is an old gag, your best bet is to give an imaginative but low-keyed buildup. For instance, saying "How'd you like me to saw your finger in half?" to a fellow diner is bound to be a real conversation stopper. On the other hand, you might arouse more interest if you casually try cutting a roll or some other food with your forefinger, muttering about a dull blade as you fail to cut through the item. When your companions stare at you as though you are peculiar, look slightly surprised and proceed to announce nonchalantly that usually you can use your finger as a saw if, for example, you concentrate on the spirits. Then offer to try it on a skeptic sitting next to you.

Props: none
Advance Preparation: none

1. Have a spectator put an extended finger on the table. Hold its tip with your left hand, your left thumbnail touching it lightly.

2. With your right forefinger, begin to saw the spectator's finger, moving alongside your left thumbnail. Distract the audience and your victim with patter so no one stares at what you're doing.

When the victim least expects it, dig your thumbnail into his finger. He should jump, since he'll feel your finger suddenly become razor-sharp.

GHOST TAPS

Among the most spontaneous ways to send chills down the spines of unwitting bystanders is to perform a version of the ghost tap. In the many versions of this trick, the magician creates an illusion through the power of suggestion. The basic concept of most versions lies in the spectator being tapped mysteriously, though previously having been convinced (in fact, having seen with his own eyes) that both magician's hands are occupied elsewhere. Of course, the spectator also must be convinced that no one in the vicinity has provided the extra hand. The nice thing about these tricks is that they require virtually no skills on the magician's part. Just try one once with a willing guinea pig to make sure you know how the routine works before regaling an audience with your command of the spirits.

GHOST TAP I

A good trick to do at the table, this one can be done about anywhere.

Props: none
Advance Preparation: none

Place the tips of both forefingers on a spectator's forehead and draw them gently down his face, over his eyes and cheeks. Repeat this in stroking fashion several times.

Then have the spectator close his eyes and, without breaking the rhythm, immediately substitute the second finger of one hand for the forefinger of the other, thereby freeing one hand for the ghost tap.

Continue the stroking motion with the two fingers of one hand, stop with your fingertips on his eyelids and tap the back of the spectator's head.

Immediately return your hand to the front so when his eyes open he will see both your hands there.

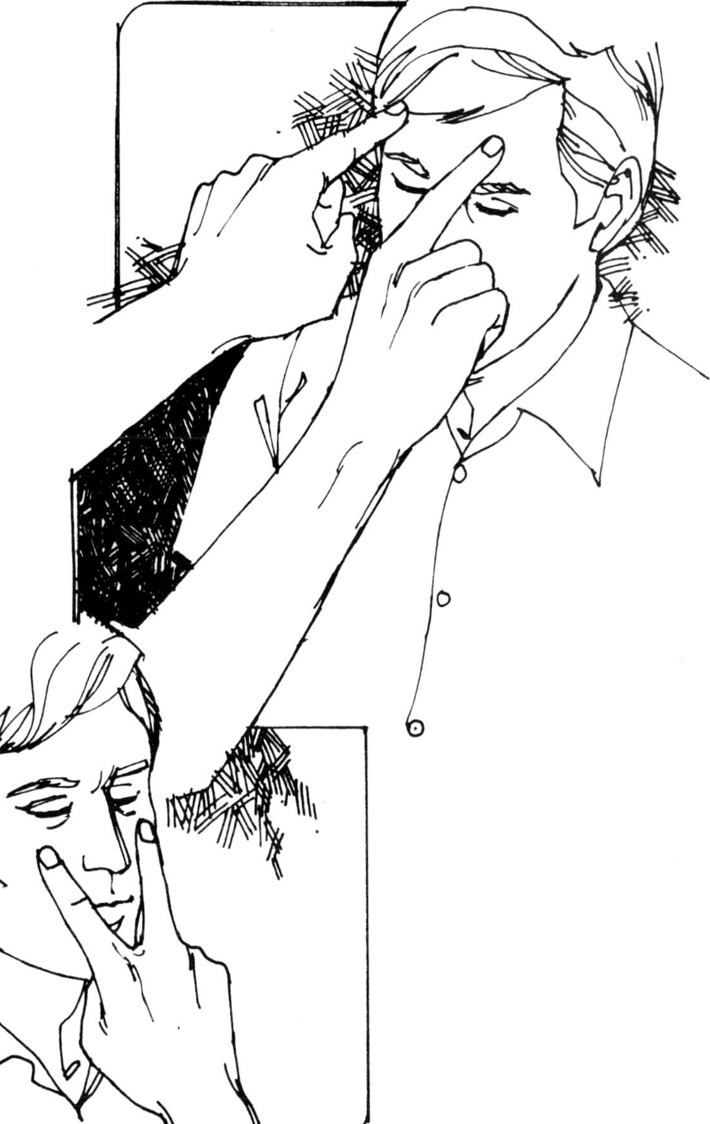

A SHOW OF HANDS

GHOST TAP II

The illusion for this tap is created through sound rather than touch, so it is trickier than the preceding; you must be sure that the switch made is not audible. Since you're supposed to stand for this trick, it's suitable for the living room. Or, you may get up and stand behind your victim's chair. Again, introduce simple tricks like this with an impressive buildup. For this one, try talking about evoking spirits to greet the victim.

Props: none
Advance Preparation: none

Stand behind your victim and begin to clap your hands to an even beat, planting the suggestion that both hands are occupied.

At a certain point, raise your hands, continuing to clap; when they reach your face, free one hand and slap the other against your face, without breaking the set rhythm. You must be sure there is no audible difference in sound. Now tap the back of the spectator's head, as though a ghost did it.

GHOST TAP III

This tap is more subtle than the two preceding, because the freed hand must be withdrawn very gently so the spectator will not feel the slightest jerk. Like the others, perform this at the dinner table or elsewhere.

Props: none
Advance Preparation: none

Have a spectator extend one forearm and grab it with both hands. The trick is to casually glasp your hands side by side around the arm and secretly insert your right thumb under your left hand. Clasp the left hand very loosely with fingers resting mainly on top of those of the right hand rather than on the spectator's arm. The right fingers and thumb press firmly against the victim's skin.

Have the spectator close his eyes, then very carefully remove your left hand. If you've clasped your hands correctly, no jerking motion will be felt and the pressure of your right thumb will simulate the pressure of your entire left hand. Now call on your favorite ghost to tap the victim's head.

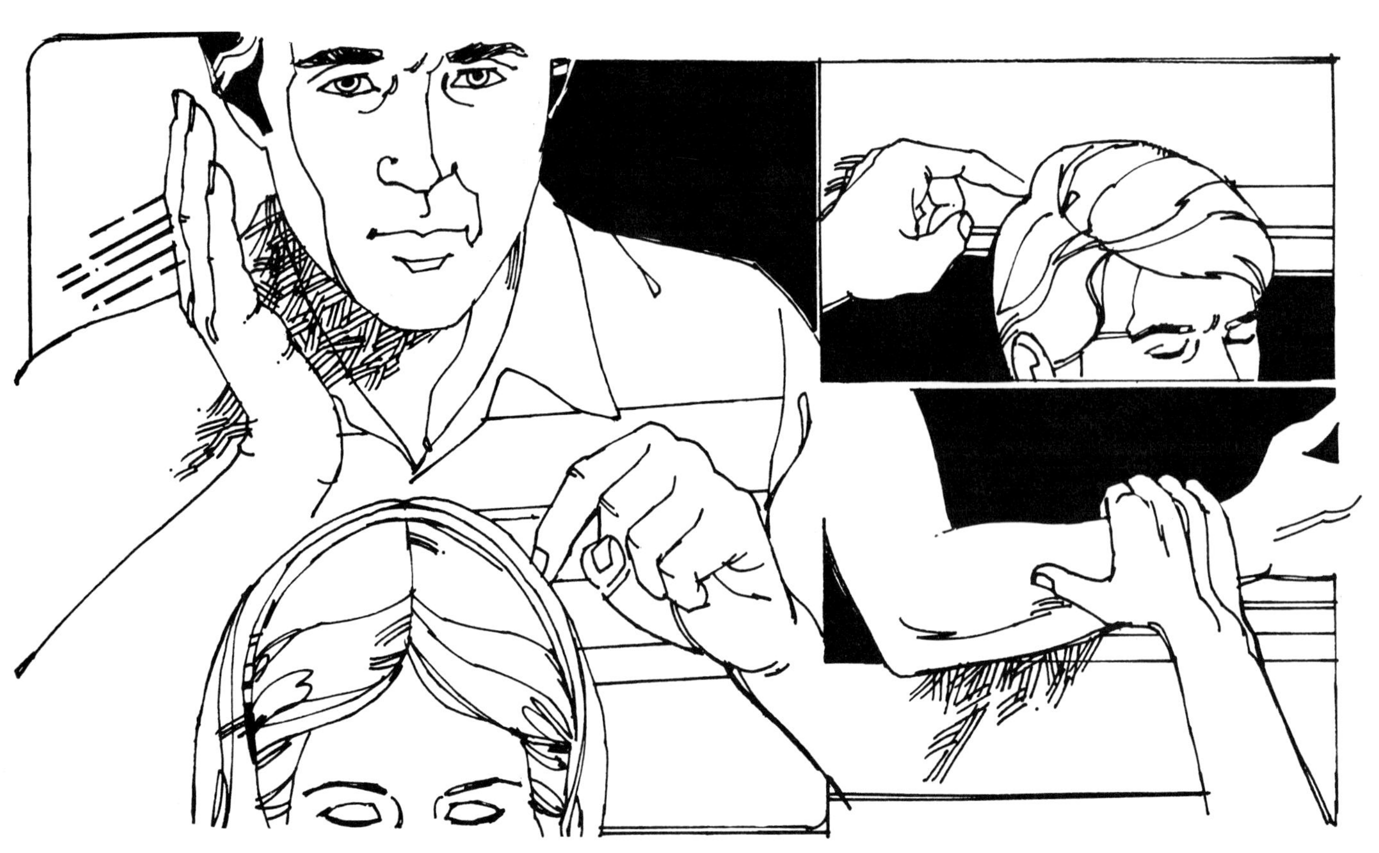

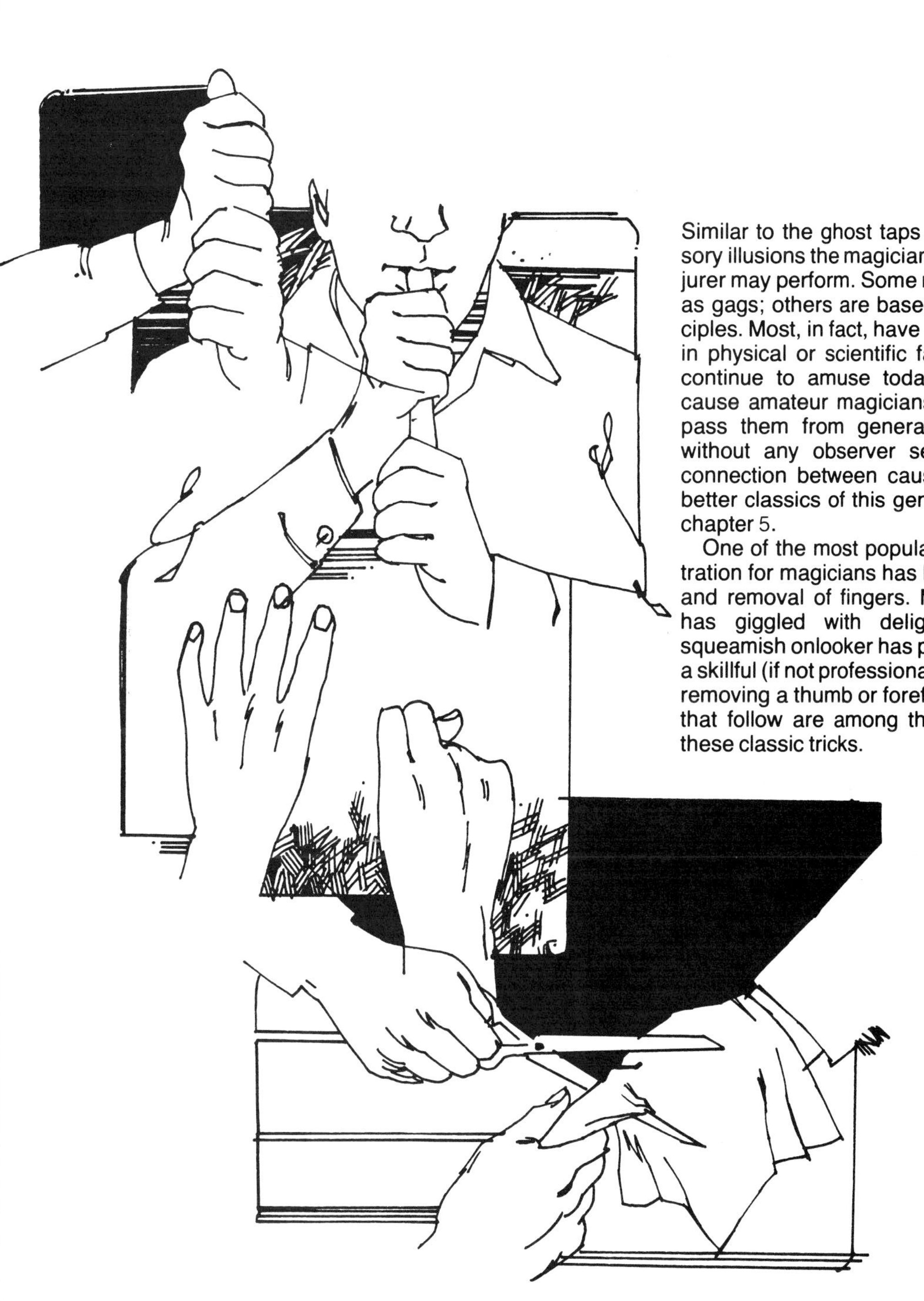

Similar to the ghost taps are the many sensory illusions the magician or living room conjurer may perform. Some may be categorized as gags; others are based on scientific principles. Most, in fact, have tangible foundation in physical or scientific fact. However, they continue to amuse today's spectators because amateur magicians often are able to pass them from generation to generation without any observer seeing the obscure connection between cause and effect. The better classics of this genre can be found in chapter 5.

One of the most popular areas of concentration for magicians has been the stretching and removal of fingers. Many a small child has giggled with delight, and many a squeamish onlooker has paled, at the sight of a skillful (if not professional) conjurer casually removing a thumb or forefinger. The routines that follow are among the best versions of these classic tricks.

THE ELASTIC THUMB

This trick, like other stretches and removals, can be done anywhere since no props are needed, but it requires practice because movements must be smooth and quick. If you're performing onstage, this thumb stretch is a good prelude to a thumb removal. (You may tell the audience you need to limber up your thumb before pulling it off entirely.) If you're doing this trick impromptu at the table or party, take a low-key approach. You can imagine the sighs of boredom that might follow the announcement, "Watch me pull my thumb out of shape!" You'll more likely get gratifying looks of shock from your audience if you wait for a lull in the action around you to draw attention to-yourself through some other ploy. Then you may really surprise your audience, since they won't at all be expecting you to do a trick.

This trick is so simple (and fairly obvious) that it's especially suitable for young children. Keep in mind that the more nonchalant your manner, the more likely your eliciting an impressed double take by a spectator.

Props: none
Advance Preparation: No props need be prepared, but it's a good idea to run through the moves in front of a mirror a few times.

1. Close both hands into fists with thumbs pointing upward. Hidden from spectators' view, put your right fist on top of the left, with the left thumb inserted into the right fist. The right thumb will appear to be the protruding tip of the left.

2. Now bite the thumb tip with your teeth and as you pretend to pull the thumb upward to stretch it, pull your right fist up a bit to expose part of the left thumb.

Quickly push the right fist down to cover the left thumb.

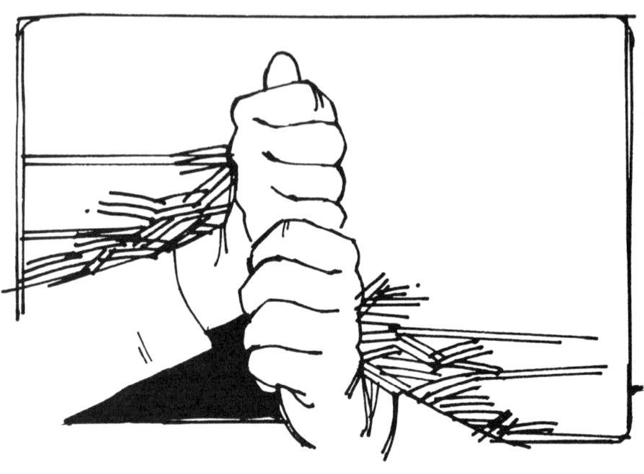

One way to improve the "sell" on this swindle is to begin biting your left thumb and acting as though you are trying to pull and lengthen it. When this doesn't seem to work, add your right hand to pull harder until you reach the position shown in figure 2. Go backwards to figure 1 and back further still until you are biting your left thumb again. For a finish you bit hard enough to leave tooth marks and show it's not just the audience that suffers when you do tricks.

THE GHOSTLY FINGER

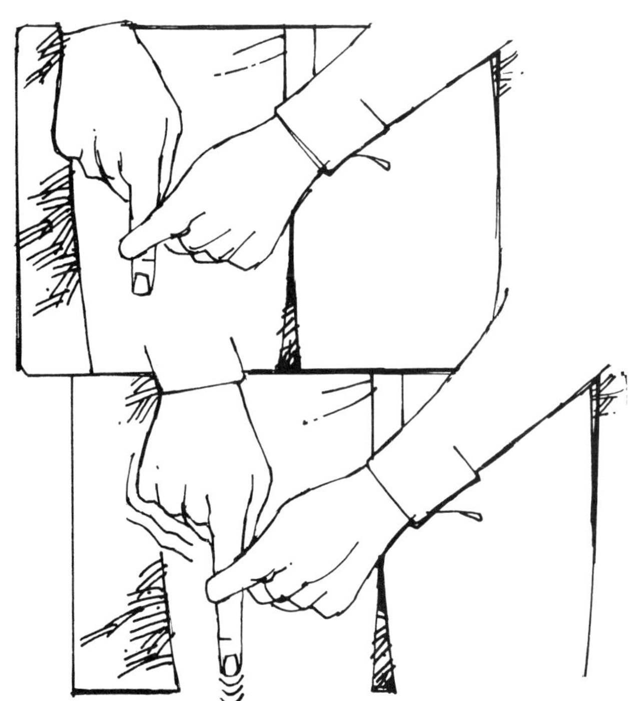

While the effect of this trick is the same as the Elastic Thumb's, the technique is totally different. This finger stretch relies on an optical illusion and need only be tried once in front of the mirror to assure the effect is correct. It can be done at home (in a standing position) or onstage as a prelude to a finger removal.

Props: none
Advance Preparation: none

1. Close your right hand into a fist and extend the forefinger. Hold your hand against your thigh (finger pointing downward) and curl your left forefinger across it.

2. By moving your right hand rapidly up and down an inch or so (leaving the left forefinger in place), you create the illusion of stretching your right forefinger.

OFF WITH YOUR THUMB!

This is not a thumb removal per se, because a prop substitutes for your thumb before it is cut off. Nor is it entirely instant, since you do need to prepare and use props. However, if you're willing to make the preparations, it can be a real shocker at the dinner table.

Props: a carrot
a paper napkin
scissors or a knife

Advance Preparation: Let the carrot soften unrefrigerated for a few days. Then cut it into the shape of your left thumb. At the table, surreptitiously slip the carrot under a paper napkin before announcing the trick.

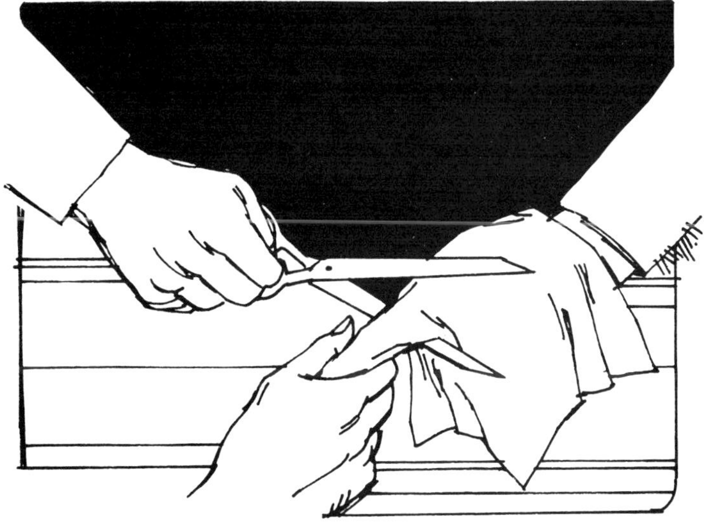

To start, close your left hand into a fist with the thumb pointing upward. Pick up the napkin with the carrot and pretend to wrap the napkin around your thumb. Instead, push your thumb into your fist and grip the base of the carrot thumb under the napkin.

Now let the spectator hold the tip of the carrot thumb. Grab your scissors and proceed to cut off your thumb, leaving it in the spectator's hand!

THE SHAKY THUMB

The advantage of the thumb removal to the inexperienced magician is that shaking the hand during the trick covers much of the hidden movement. The wiggling hand also enhances the effect, since the magician continues to shake the "removed" thumb after it has been "severed."

You must be standing to do this trick, as it's difficult to do at the table, but you may try it just about anywhere else.

Props: none
Advance Preparation: A little practice in front of a mirror is all it takes.

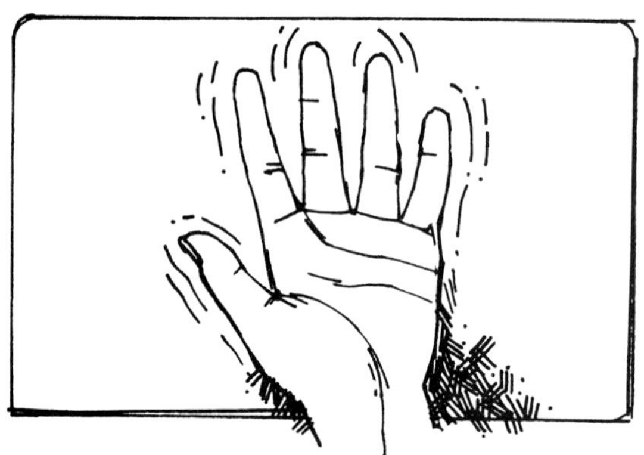

1. Start by holding your left hand in front of your thigh, palm toward the audience. Shake fingers and thumb as you announce the trick. (You may even suggest that the ghostly force you have evoked to assist in the removal is wiggling your hand.)

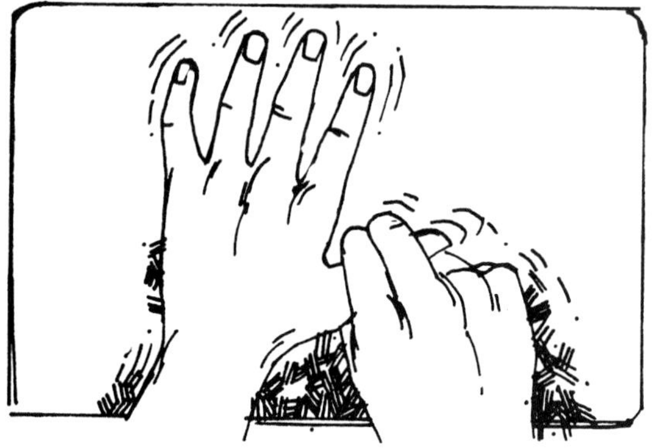

2. Now turn your hand so the back faces the audience; continuing to shake it, grasp the thumb with the first two fingers on your right hand.

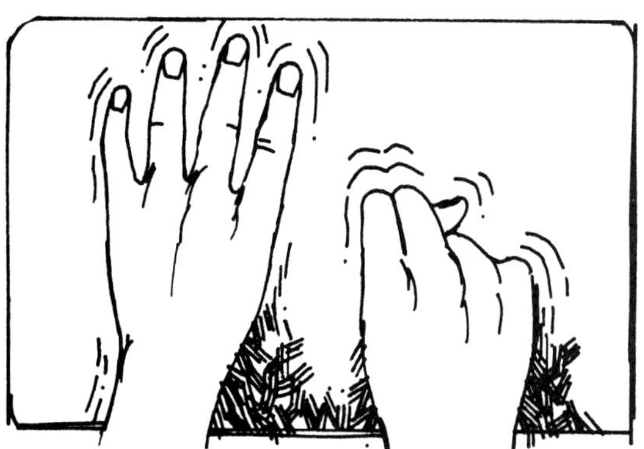

3. Next, in one smooth motion, separate your hands, quickly and unobtrusively bending your left thumb behind your hand and inserting your right thumb between the second and third fingers of your right hand. It is very important to continue shaking your left hand and to begin wiggling your right thumb immediately after the hands are separated.

Quickly put your hands back together, pretending to replace the thumb. Obviously, the most effective part of the trick lies in wiggling the apparently removed thumb so it appears to have come from the shaking hand.

THE SLIDING THUMB

You don't need a pair of scissors, a paper napkin and a slightly soft carrot to remove your thumb.

Props: none
Advance Preparation: You probably should practice the entire routine several times before presenting it to an audience.

1. Start by holding your left hand in front of you with the fingers pointing to the right. Grab your thumb knuckle from above with your right thumb and forefinger.

2. In this position, twist your thumb around and use your imagination to come up with amusing contortions to try pulling off your thumb.

After several unsuccessful attempts, close your right fingers over the thumb.

3. Under their cover, bend your left thumb back and your right thumb forward to resemble the left thumb tip. You should practice this step in front of a mirror until you can place your right thumb at the most realistic angle.

Then lift the last three fingers on the right hand to show the audience the right thumb tip (which looks like the left thumb tip to them).

4. If you find it difficult to hide your bent left thumb tip with your forefinger alone, try doing the trick by lifting only the last *two* fingers.

5. Now slowly slide your right thumb along the top of the left forefinger. Then slide the thumb back to its original position.

6. Here is the trickiest step in the trick: When your thumb knuckles touch each other, quickly separate your hands by moving them up and then down again about 6 to 8 inches. As you do so, you switch thumbs again by leaving your hands in position but pulling the right thumb back and extending the left, grasping it with the right thumb and forefinger (or right thumb and two first fingers). If done correctly, your audience will be unable to see your thumb switch.

As your hands descend to the original position, you will be grasping your left thumb tip (as the audience thought you were at the beginning of the trick), and you can astound the spectators by displaying your restored thumb.

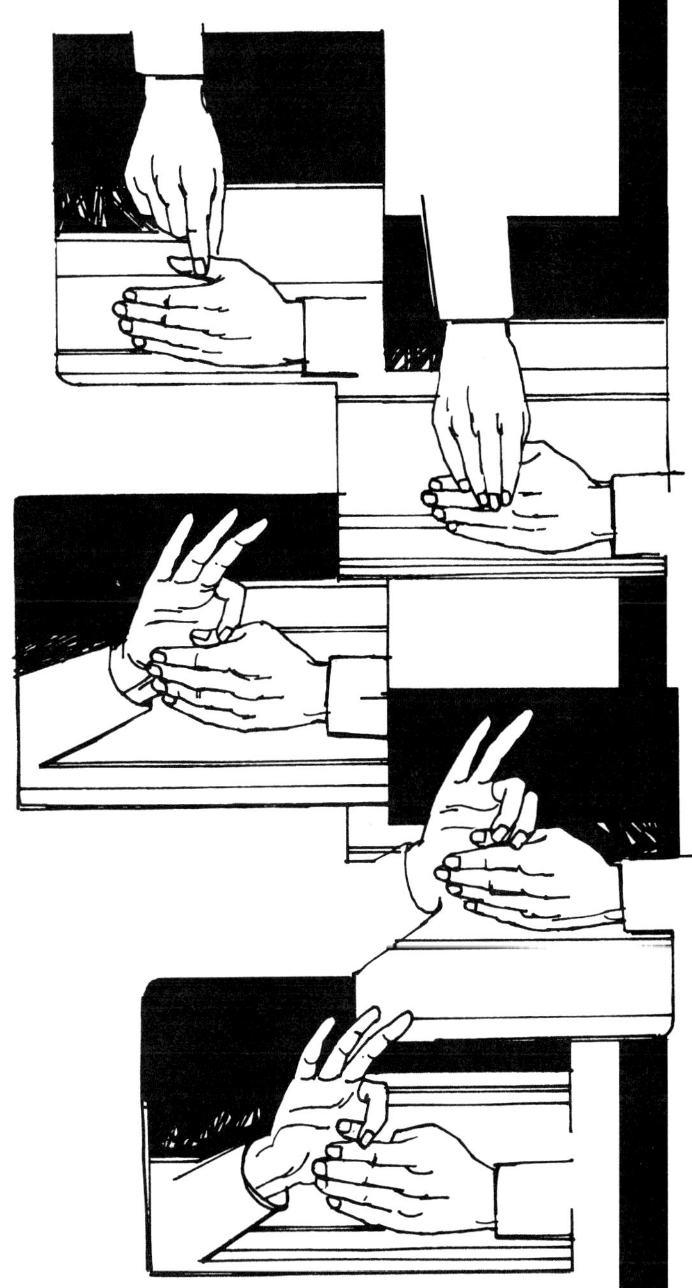

Some audiences find vanishes the most fascinating magic tricks. There is something particularly alluring about the illusion that a concrete, tangible object can be made to disappear "into thin air" with the mere flick of a magician's wand, wave of a skillful hand, or simple recitation of some other-worldly invocation. Often even the most stubborn skeptics secretly want to believe that your powers have dispatched an object from this world to another. Beware of these vocal doubters, however; you may have to go to great lengths to turn them into true believers in sorcery. Children may exhibit uncritical delight, but you may find mature spectators crawling under the table, peeking under plates and even attempting to frisk your person in order to expose you for a fraud.

The best way to handle vanishes is to put all your acting abilities into them. Spare no histrionics in your performance and you might be rewarded with unqualified applause for your showmanship—even when your audience is composed of down-to-earth types who always think they know the secret behind your wizardry.

SIMPLE KNIFE VANISH

This trick is so simple that it may not fool a discriminating audience, so ham it up. The trick must be done at the dinner table. Casually pick up a knife and tell your audience you are going to wrap the knife before trying to bend the blade at the handle.

Props: a blunt table knife
a cloth napkin

Advance Preparation: None is necessary, but you might want to practice until you can do the trick smoothly without a hitch. You may substitute a handkerchief or scarf for the napkin, but make sure in advance that the cloth is large enough to conceal the entire length of the knife.

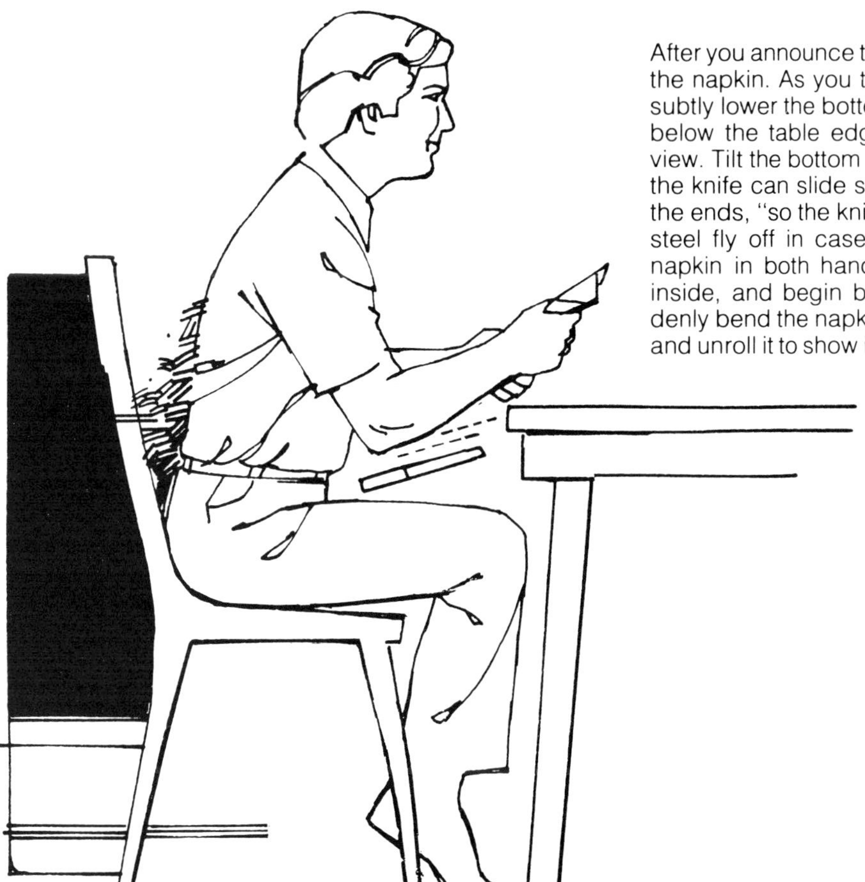

After you announce the trick, roll the knife loosely in the napkin. As you talk to distract your audience, subtly lower the bottom end of the roll until it is just below the table edge and out of the audience's view. Tilt the bottom of the loosely rolled napkin so the knife can slide silently into your lap. Fold over the ends, "so the knife can't get out, and no bits of steel fly off in case the blade snaps." Hold the napkin in both hands, as though the knife were inside, and begin bending apprehensively. Suddenly bend the napkin roll double, straighten it out and unroll it to show it empty!

THE DISAPPEARING DAGGER

This trick, another knife vanish, is more impressive in some ways than the "Simple Knife Vanish" (page 25) and also takes more practice to carry off well, but it is worth the extra effort.

Props: a table knife
a cloth napkin
Advance Preparation: Practice until you are satisfied with your performance. Also, make sure the napkin or other cloth you have chosen is large enough to cover the knife entirely when draped over it.

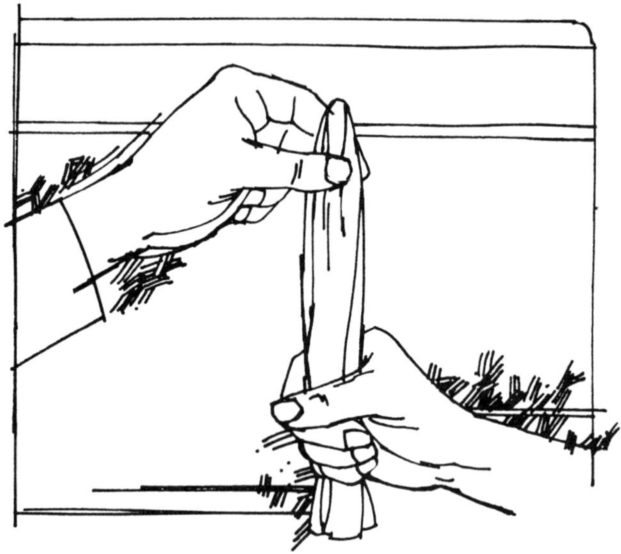

To begin, drape the napkin over your left arm, with most of the cloth hanging in front, toward your audience. Hold the knife in your right hand.

Move the knife behind the napkin and immediately slip it up your sleeve, putting your right forefinger tip against the middle of the napkin (X in the drawing) to simulate the knife point.

Lift the napkin with that finger so that it drapes over your hand. With the left hand, grab what looks like the knife point but is actually your finger.

Now remove your right hand from the napkin and grab a corner of the cloth with it. To finish, release the napkin from your left hand and shake the cloth to show that the knife has disappeared from it.

For an alternate ending, grab the middle of the napkin with your right fist while the left hand grips the phony knife tip. Then pull the cloth upward with your left hand, the right fist remaining around the napkin. Let go with your left hand; the typical linen napkin will remain standing as though the knife were inside.

Next, place your left hand into your lap, sliding the knife from the sleeve and into your hand, leaving the hand in your lap so the audience does not suspect.

Now catch everyone off guard by turning to the person seated to your left and stabbing him suddenly in the chest with the napkin that supposedly holds the knife.

As everyone recovers from the shock, immediately reach behind your victim with your left hand and pull out the knife as though it had penetrated the chest and come through the back.

TO BURN OR NOT TO BURN?

This paper napkin vanish fools everyone.

Props: a paper napkin
a book of matches

Advance Preparation: Keep the matches in your jacket pocket. Also, wet the curve between your left thumb and forefinger. Using saliva is the easiest if not the most pleasant method.

(If you have just done the Wishing Well (p. 28), you have a paper napkin crumpled from corner to corner and you have a matchbook with a coin in it in your right coat pocket. Follow these directions except that you use a corner of the crumpled wishing well instead of the center of a fresh paper napkin.)

Start by letting the napkin drape from its center. With your left hand, hold it about an inch or two from the tip.

With the thumb and forefinger of your left hand, push the napkin tip upward. The moistened spot on your hand will tear the tip from the rest of the napkin, although the spectators will not see the tear since your hand will hide it.

With your right hand, roll the napkin upwards toward your left hand. When it appears that you have rolled it into a ball in your left fist, actually palm the paper wad in your right hand.

Put your right hand into your pocket, leaving the paper ball and removing the matchbook. Chatter about whether it would be dangerous to burn the napkin supposedly in your left fist. Finally decide against it and tell the spectators you have hit upon another method to vanish the napkin.

Pretend to tear off the tip of the napkin (although the tip is all that is left in your hand). With the torn tip in your right hand, wave it around your left fist and chant a spell over all.

Open your left fist and exclaim "Voila!" as you show that the napkin has disappeared from your hand.

"Oh well, all's well that ends well." Open the matchbook and reproduce the borrowed coil which is re turned to the spectator.

THE WISHING WELL

This easy and effective trick uses a paper napkin to vanish a coin tucked into it.

Props: a book of matches in your left coat or
pants pocket
a paper napkin
a coin

Advance Preparation: none

A fellow once stood by a wishing well with a mortal enemy. He tossed a coin into the water and made a wish. Just then his enemy fell into the well and drowned. The fellow said, "I didn't think those things worked."

Introduce the trick by saying you intend to make a wishing well from the napkin.

Make a fist with your left hand and spread the napkin over it. Push the paper into the fist to make a well and secretly poke a hole in the bottom with your finger. Borrow a coin from a fellow diner and say, "When I drop the coin into the well I want you to make a wish." Often the spectator will say, "I wish I had my coin back." Say, "I once did this Wishing Well trick for a doctor and he lost his money. It was really his own fault; he should have tended to the sick and left the well alone."

While you are telling these bad jokes you have dropped the coin into the napkin and through the hole into your left hand. "And now I need some matches." Reach into your right coat pocket and there are no matches. Reach under the edge of the paper napkin apparently to hold the coin in the well with the right hand. The left hand (with the coin) goes into the left coat pocket putting the coin into the matchbook and immediately bringing out the matchbook to fan the napkin wishing well. After fanning, put the matchbook on the table and take a corner of the paper napkin with the left hand and straighten it out above the right hand and straighten out the diagonally opposite corner below the right hand which is apparently still holding the coin. Squeeze the middle with the right hand so they won't notice the hole in the napkin and say, "If the coin is gone it is said that your wish will come true."

Show the hands empty and feel up and down the straightened napkin. Smile and say, "Congratulations." Follow this trick with To Burn or Not To Burn (p. 27). Begin by putting the matches in your right coat pocket. The coin is still in the matchbook.

VANISHING SALT

Similar to the Wishing Well described on p. 28, this trick is simpler to perform. Keep in mind as you vanish the salt that anyone sitting next to you at the table may see every move you make.

Props: a paper napkin
a salt shaker
Advance Preparation: none

Rest your left fist half on and half off the edge of the table in front of you. Drape a paper napkin over it and push the napkin into your fist, subtly poking a hole in the bottom of the paper.

With your right hand, sprinkle salt from the shaker into the well. To make the trick convincing, be generous with the amount of salt, continuing to shake it into your fist as you talk to the audience. Be sure that your fist is open a little so the salt pours into your lap.

Here is a second version if you don't want salt in your lap.

When you drape the paper napkin over your left fist, DON'T poke a hole in the bottom of the well. Actually pour salt into this well, and let your audience see the salt there. Put the shaker on the table and reach under the napkin with the right hand and twist the paper around the salt. You know if you moisten your thumb the paper will tear easily, so tear off this small bag of salt, holding it in the right hand.

Move the left hand up and away from the right as though it still had the salt. Shake the left hand and then move the right hand over an ashtray. Break the thin paper bag and let the salt trickle into the ashtray from the right hand.

When the pour ends, you will still have a small piece of the paper. Reach up to the left hand and crumple *all* the paper and roll it into a ball, putting it into the ashtray on top of the salt.

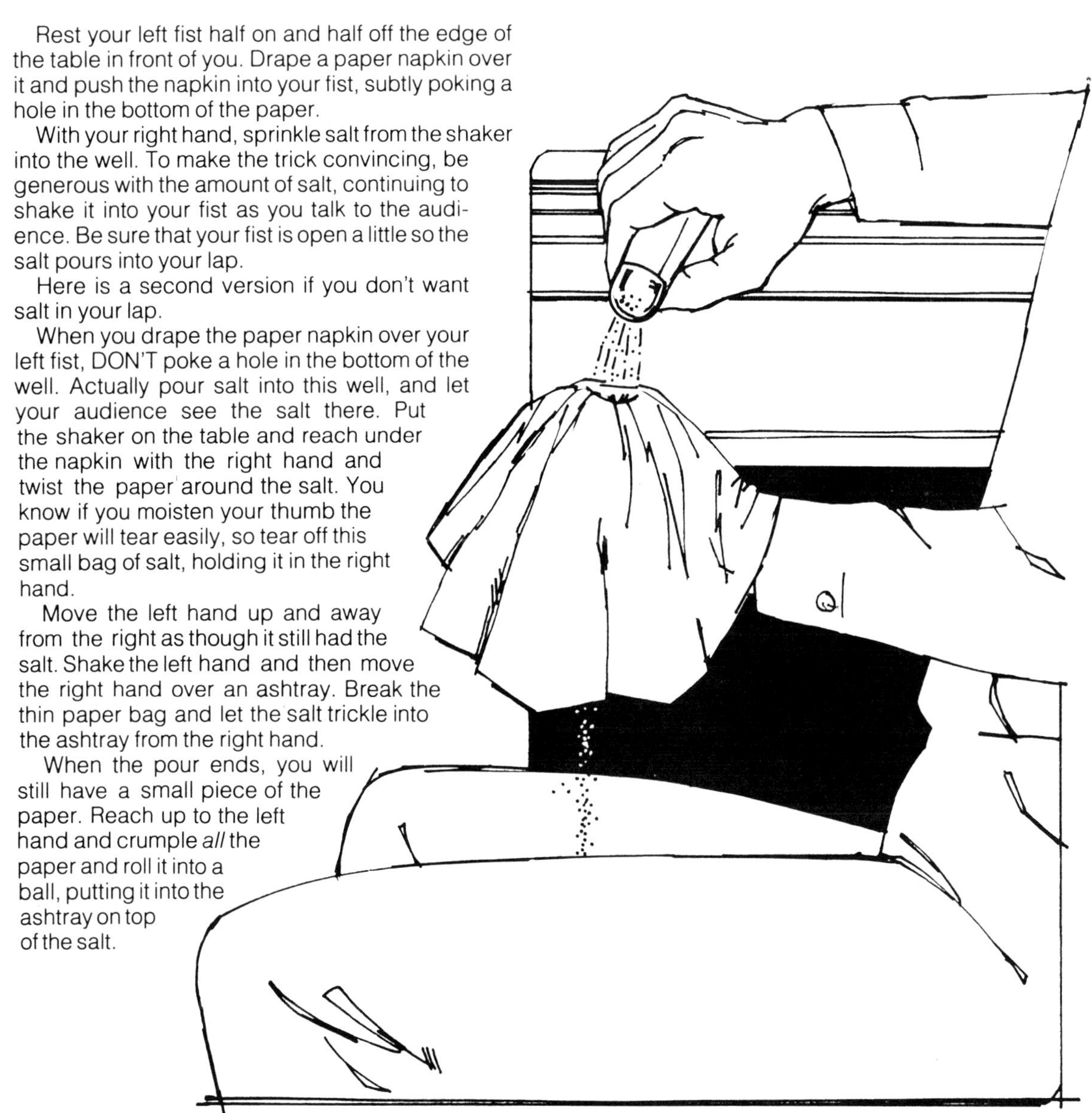

In the following tricks, the magician uses standard household items, especially those commonly available at the dinner table, to magically transform one prop into another. There are no gimmick props here; your success depends on sleight of hand and sometimes a little advance preparation.

SILVERWARE SWITCH

Using the same moves as in the "Silverware Penetration" (see p. 48), you can magically transform a spoon into a knife, a fork into a knife, and so on.

Props: 2 different pieces of silverware (or 2 different-colored pencils or pens)
a cloth napkin or handkerchief

Advance Preparation: Secretly lay one piece of silverware or one pen underneath the napkin, pointing east to west, as you lay the napkin on the table.

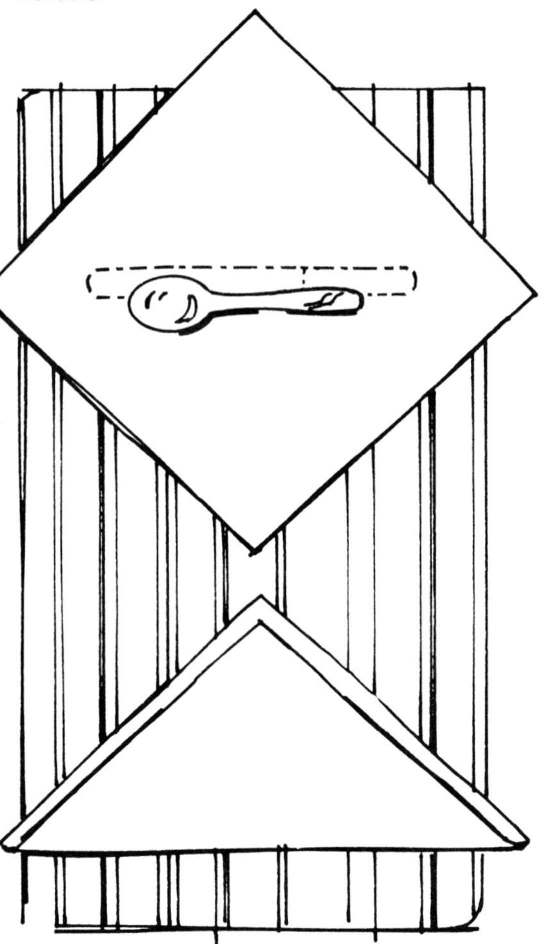

1. Direct attention to the spread napkin. Put the second piece of silverware or the second pen in the center of the napkin, roughly on top of the hidden one.

2. Fold the south corner to the north corner, stopping about an inch short.

3. Place your palms over the silverware and begin to roll the cloth under or toward you, letting the south corner rotate once around the roll, without drawing attention to this fact.

4. Now have your victim press a finger on the lower corner to hold it there. Grasp the upper corner and pull it toward you. The top piece of silverware will roll off the table edge and into your lap as the piece of silverware originally hidden underneath appears on top of the napkin.

SHARPENING A KNIFE

The effectiveness of this trick depends heavily on the performer's acting and pantomime skills.

Props: a table knife
a round plate with no pattern
Advance Preparation: none

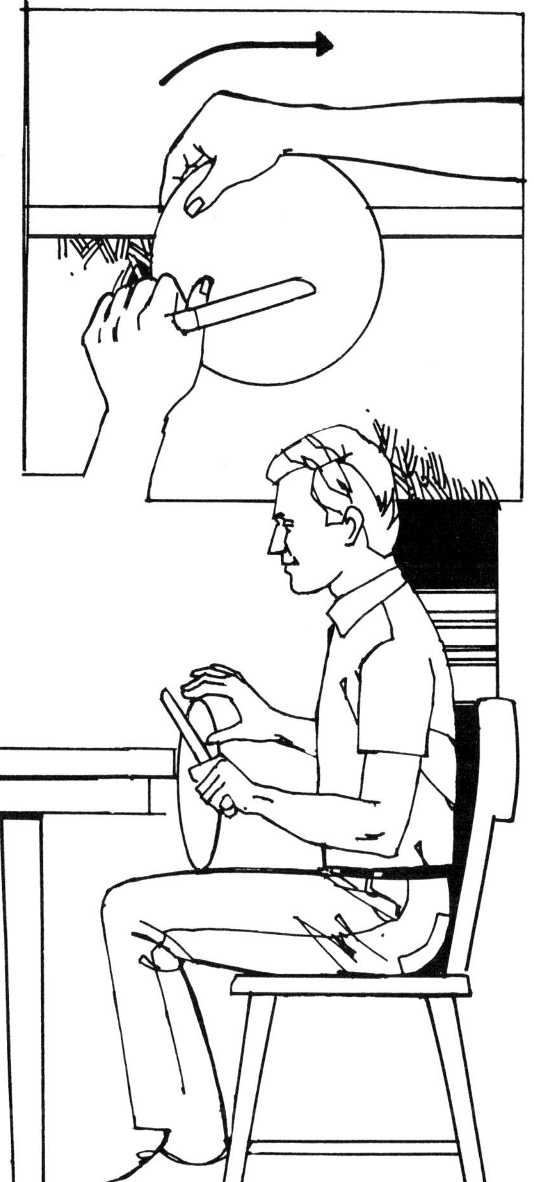

Remark that the table knife seems dull and run your thumb over the edge to prove it. Take the plate and put it on your knees at a right angle to the table top so that about a third of the plate shows above the edge of the table. Hold the knife in the left hand and hold the left thumb against the back of the plate to keep it from falling into your lap. With the right hand pretend to start the plate spinning. Now you have to jiggle your knees a bit in order to make the plate look like it is in motion and the right thumb is now used to hold the plate upright as the left hand moves the knife blade across the edge of the "spinning" plate. If you can handle it, you can also make a hissing sound when you touch the knife to the edge of the plate. After three or four passes put the plate back on the table and try the knife blade against your thumb again, this time reacting as though it has become sharp. Pretend to remove a hair and split it with your newly sharpened knife. What you need is a round dinner plate without decoration. A floral pattern or a scalloped edge will destroy the illusion.

FROM SUGAR TO IVORY

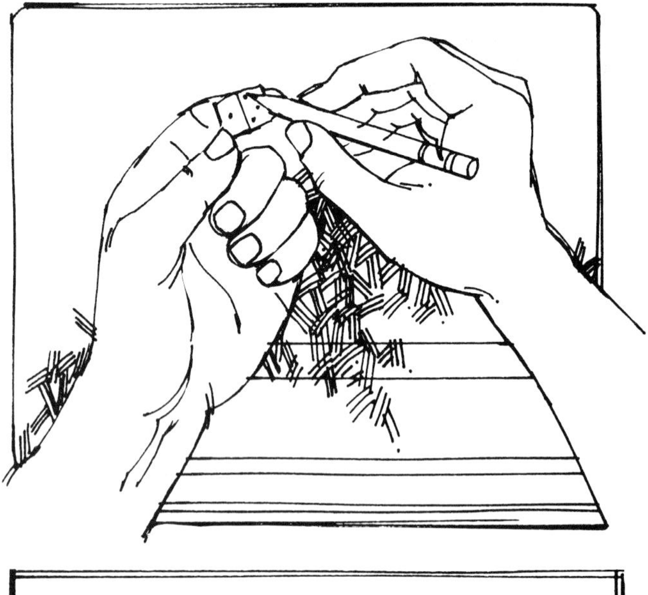

This sleight-of-hand trick allows you to transform sugar cubes marked like dice into real dice.

Props: 2 sugar cubes
a pencil
a pair of white dice with black dots

Advance Preparation: Keep a pair of real dice in your lefthand pocket.

To begin the trick, either announce what you intend to do or, perhaps even better, start to mark the dots on the sugar cubes and wait for someone to ask what you are doing.

With your left hand, casually return the pencil to your lefthand pocket. As you withdraw your hand from the pocket, finger palm the real dice in it.

Put the sugar cubes in your right hand and pretend to drop them into your left, but actually palm them in your right hand. After the transfer has apparently been made, immediately roll the real dice across the table from your left hand. At the same time, while the spectators' attention is on the real dice, drop the sugar dice into your lap.

When the dice stop rolling, the audience will see that sugar cubes have magically been transformed into real dice. If you have not announced the result you expected, you may wind up the trick by looking just as surprised as the audience.

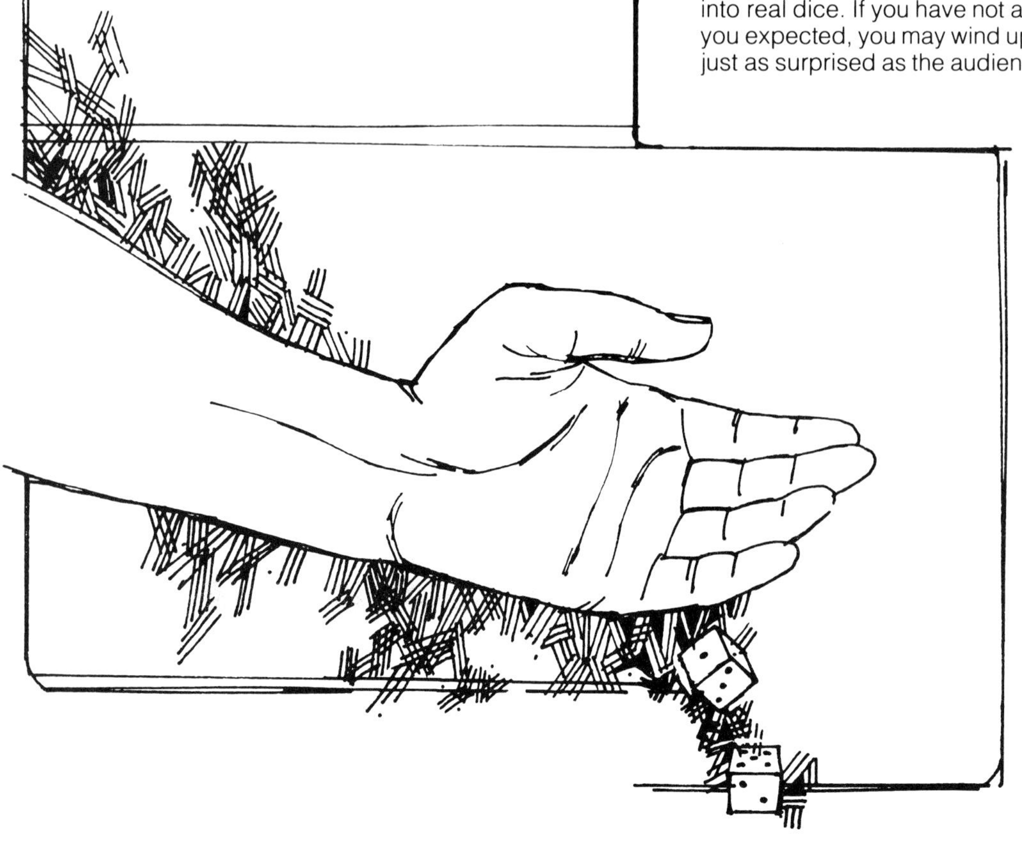

SWIZZLE SWITCH

This sleight is especially confusing to an audience that has seen the elastic pencil trick, because you appear to use the same technique but surprise your audience by proving the illusion was no illusion at all—the prop really is bent.

Props: 2 swizzle sticks
Advance Preparation: Bend one swizzle stick slightly in the middle by heating it. If made of glass, the stick will need a fairly hot flame. If the stick is of the plastic variety, a match flame will soften it enough to bend it. Keep the bent swizzle stick in your lap as you begin the trick.

Rather than announce the trick at all, merely wave the straight swizzle stick as you would for the Elastic Pencil trick (p. 37).

To increase the effect, consider letting another diner imitate your movements. As your victim hands the stick to you do a quick switch for the one in your lap and repeat the waving action with the bent stick.

Say abracadabra over the stick, explaining that this will freeze the stick in its bent state.

Stop shaking the swizzle stick and show your audience that it remains bent. Dispose of the straight swizzle stick in your lap by dropping it to the floor beneath the chair or slipping it into your pocket under cover of some other action.

If you don't care if they know how you did it, you can heat a plastic swizzle stick in the middle with a match and bend it over double; when it cools, it makes a practical tie clip.

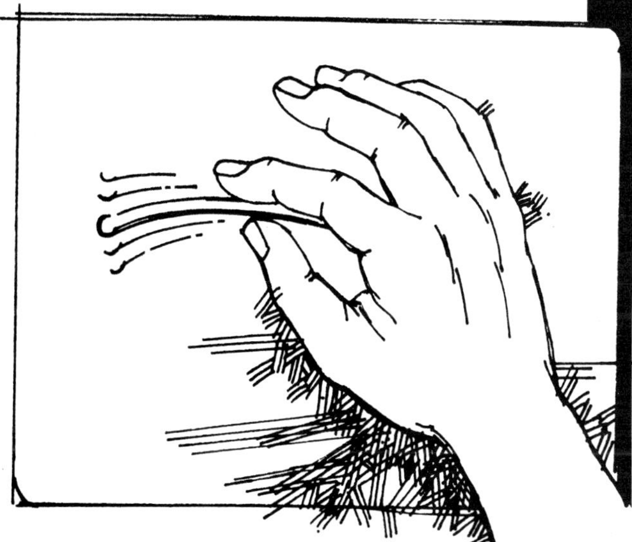

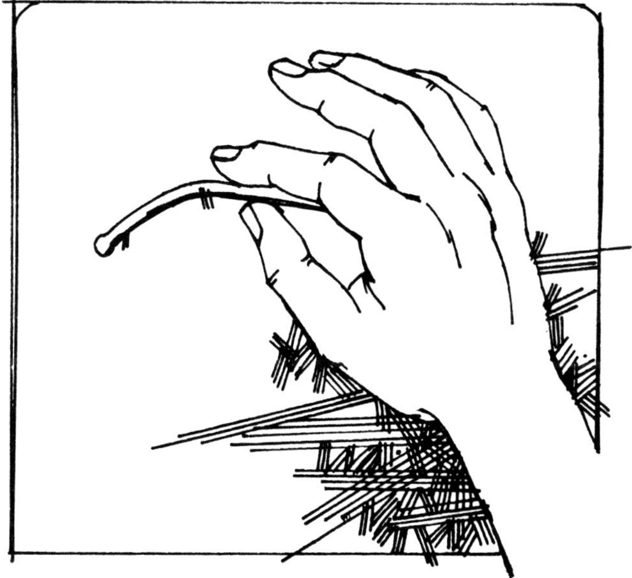

Most diners find it impossible to resist toying with paper placemats in restaurants, either by doodling on the paper or by ripping it into shreds absent-mindedly. Here you can show your inventiveness by coming up with new ways to annoy the waitress and amuse your dinner guests. Of course, you may do the following tricks with another sheet of paper if a placemat is not available.

RETURN OF THE X'S

With a little advance preparation, you can do this easy trick in which you force Xs drawn on paper squares to jump to blank squares of paper.

Props: a paper placemat (or other rectangular sheet of paper)
a pen or pencil (or other marker)
a match or lighter
an ashtray

Advance Preparation: Before announcing this trick, make four Xs on half the backside of a placemat or on the underside of another sheet of paper. Make sure that the Xs cannot be seen through the paper from the top.

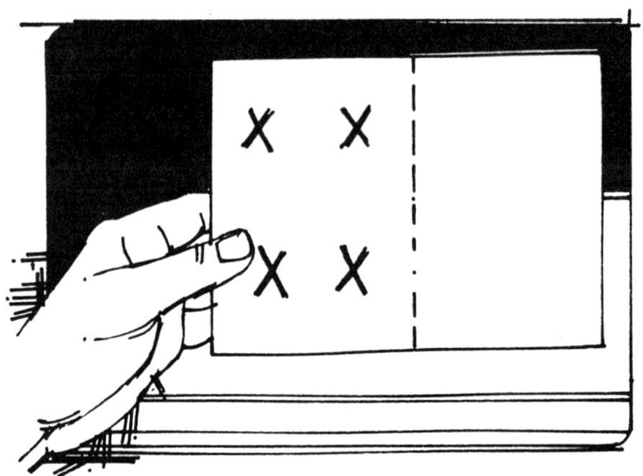

To start, explain what you intend to do and hold the previously marked paper just above the table so that your audience cannot see the Xs on the other side.

Now tear the paper in half so that all the Xs are on one half. Flip the unmarked side over to plant the suggestion that both sides of both halves are blank. However, it's a good idea not to draw attention to this verbally, or you will risk eliciting a request to show the other side of the marked paper, which would obviously kill the trick.

Place the unmarked half under the other half, then turn both pieces over.

Now tear the sheets in half and place one stack on top of the other.

Turn the stack over again and tear in half once more.

Stack one group of squares on top of the other. This gives you eight squares of paper, with alternating squares marked with an X.

Separate the squares into two piles again by dealing them one at a time from left to right. This places all the Xs in one stack.

Have a spectator choose one of the stacks of paper. If the victim chooses the lefthand pile, instruct him to hold the stack in a fist. If he chooses the righthand pile, make an X on each sheet in the stack and have the spectator hold the lefthand pile in a fist.

Now burn the pieces you have just marked with Xs (using the match and ashtray) as you incant over them.

Finally, have the spectator open his fist, where he will find the Xs mysteriously transferred to the alleged blank paper.

THE SECRET SIX

Props: a long strip of paper
a writing tool
Advance Preparation: Practice the trick a few times until you are sure you can remember the precise sequence of moves.

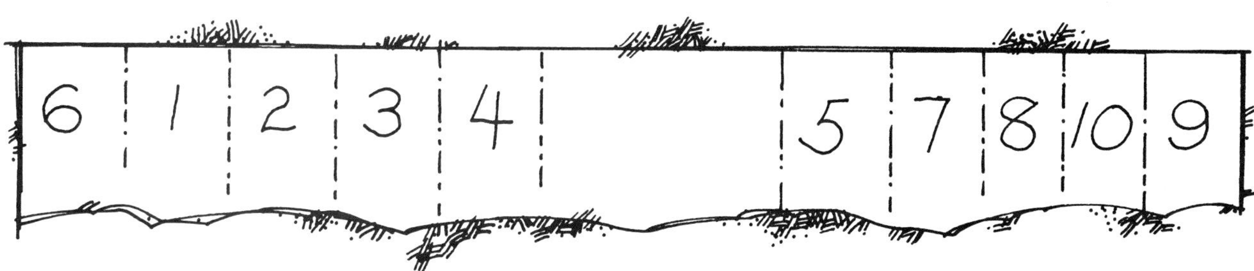

It tells you what to do just under the title. Look at the spectators and write the word "six" on a piece of paper, but don't let them see it. Tell them they are going to make a selection of a number by the process of elimination and you have one chance in eight of being right. Fold the prediction in quarters and cover it with a glass so everyone can see it but cannot touch it. Say, "I'll take a chance and make the odds more difficult for me. I'll make it one chance in ten that the prediction is right."

Tear a strip from the long edge of a placemat or otther paper sheet. Tear five small squares from each end.

Note that the two squares torn from each end will differ from the others in that two of their sides will be smooth; the others will have only one smooth side and three ragged ones.

Number the squares from 1 to 10, being sure to write the 6 and 9 on the two end squares. Also make sure you draw the 6 and 9 so that they are identical when one is inverted.

Turn the squares upside down so the numbers cannot be seen; then have your victim mix them around on the table.

Divide them into two piles of five squares each, making sure that the 6 is in one pile and the 9 in the other, using the two smooth edges as indicators.

Now have the victim tear up the squares in one of the two piles and throw them away. Either the 6 or the 9 will be in the remaining pile.

Have the spectator mix the five squares on the table again.

Now divide the squares into two piles—one of three and one of two squares. Make sure that the 6 or 9 is in the pile of two squares.

Tell the spectator to point to the pile of his choice. If he points to the three-square pile, tear it up. If he points to the two-square pile, tell him to keep a finger on it while you tear up the other.

Now turn the two squares face up so that the 6 or 9 appears to the spectator as a 6 only. Have the spectator choose one or the other of the two squares. If he chooses the one that is not a 6, tell him to tear it up. If he chooses the 6, tear up the other.

Now have one of the spectators lift the glass and read your prediction. Unless one of the spectators has switched predictions, the slip of paper will say "six."

You can use the smooth edge principle in several ways. Hand out about seven sheets of paper with rough or torn edges and one sheet from the corner with two smooth edges. Have the spectators write their phone numbers on the sheets. If you have handed the smooth sheet to a lady you want to know better, you can tell her phone number from the rest, and can hope her husband is not annoyed.

PLACEMAT PRANKS

HOW MANY HOLES?

This guessing game is for the table. It can be done with a large square of paper torn from a placemat or with a paper napkin. Announce that you intend to fold the paper, cut off a corner, and ask the spectators to guess the number of holes your cut has made in the paper.

Props: a paper napkin (or a placemat cut into a large square)
scissors

Advance Preparation: Memorize the exact sequence of folds described below to make sure you come up with the correct result every time.

This trick is interesting only because you must offer to make the folds slowly enough to allow the spectators to watch your every move. This is not a bluff; no sleight of hand is involved. However, this trick still fools most people.

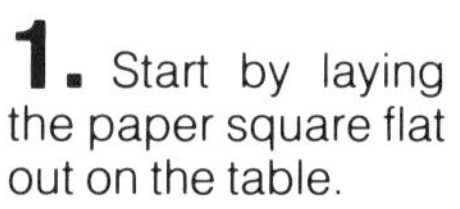

1. Start by laying the paper square flat out on the table.

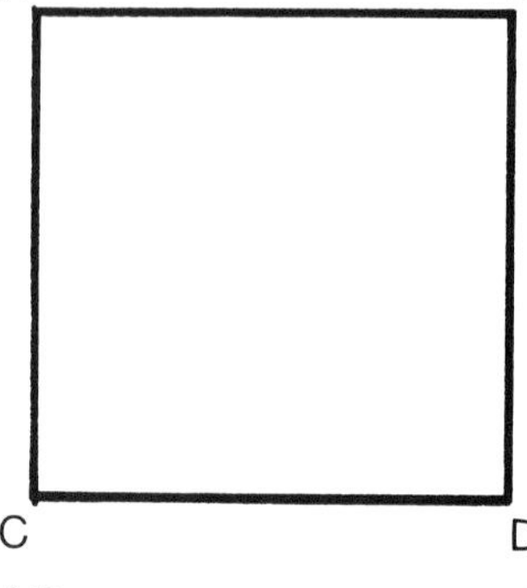

2. As shown in the diagram, fold corner D up to corner A.

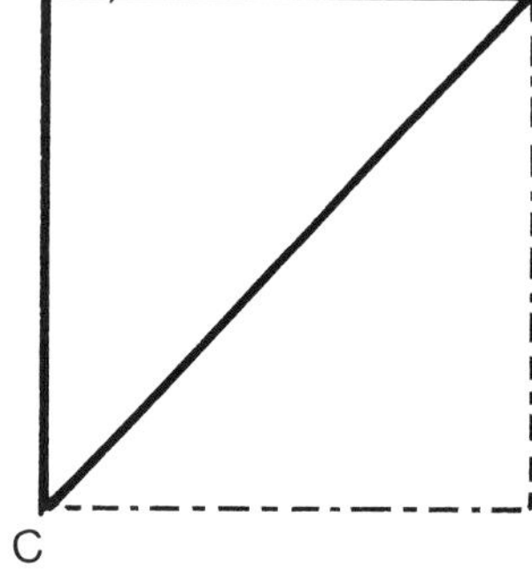

3. Now fold corner C up to corner B.

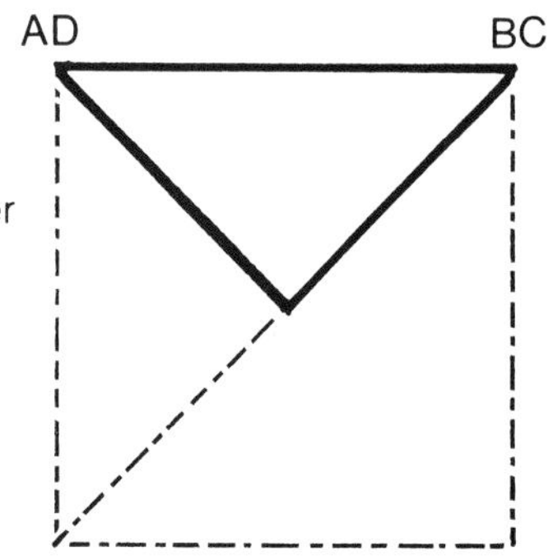

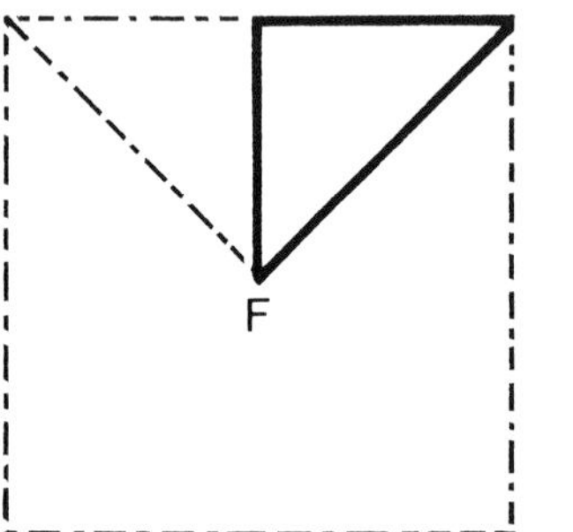

4. Next, fold the corner AD up to corner BC.

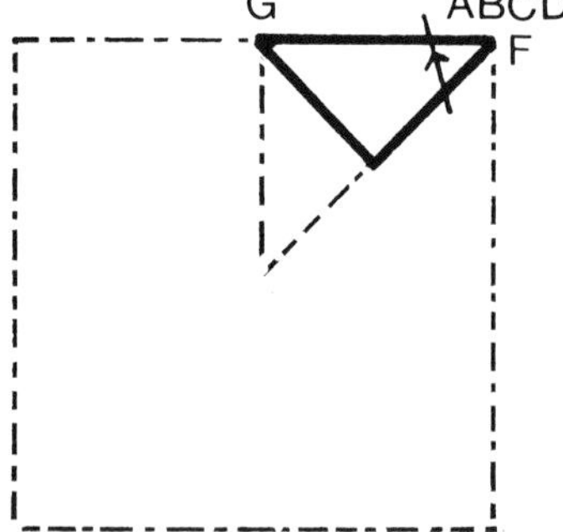

5. Finally, fold the new corner F up to corner BCAD.

6. Now snip off corner BCADF and ask the spectators to guess how many holes have been made in the paper. Hardly anyone will guess one, so open the sheet to amaze them all.

7. Now refold the same paper in the same sequence, remembering to proceed slowly so that your audience has every chance to guess correctly. Snip the corner marked G. Ask the audience how many *new* holes have been made. The answer is zero, but again, most people will be fooled.

THE ELASTIC PENCIL

Properly done this gives the amazing visual illusion of being a totally rubber pencil. People will pick up the pencil to be sure it is really wood.

Prop: a wooden pencil about 7 inches long
Advance Preparation: none

You pick up an old-fashioned wooden pencil and shake it so it looks like the whole thing is made of rubber. To do this, you hold the pencil loosely so the point hangs down slightly (Fig. 1). Now move the whole forearm up and down about 4 inches each way while retaining a loose hold on the pencil. The way it flops up and down is a great visual illusion (Fig. 2).

For a finish, drop the pencil on its rubber eraser end on the table and it will bounce. "It's not much good for writing, but it's great for erasing mistakes."

THE SHRINKING PENCIL

This illusion is similar to the trick above, but this time you make the pencil shrink. The moves are a little more difficult to execute, so you might want to practice in front of a mirror.

Prop: a pen or pencil (or any other long, uniform object such as a comb or a ruler)
Advance Preparation: The to-and-fro movements of the hands required for this trick must be uniform to obtain the desired effect, so some practice might be necessary.

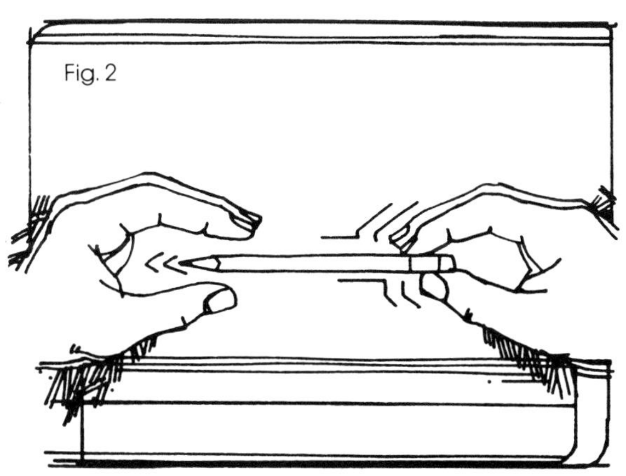

Tell your audience what you intend to do, then grab the pencil with one hand at each end. Your thumb and fingers should grip the pencil, with fingers pointing to the middle of the pencil.

To create the illusion, pass the pencil from one hand to the other, back and forth horizontally. The faster you pass the pencil, the more it will appear to shrink, but in general, your prop will appear to be reduced in length by about half.

Some of the most amusing—and sometimes shocking—tricks to do instantly at the dinner table are the body penetrations. The magician seems to push an object through one part of the body and reproduce it through another. Most should be performed without introduction to catch the audience by surprise, since these routines are intended to provoke a double take.

EAR-TO-EAR STRAW WRAPPER

Through this comic illusion, you can make your audience think you have unwrapped a standard soda straw by pushing the paper through one ear and out the other.

Props: 2 paper-wrapped soda straws

Advance Preparation: Unwrap one of the straws by sliding off the paper and compressing it into tight accordion-type folds. Secretly insert the paper wad into one ear.

Do not announce the trick, but keep in mind that you will not be able to repeat it without also repeating your secret preparation, so be sure you have everyone's attention before you begin.

Tear off the end of the second straw's wrapper and insert the unopened end of the straw in the ear opposite the one prepared with the wrapper. With one hand, slip the wrapper off the straw toward your ear, at the same time pulling the concealed wrapper from the other ear with the other hand.

Your timing must be correct, so that when the straw is unwrapped as far as possible, the whole wrapper has been withdrawn from the other ear.

Note that plastic straws may be the best props for this trick, since the paper wrappers will slide off smoothly.

BODY PENETRATIONS

THE PENETRATING PICK

This instant gag can be performed for friends at the dinner table or, obviously, at a cocktail party.

Props:
Advance Preparation: Hide one of the toothpicks in your right hand. A good method is to finger palm it as in the olive balancing trick (p. 51).

This trick needs no introduction. It may be repeated as many times as you like, as long as you do not dispose of the second toothpick at the end of the trick.

Start by casually placing one toothpick between your lips. As you talk casually about any subject of your choice, reach for the toothpick with your right hand. Pretend to remove it, but actually flip it into your mouth by tonguing it and substitute the finger palmed pick between your lips.

Immediately pull this toothpick out of your mouth, leaving the concealed one on your tongue, and put the toothpick point against your chin.

Now pretend to push the pick through your chin by moving your hand toward your chin and letting the pick slide back into your hand, where it should remain hidden. At the same time, let the tongued pick emerge from your mouth as though the toothpick penetrated your chin and came out through your lips.

To finish the trick, remove the pick from your mouth with your left hand. If you do not intend to do an encore, surreptitiously drop the right hand to your lap and let the second toothpick fall to the floor. If you do want to repeat the trick, merely keep the second pick palmed in your right hand and start over.

SEEDY EARS

This easy one can delight children at a picnic table. Simply pretend to empty your ears of watermelon seeds that supposedly have stuck there as you ate a slice of melon.

Prop: a slice of watermelon
Advance Preparation: As you eat the melon, secretly palm a pile of the seeds.

Announce the trick by shaking your head a little and grumbling about the seeds that somehow became stuck in your ears.

Tilt your head to one side and cup your hand with the palmed seeds at your ear. Pretend to wiggle your ear with the hand to loosen the seeds, then let the seeds pour out as if they came from the ear.

THE GREAT GRAPE ESCAPE

This real oldie is as effective as it is easy to perform. You create the startling illusion that a grape slapped into the top of your head penetrates your skull and pops out of your mouth.

Props: 2 grapes, cherries or shelled peanuts

Advance Preparation: Before anyone notices what you are doing, secretly put one of the grapes into your mouth and conceal it there.

To start, pick a grape from a bunch on the table and make a point of examining it in your right hand to attract the other diners' attention. Glare at the grape with disgust as though you have decided not to eat it for some reason.

Then pretend to drop it into your left palm, but palm it in the right. Drop the right hand with the grape into your lap.

Smack the top of your head with the left hand, which spectators think holds a grape. As soon as your hand touches your head, open your jaw and let the concealed grape fall out.

To vary the trick, show the grape in your mouth at the end, then pretend to remove it with your right hand, which holds the other grape. Suck the first grape back into your mouth as you open your right hand to show the second. This allows you to repeat the trick from the top if you did not catch everyone's attention the first time around.

SWORD SWALLOWING FOR THE DINNER TABLE

The classic conjurer's stage trick in which a three-foot sword is swallowed in toto is easily adapted to a common, blunt table knife. It is a simple trick but must be done with flair for the proper effect.

Prop: a table (butter) knife
Advance Preparation: Practice in front of a mirror. If you aren't convinced, no one else will be.

To begin, lay the knife along the edge of the table in front of you and cover it with your hands, the fingers of one hand overlapping the fingers of the other slightly.

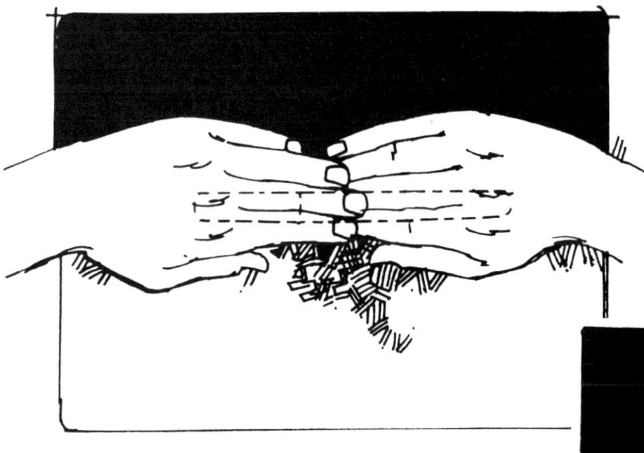

Holding the knife with your thumbs, lift your hands and tilt your head backward to a position you would adopt if you really did intend to swallow the knife.

Pretend to swallow the knife, choking and gasping as you do so. Then replace the knife on the table edge and proceed to prepare the knife in some way to make it suitable for the trick—salt it, warm it in your hands, wet it with water or come up with some other ploy that you can claim will help you do the trick correctly the next time.

Now try it again, lifting the knife from the table edge in the same way, but this time, when you slide your hands off the table, ostensibly to lift the knife, let the knife slide into your lap.

Now raise your hands to your mouth, holding them so that the audience cannot see they hold no knife.

Slowly lower your hands toward your mouth as though you are pushing the knife into it; accompany your actions with convincing sound effects.

End the trick by reproducing the knife through one of the various methods, so the audience does not just watch as you pull it from your lap, giving away your magic secrets.

For instance, a few minutes later, you may reach for your napkin in a nonchalant manner, at the same time picking up the knife and placing the napkin (with knife underneath) on the table after wiping your mouth. Or, you may sleeve the knife and then find it—to your surprise. Or, you may slip it up and inside your jacket, pretending to pull it from an inside pocket with the other hand.

Many instant tricks are based on unexplained movement of an object, or mysterious magnetic forces, and on other supernatural influences that come to bear on your props. For the most part, the simplest versions actually rely on down-to-earth preparation by the magician. Following are some of the easiest tricks for the beginner to perform.

THE MAGNETIC PENCIL

This trick, known in magic circles, still may fool the uninitiated.

Prop: a wooden pencil with hexagonal sides

Advance Preparation: Try this at home, and if you find you need a little help from the "spirits," secretly moisten the fleshy part of your palm at the base of your fingers before starting the trick.

To start, boast that you can train the pencil to adhere to your hand without holding it with your fingers. Put the pencil on the table and then lay a hand across it so that the pencil lies in the crease between your palm and fingers. Quickly raise your hand and show the audience how the pencil clings to it. If your hands are naturally damp, or if the palm is particularly fleshy, you won't need any assistance from the water.

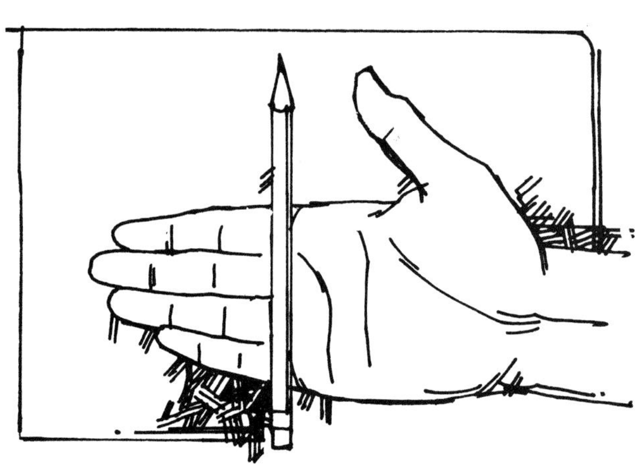

KNIFE WITH INVISIBLE GLUE

This trick and the alternate versions following resemble the preceding trick. Vary this concept to your liking, even combining several of the methods in one performance.

Prop: a blunt table knife
Advance Preparation: none

1. Lay the knife across your left palm and point the fingers toward your audience. Then grab the wrist with your other hand.

2. Grip the knife with your thumb, then raise both hands toward the right side of your body, turning the back of the hand that holds the knife toward your audience. Now lift your thumb and let the knife drop to the table or floor.

Apologize for your failure and attempt to put a spell on the knife to magnetize it.

3. Start the routine again, but this time, as you raise and turn your hands, quickly and secretly extend your right forefinger across the left palm to hold the knife where it is. Now you can lift your thumb and the knife will remain glued to your hand.

4. You can end the trick with a laugh by pretending you cannot shake the knife off your hand, finally loosening the pressure of your forefinger to let it drop.

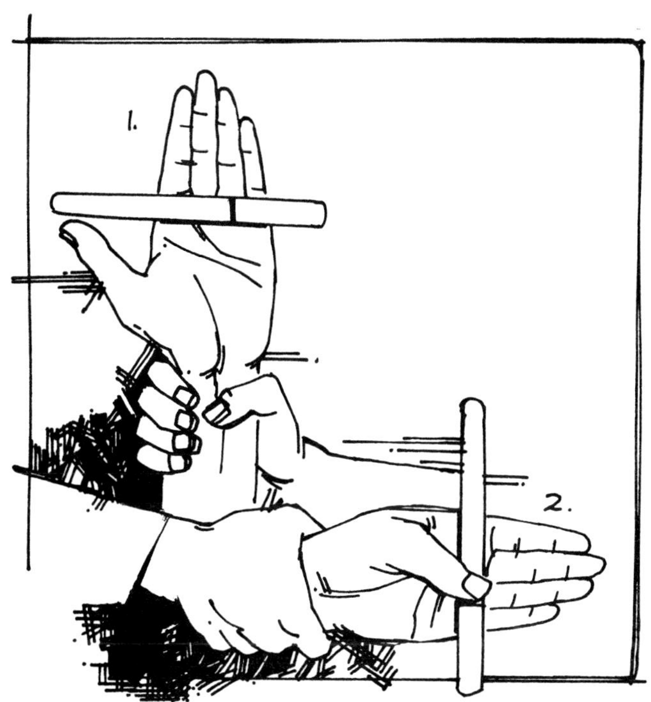

MAGNETIC KNIFE II

In this version, you need an additional prop, so it is not quite as instant.

Props: a blunt table knife
a pencil
a wristwatch (preferably with an elastic band)
Advance Preparation: Wear a long-sleeved jacket or shirt and insert the pencil into the watch band so that most of it is hidden by the sleeve.

Run through the same routine as in the previous trick, but just before turning your hands, use the hand around the wrist to extend the pencil far enough forward to hold the knife in place. Then astound the viewers by removing your hand from the wrist without letting the knife drop.

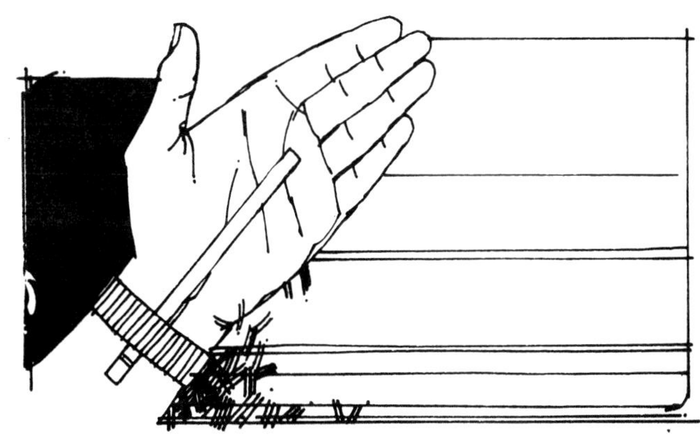

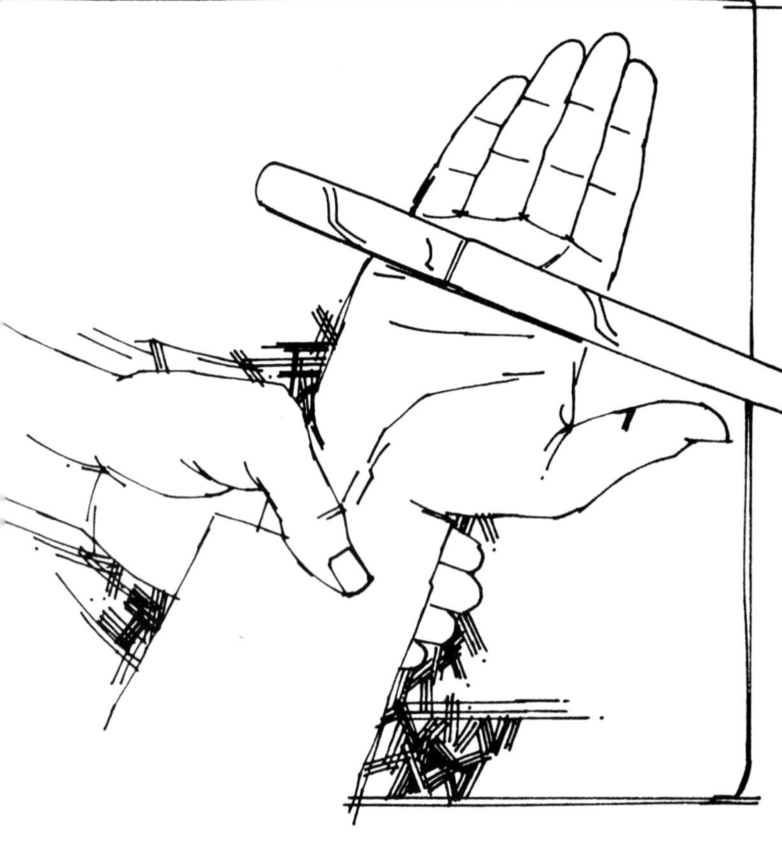

MAGNETIC KNIFE III

This is possibly the oldest known version of the trick.

Props: 2 blunt table knives
Advance Preparation: Before announcing the trick, conceal one knife up your sleeve.

1. Start by holding the knife across your palm as in the preceding versions, but when you grip your wrist with the other hand, make sure the thumb is on the inside and all four fingers are across the back of your wrist.

2. Now raise your hands and flip them so that the backs of the hands face the audience. As you do so, slide the fingers and thumb along your wrist to "magnetize" your hand, secretly sliding the sleeved knife down to hold the other knife in place.

3. To finish the trick, slide the hand without the knife slowly up the wrist as if to demagnetize it, but actually resleeve the second knife.

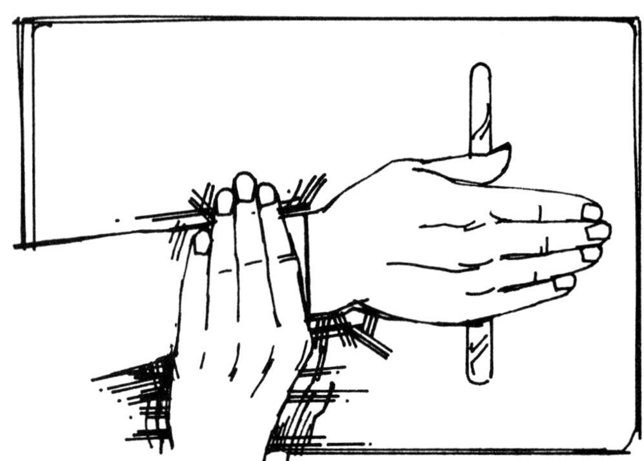

SPECTATORS' VIEW

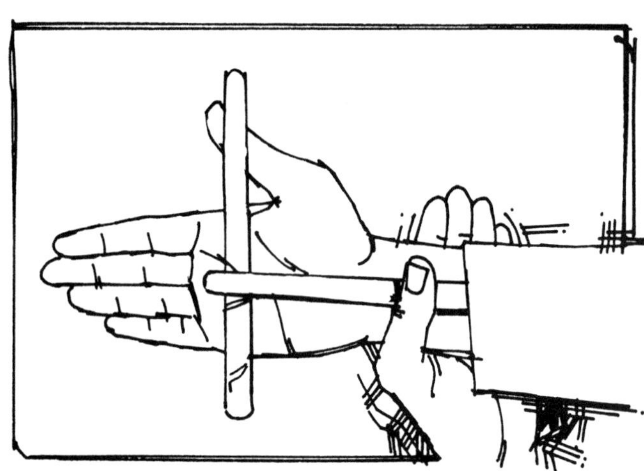

MAGICIAN'S VIEW

MAGNETIC KNIFE IV

In this version, clasped hands create an illusion for the audience.

Prop: a blunt table knife

Advance Preparation: You may need some practice to do this trick, because success depends on intertwining all fingers of both hands alternately except for a middle finger, which is left against your palm out of the audience's view. This finger holds the knife in place. It is amazing how few people will notice from the outside that a finger is missing, but don't press your luck—do the trick quickly.

1. Hold the knife in one hand by pressing it against your fingers with your thumb. Show this to the audience.

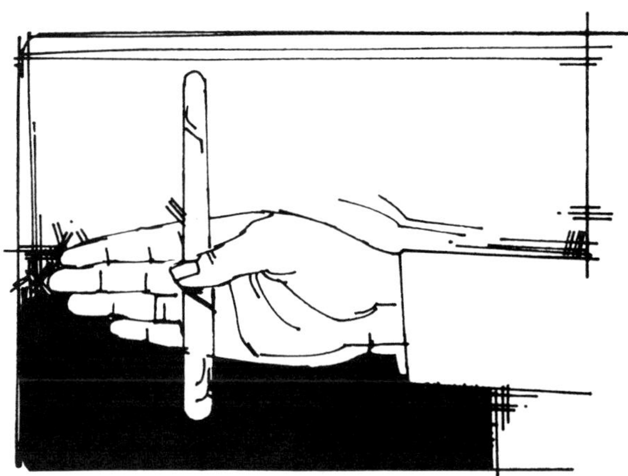

2. Still holding the knife with your thumb, intertwine your fingers as shown in the picture. With your middle finger holding the knife, lift your thumb to show that the knife is adhering to your hand. Note that the middle finger must go over the knife as you clasp your hands.

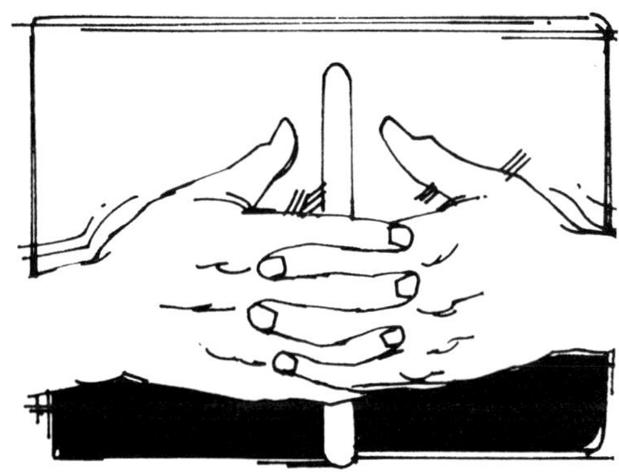

3. To end the trick, try to shake off the knife, never showing your palms to the audience, and finally succeed by bending your middle finger toward its palm (at the large joint) to release the knife.

MAGNETIC KNIFE V

This simplest version may seem a cheater to purists.

Prop: a blunt table knife with a bulge or ridge at the beginning of the handle (where it meets the blade)

Advance Preparation: Try the trick beforehand to make sure the knife you plan to use is the correct shape and weight.

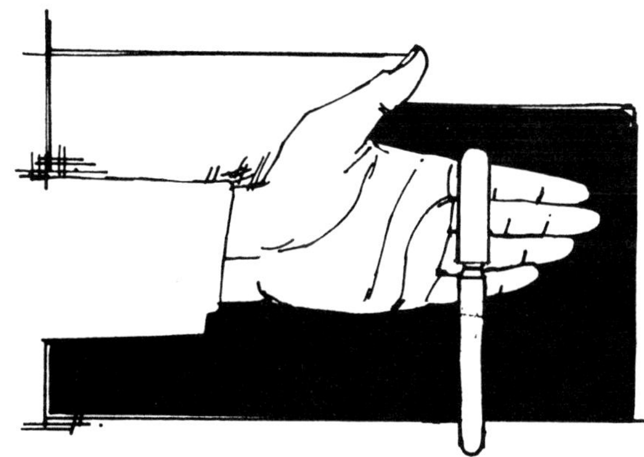

Lay the knife across your palm, with the blade pointing toward your little finger. Slowly tilt your hand until it is almost vertical. The knife will be held there by the ridge against your pinkie.

THE SPIRIT RING

This interesting trick attributable to the forces beyond is most effective when accompanied by much buildup and constant patter. A ring on a rubber band moves back and forth in a mysterious way. This allows you to use the ring as an indicator of all sorts of things. For example, you can say that when the ring moves to the left, your chosen victim is telling the truth; when it moves to the right, he is lying. Or, use it as a fortune telling device in which the direction of the movement indicates either a yes or no answer to a question posed by a spectator.

Props: a narrow rubber band
a ring
Advance Preparation: none

Announce the trick, tear the rubber band at one point, and make it into a rubber string. Slip any ring (a borrowed wedding band is suitable) onto the band and grasp each end of the band in a hand.

Stretch the band as far as possible without breaking it again. Then shift the ring into the middle of the band.

To move the ring, lessen the pressure of one hand. If you loosen the grip of your left hand, for instance, the ring will move toward your right hand.

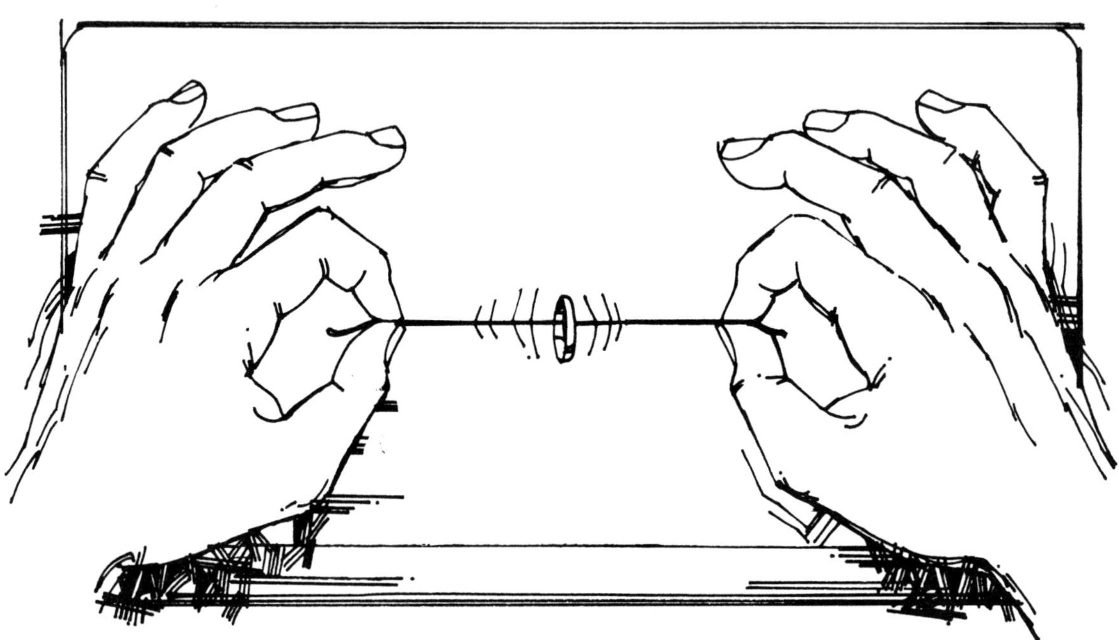

In the following tricks, the magician forces one prop to penetrate another for intriguing results.

ROD AND NAPKIN PENETRATION

A great instant trick occurs when any rod-type object is apparently pushed through a cloth napkin without puncturing a hole in the napkin. It is particularly good for beginners.

Props: a pen, pencil, table knife, cigarette, or any other rod-like object
a cloth napkin or handkerchief
Advance Preparation: none

1. After introducing the trick, spread the napkin over your left hand, which is closed into a fist. Have a spectator form a well in the cloth by pushing the cloth into your fist with a finger. Make an excuse for making the well deeper and insert your own forefinger into your fist, pointing your middle finger downward and resting it in the angle formed by your closed fingers and thumb of the fist.

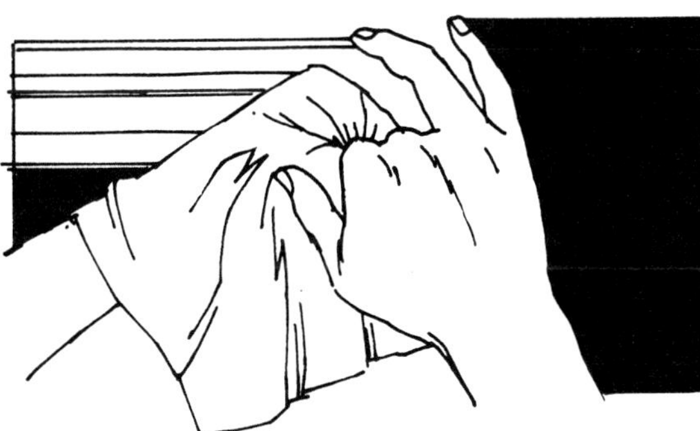

2. Now secretly open your fist a bit and grasp the middle finger through the napkin, closing your fist again around it.

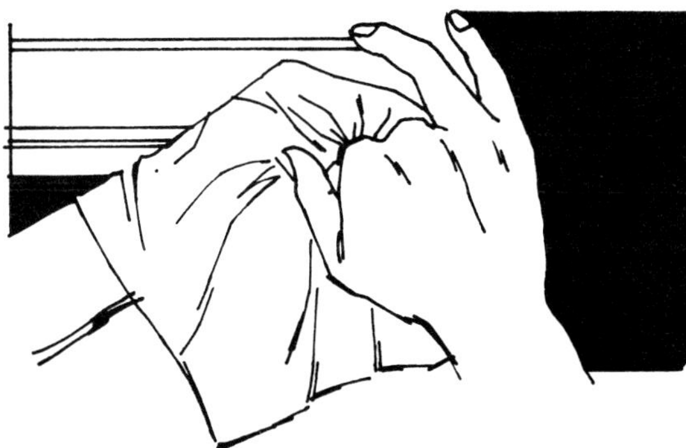

3. Now take your forefinger out of the cloth well.

4. Pretend to smooth out the sides of the well with your middle finger, using this excuse to twist your hand around the middle finger. This creates an extra cylinder in the cloth with open ends, which is invisible to the audience.

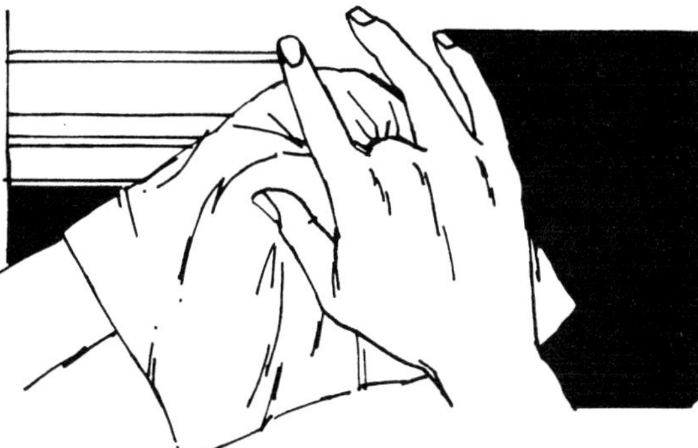

5. Now insert the pencil through the top of the well and with a flourish let it fall to the floor through your cloth-covered fist. Open your hand and show the napkin to the audience; there will be no hole in it.

DINNER TABLE PENETRATIONS

SWEETENING YOUR COFFEE

This is a good quicky for the dinner table, especially when you have reached the dessert course and are about to drink coffee or tea.

Props: 2 paper-wrapped sugar lumps
a cup of coffee or tea

Advance Preparation: Secretly remove one sugar lump from its wrapper and then refold the wrapper carefully so it will look as if the sugar is still inside. Palm the unwrapped lump in your left hand. Put the empty wrapper back into the sugar bowl, but remember which is your prop.

To start the trick, take the rigged sugar wrapper from the bowl and place it on the back of your left hand, which is poised above your coffee cup. Make sure that no one can see the palmed sugar lump in that hand.

With your right hand, smack the back of the left hand with vigor, simultaneously dropping the palmed lump into the cup.

SILVERWARE PENETRATION

This penetration, using a slightly different technique, is relatively foolproof for beginners. After rolling a piece of silverware in a cloth napkin, you unroll it to discover it has penetrated the cloth to appear on the outside of the napkin.

Props: a piece of silverware (or a pen or pencil)
a cloth napkin or handkerchief

Advance Preparation: none

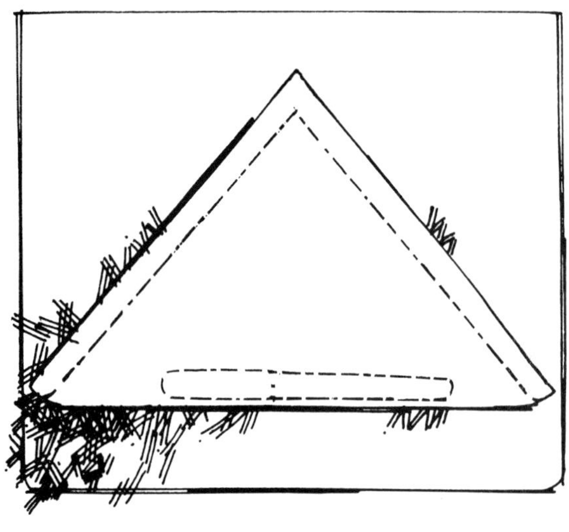

Announce the trick, then lay the napkin on the table, with corners pointing north, south, east, and west. Place the silverware across the napkin from east to west.

Now fold the south corner of the napkin up to meet the north corner, but be sure to extend the south corner about an inch above the north corner, without letting your audience notice this move.

Now lay your palms flat on the pencil through the cloth and roll the napkin with them all the way up to the corners, allowing the north corner to rotate around the roll once, but hiding this move with your palms.

Let the spectator you have chosen as a victim hold both the north and south corners on the table with a finger as you unroll the napkin toward you. The silverware will appear on the outside of the napkin, and the napkin remains whole and unpunctured.

THIMBLE PENETRATION

Another good penetration for instant magicians, this is best suited for the living room, where it may be more convenient for your host or hostess to get up and find a thimble.

Props: a thimble large enough to fit on your middle finger
a cloth napkin or handkerchief

Advance Preparation: none

Announce the trick, then put the thimble on the tip of your right middle finger. Hold up the edge of the napkin, gripping it between the left forefinger and middle finger.

Place the napkin in front of your right hand, lowering the middle finger with the thimble to point toward you, and raising your forefinger in its place.

Drape the cloth over the forefinger, which the audience will think is your middle finger with the thimble. At the same time, the left hand that holds the cloth moves so that the crease between your thumb and forefinger can pull the thimble off your right middle finger.

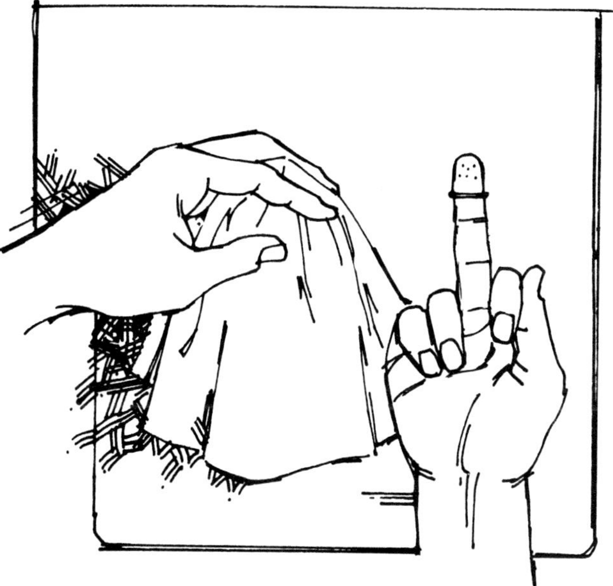

Now move the left hand (with the thimble) away and make a fist to grab the right forefinger through the cloth. Under cover of the fist, slip the thimble over your right forefinger and the cloth, then squeeze your fist as if to effect the penetration.

Now remove your fist to show the thimble on the outside of the napkin.

Perhaps the most effective tricks of the instant variety are those that do not fall into any other category of magic skills. These are the spontaneous gags and pranks you can do at the dinner table or in the living room on a moment's notice, and for the most part they are guaranteed to elicit a laugh, a double take or at least a raised eyebrow. To perform these tricks, it is best not to say anything at all in the way of announcement, because this has a tendency to lessen the effect.

While the props required for the following tricks can all be found on the dinner table or somewhere in the average household, the techniques often are based on some type of gimmick or scientific property. For this reason, and because of the tricks' simplicity, a big buildup will usually lead to just as big a letdown. The key to success in this type of instant magic is the element of surprise.

DINNER TABLE STRONGMAN

This simple trick can be introduced as a boast. Claim to be the strongest person at the table and proceed to prove it by demonstrating that only you can tear a twisted paper napkin in half by pulling on its ends.

Props: a paper napkin
a glass of water (or a glass covered with condensation)

Advance Preparation: Make sure the water glass is within reach before starting.

As you expound on your magnificent strength, twist a paper napkin into a tightly rolled length resembling a rope.

After one or more victims have been humiliated, take the napkin back by grabbing it in the middle with your wet fingers.

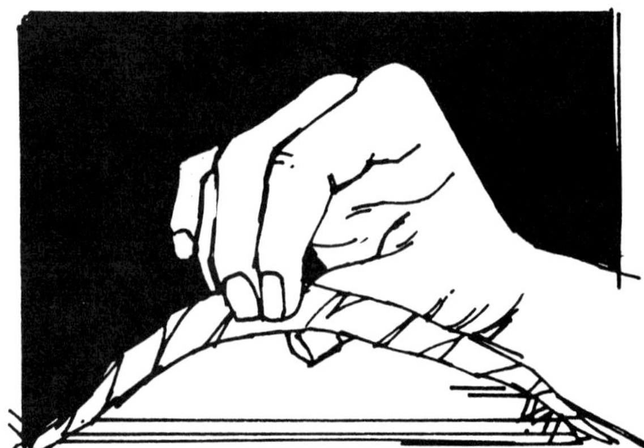

Hand the napkin to your first challenger and have him try to tear it in half by tugging on the ends. As you and the other diners laugh at the victim's failure, wet the fingers on one hand by subtly dipping your fingertips into a water glass as you drink from it, or by merely gripping the glass if it is covered with a healthy coating of condensation.

Now, before anyone notices the moisture on the paper, quickly pull apart the napkin ends and, with the appropriate groans of exertion, tear the napkin in two.

THE AMAZING OLIVE BALANCE

Another challenge trick, this is more impressive if others first try the feat. Merely suggest you can balance an olive on your fingertip for an indefinite period of time. Then let your fellow diners (or drinkers) try it so they will be suitably impressed when you succeed after they fail.

Props: an olive (any type)
a toothpick

Advance Preparation: Secretly hold a toothpick behind your forefinger before starting the trick. But keep in mind that diners to either side of you may be able to see it.

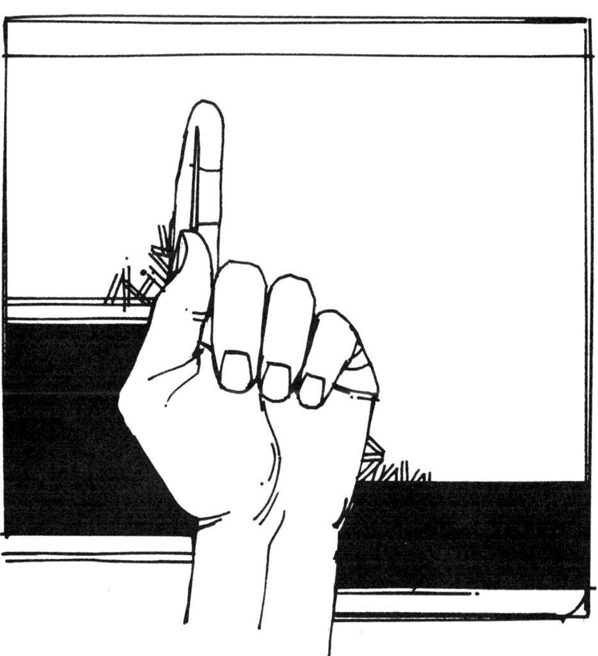 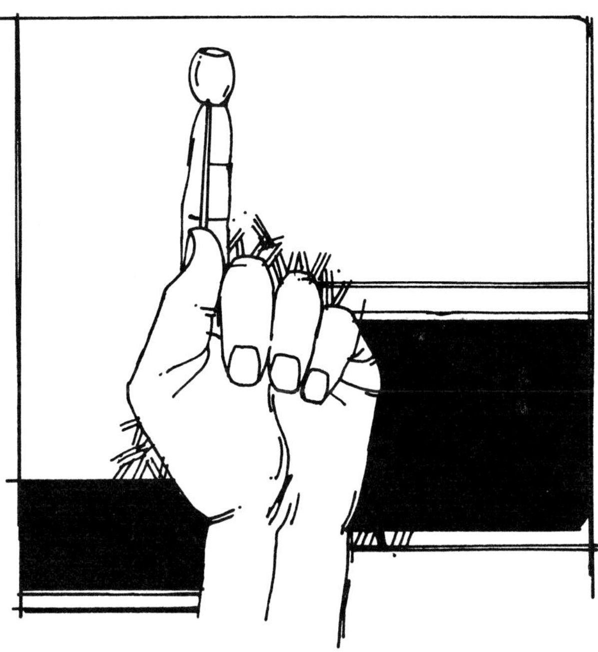

To start, pick up an olive from a bowl on the table or from the bottom of a martini glass and make your challenge. Note that other bits of food may be used but should be tested ahead of time for suitability. The olive is particularly appropriate because the toothpick pierces it easily.

When your victims fail to balance the olive on their fingertips, take it in your hand and point the forefinger of the other hand, which is equipped with the toothpick, upward with the back of the hand facing your audience.

Stick the olive on your fingertip, holding it there by subtly sliding the toothpick up and into it a fraction of an inch.

To increase the effect, move your finger around while the olive is balanced on it. For a nifty finish, you might even dip the finger toward the floor. Watch the looks of shock as the olive remains on your fingertip, and then expose the toothpick for a laugh.

SEASICK (OR TIPSY) PUPPET

Stage this for the amusement of your fellow diners; it makes use of standard table items.

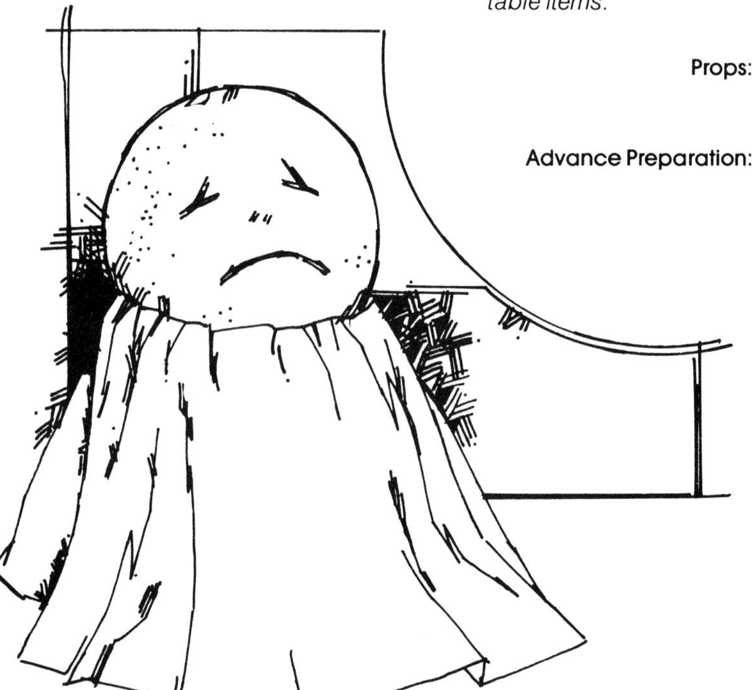

Props: an orange (or other spherical fruit)
a sharp knife
a glass with an opening narrower than the orange
a cloth napkin (or placemat)

Advance Preparation: No preparation is necessary, although you can create the puppet and bring it into the room for the performance.

To start, tell your audience some story about the puppet as you create it at the table. Say that the puppet is either seasick or drunk. Cut appropriate facial features into the orange skin with a knife, depending on the expression you want the puppet to take on. Drape the napkin over the mouth of the glass and rest the orange head on top.

To simulate a seasick or drunken sailor, pull the edges of the napkin back and forth, causing the orange head to roll on the glass. With a little experimentation, you can make the puppet execute other movements. For instance, try pushing the glass across the table in a zigzag pattern while pulling the napkin, to simulate drunken stumbling.

RADISH SUCTION CUP

This simple but startling feat needs no introduction. However, you might introduce the trick as a strength stunt, asking fellow diners how much they would bet that you cannot lift a clean plate with a radish.

Props: a radish (preferably with stem on)
a dinner or salad plate
a sharp knife

Advance Preparation: Try this several times in advance to determine how much weight you can lift with the radish.

After all bets are in, cut the radish in half crosswise, hollowing out one of the cut sides to make it slightly concave.

Press the radish half into the middle of the plate and then amaze your friends by lifting the plate with the radish stem.

THE FLOATING ROLL

This impromptu trick needs no introduction as you magically make a bread roll or other food rise from the table, as if possessed by some occult force, and wait for others at the table to notice.

Props: a hard roll or a piece of fruit
a cloth napkin
a fork

Advance Preparation: While no one is paying attention to you, put the roll or fruit on the table next to your plate and fork. Place the napkin over the roll and the fork, then subtly stick the fork into the roll.

To start, wait until at least one person is looking your way, then grab the corners of the napkin near you (corners A and B in the diagram), one corner with each hand, secretly holding the fork with one hand as well. Note that the fork should pierce the roll so that the handle tilts downward a bit. At this angle, the fork will not be seen when the roll is raised.

Slowly lift the fork and napkin corners off the table. Corners C and D will drape over the roll, hanging in front of it so that anyone across the table from you will have a hard time seeing the fork outline anyway.

The best way to carry off this trick is to act as though the roll is pulling the napkin upward, taking your hands along with it. Ham it up by actually standing up as the roll continues to rise higher and

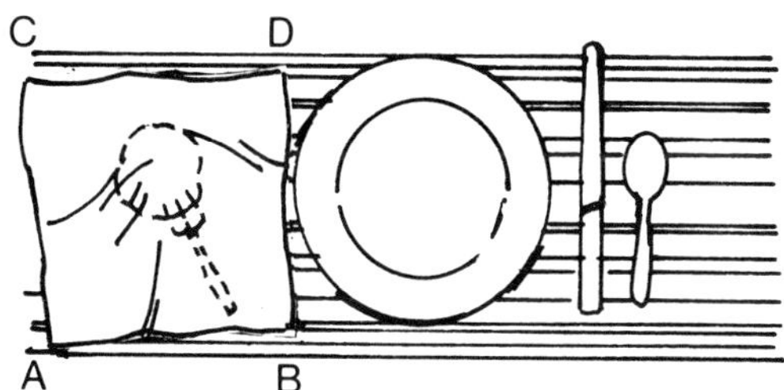

higher, then sitting down when it takes a sudden plunge.

To finish, pretend you are exerting tremendous pressure on the roll to push it back to the table. When you have done so, slip your hand under the napkin as if to hold the roll down while you remove the napkin, secretly pulling the fork out and leaving it beside your plate again.

THE WANDERING SHOES

Though a funny gag to pull on your friends, it is sure to elicit disapproving glances from diners at an elegant soiree. The whole trick lies in magically transferring your shoe from your foot to the dinner table. As such, it requires no introduction. The effect is enhanced when the magician looks just as surprised and embarrassed by the discovery as the audience.

Props: a shoe
a cloth napkin

Advance Preparation: At an opportune moment during the meal, subtly remove one shoe and put it on your lap.

To start, talk about the Hindu mango tree trick—or was it the Hindu rope trick? With the right hand, drape the table napkin from the left shoulder over the curved left arm. As you are doing this, the left hand is grasping the toe of the shoe in your lap and pivoting it under the napkin undetectably. The right hand brushes under the left as though to clear the table. The left hand lowers the shoe onto the table.

With either hand, whip the napkin up and away to display the shoe, immediately looking shocked and embarrassed, and quickly place the shoe on the floor and put your foot in it—if you haven't already.

THE RISING THREAD

This miniature version of the Hindu rope trick is especially simple since it is based on the nature of static electricity. Again, announcements are not needed. On the other hand, it is important to develop amusing narrative while doing the trick, since most adults will catch on to the technique.

Props: a comb
a small piece of thread

Advance Preparation: Keep the comb and thread in a pocket. Before doing the trick, charge the comb with static electricity, done easily by combing your hair. Since hair combing at the dinner table is usually frowned upon, you might excuse yourself for a moment; this will also make the static electricity more baffling.

When you return to the table, casually pull the comb and thread from your pocket. Either hold onto the thread with one hand and the comb with the other, or leave the thread hanging out of your pocket when you leave the room. You may then look amazed when the thread follows the comb as the comb is taken from the pocket.

With the comb a few inches above the end of the thread, you can make the thread stand up straight. Moving the comb in various directions makes the thread move likewise.

If the comb retains enough electric charge, you may proceed to pick up other lightweight objects with the comb, such as shreds of paper, or, at a child's party, floating balloons.

SPOON MOVIES

Some amazingly realistic moving pictures can be created by wiggling your fingers in front of a spoon. The reflection created on the spoon's back bears a striking resemblance to the movements of a human body. This is a puppet-type trick that must be accompanied by bright chatter for the best effect.

Prop: a metal spoon

Advance Preparation: It is a good idea to practice these routines so the position and movements of your fingers will create the desired effect. The following are just two common scenes you might create.

Start by announcing the title of your movie. Hold the spoon handle in your left fingers with the back of the spoon toward you. Spectators must be at your side to see the movies.

To create a diver going into a pool, put the middle and ring fingers of your right hand on the table edge, with the forefinger and pinkie straight and aimed up and out to the sides. Hold the spoon 6 to 8 inches in front of your hand, adjusting its position until the image of the diver is centered in the spoon. Your thumb should not appear in the reflection.

Move the two straightened fingers up and down in unison to simulate the diver's arms swinging for momentum on the dive. To make the subject dive, move your entire hand up and back (toward the back of your wrist).

Embellish on the routine by adding other movements, using your imagination and various small items from the table if you wish to add props to the movie.

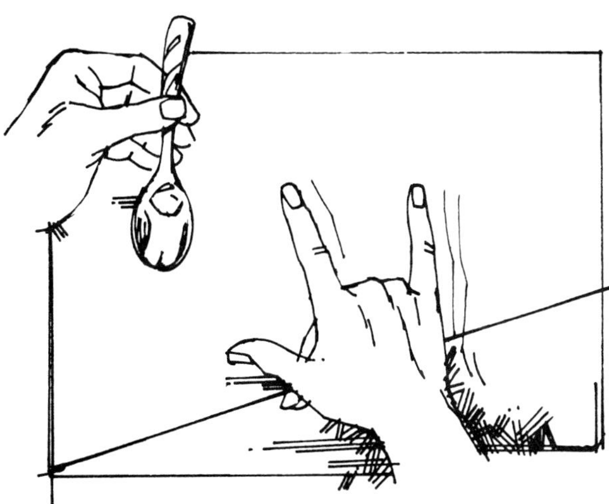

A similar movie can be made of a person bathing in a tub. Close your right hand into a fist, then lift the forefinger and pinkie but keep both bent at the knuckles. Place the back of the spoon against your hand.

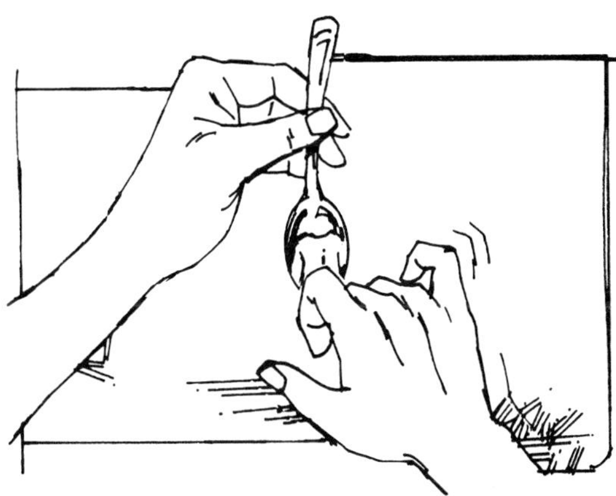

This will create a picture of a bather bending over in the tub, as viewed from behind. By moving the forefinger and pinkie alternately, you simulate arms scrubbing the body. Tilt your hand and move your forefinger and pinkie in different directions to make the bather drop and pick up the soap, bend over to wash feet, and so on. Use the same move as described for the diver to make the bather leap from the tub.

THE MYSTERIOUS RICE BOWL

This old trick, said to have originated in India, can be done by anyone anywhere. It is perfect for the dinner table and adapts itself to a challenge or wager. Claim that you can lift a bowl of rice off the table by plunging an ordinary knife into it.

Props: raw rice
a table knife
a bowl or jar with mouth narrower than the sides

Advance Preparation: You may incorporate this preparation into your introduction of the trick, although it may be more effective to prepare your props before you confront your audience. Fill the bowl with rice a little at a time, constantly packing the grains close together by pressing with your fingers. Continue adding rice until it reaches the brim and you cannot press it down further.

After announcing the trick, start poking the knife into the bowl in shallow jabs. Give a phony reason for this; actually, this helps to back the rice more firmly. Keep your commentary going as you do so, because it may take quite a few thrusts of the knife to pack it as tightly as required.

After you have given about twenty jabs, try to lift the bowl by plunging the knife deep into it. If the rice is packed firmly enough, the knife will catch and the bowl will be lifted along with the knife. If it does not work this time, do a few more shallow jabs with the knife, then try the deep plunge again.

To finish the trick by completely baffling the audience, twist the knife imperceptibly and then allow a spectator to pull it out. It will withdraw with ease, forcing the audience to conclude that you really do have some magical power over your props.

THE REFORMED PENCIL

*This classic impromptu trick can be done nearly anywhere, so long as some-
one in the vicinity has a wooden pencil. Pretend to break a pencil in half, then
proceed to restore it to its original state—without scars.*

Prop: a wooden pencil
Advance Preparation: Before making empty boasts, make sure your fingernails are long and strong enough to make an audible snapping noise when one thumbnail is clicked against the other.

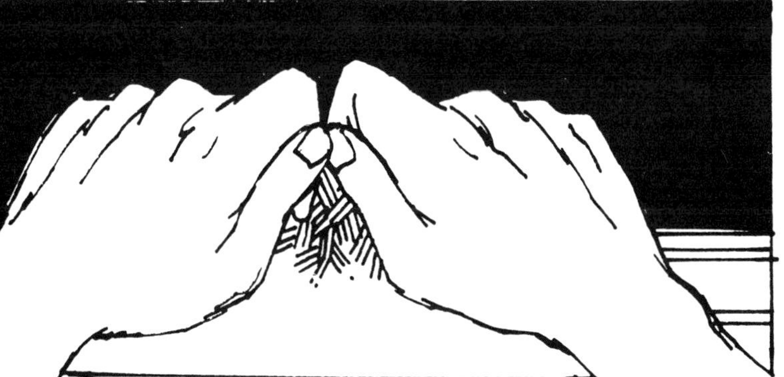

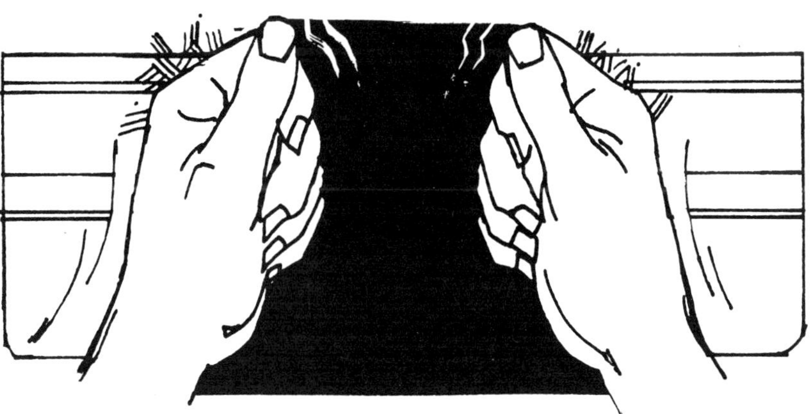

After announcing the trick, place the pencil a few inches from the table edge
and parallel to it. With palms downward and thumbs overlapping a bit, pretend
to lift the pencil from the table, but actually roll it off the edge into your lap.

Lift your hands off the table in the same position, as if you are holding the
concealed pencil. Pretend to break the pencil in half by twisting your hands
quickly, simultaneously snapping one thumbnail off the other.

Now open your hands to show that the pencil has disappeared.

Naturally, a discriminating audience will want to see the pencil again, so you
may finish by reproducing it in its whole state by various methods. A traditional
move that fools them every time is to secretly pick the pencil up from your lap
with your left hand and shove it up inside your jacket as you open that side of
the jacket with your right hand to remove it.

THE PAPER CLOCK

This little parlor invention is suited to children. Draw a clock on a sheet of paper, then produce a realistic ticking sound as you hold the clock to a child's ear.

Props: a sheet of paper
a pen or pencil
Advance Preparation: none

Tell your young audience you will make a clock for them; draw a clock face on the paper.

Hold the paper between forefinger and middle finger of one hand, with the thumb hidden behind the paper.

Now prove that the clock really works by holding the paper to a child's ear and reproducing the ticking sound by clicking the nail of the middle finger against the nail of the thumb.

RUBBER BAND TRANSPOSITION

This nifty trick can be done anywhere with just two rubber bands!

Props: two rubber bands
Advance Preparation: none

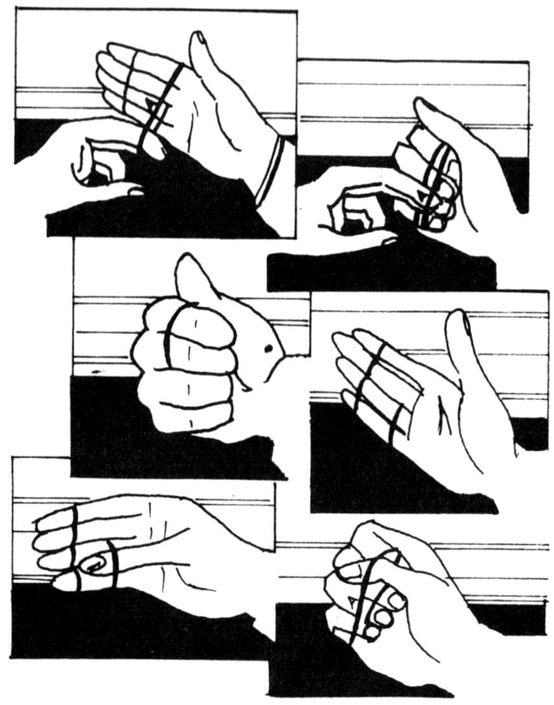

Place one rubber band around the first and second fingers of your right hand as shown at upper left. Then twist a second rubber band around all the fingers of your right hand.

Slip the index and second fingers of your left hand under the first band and pull it out from your hand. Then close your right hand while pushing all four fingers through the first band. Now work from the inside of your palm so that the audience will see the rubber band still in position on the back of your hand as shown at center left. Then open your hand, beginning by stretching out the first and second fingers. The rubber band will jump down onto the third and fourth fingers below the other band. Open your hand.

To make the rubber band jump back to the first two fingers, slip the thumb of your right hand under the band and pull it away from you hand as shown at lower left; then put all four fingers through the loop.

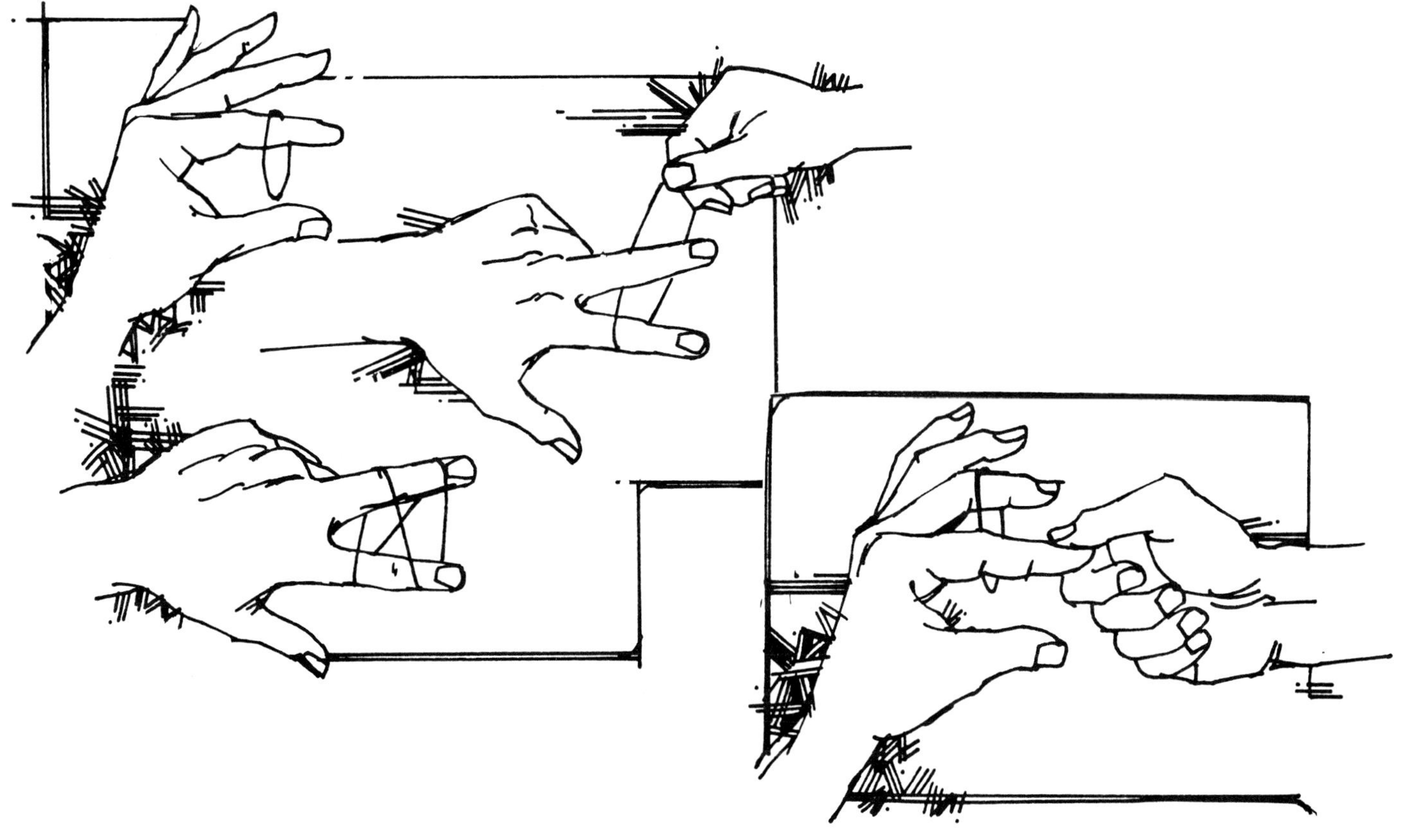

RUBBER BAND TRANSPOSITION II

This nifty little trick can be done anywhere; the prop couldn't be simpler. The trick requires a bit of coordination, but if you have trouble executing the moves, keep in mind that it is said to have been created by the five-year-old nephew of famous conjurer Martin Gardner.

Props: none
Advance Preparation: a rubber band

Loop the rubber band over the fore and middle fingers of your right hand, hooking your right thumb over it to hold it in position. Then, loop it over all four fingers near the first knuckles.

Now cover the portion of the rubber band that is over all four fingers with your left hand and point your left fingers toward the audience so they cannot see what your right thumb is doing.

Announce the trick, then command the rubber band to leap from the first two fingers to the last two fingers of your right hand. The rubber band will respond when you release your thumb, causing it to jump magically.

A SUGARY MESSAGE

This is an old trick that was always passed up until a Chicago bartender magician nicknamed "Heba Habba" started fooling magicians with it.

The effect states: A mark made on a sugar cube is transferred to a spectator's hand. That may not sound too thrilling, but if you try it a couple of times you'll be surprised by the reaction.

Props: an ordinary lead pencil
a sugar lump or cube
a glass of water
a napkin

Advance Preparation: none

Al "Heba Habba" Andrucci begins by having the spectator select a cube of sugar from a bowl. He uses the unwrapped cubes, so if yours are wrapped remove the paper. He asks the spectator for his first name. We'll say his name is Sandy, so Al would say, "We're going to write your initial 'S' on this sugar cube. We have to trace it several times so we get a heavy image."

He leaves the sugar cube on the bar and goes for a glass of water. "It can be clean, dirty, hot or cold, just so long as it's water."

It's when he comes back with the water that he does the dirty work. He moistens the tip of his right index finger as he puts the glass in front of the spectator. He gestures as though to indicate what to do, but this idle gesture makes the trick work.

He touches his wet right index finger on the S and points to the glass. "Pick up the sugar cube and drop it in the water." It doesn't matter where the S lands—he just watches it start to dissolve. He takes Sandy's right hand in his left hand and points to the palm. "Cover this glass with the palm of your hand."

As he turns Sandy's left palm down over the mouth of the glass he taps the palm with the right forefinger. "Now put your other hand on top." As he says this, he taps the back of Sandy's hand on the glass just as Sandy covers it himself. He taps the back of the left hand as he says, "Repeat after me, 'Hocus Pocus, out of focus.' " (If there is someone close to Sandy, Heba will touch the back of his or her hand leaving another mark as he asks, "Have you ever seen this trick before?").

Then, "O.K., Sandy, look at the palm of your hand. Did the S come up through the water? . . . If it did blow on your hand. . . . Look at the back of it. . . . Is there a mark there? . . . Look at the other hand, on the back. . . . Touch the shoulder of the fellow next to you. Do you have a mark on your hand? . . . I'll bet you've got another S on your hip. . . . Take the flashlight and go in the washroom." Surprisingly enough, quite a few head for the washroom so you know it's an effective trick—and you were gonna pass it up.

Oh, yes, the napkin you find listed among the props is so you can wipe off the marks. If there happens to be one on the spectator's hip, please write and tell the publisher how you did it.

THE MAGIC CIRCLE

This impressive and relatively easy mind reading act is best suited for the dinner table. The drama lies in the fact that all evidence apparently has been destroyed. Tell a spectator or fellow diner that you are going to "read his mind" so you can tell him the exact words he writes on a paper, which you subsequently burn.

Props: a pen or pencil
a small (about 4 inches) square torn from a paper placemat (or other colored paper)

Advance Preparation: You don't have to slip anything up your sleeve before confronting your victim, so the trick may be done on a whim. However, you may want to devote a small amount of time to practicing the simple palming technique required.

Start by drawing a rough circle or horizontal oval on the paper's center.

Hand this to a fellow diner and ask him to write any word(s) or name(s) he wishes within the circle.

Then tell the victim to fold the paper in quarters to conceal his writing and return the paper to you.

Proceed to tear the folded paper in quarters as shown and pretend to drop all scraps into an ashtray; light them with a match. Actually, drop all but the piece of paper with the circle on it into the ashtray.

No matter how the victim has folded the paper, the circle always will be in the corner showing no more than two leaves of paper. Try it beforehand with white paper and a dark pen, so you can see the circle and writing from the outside.

Then stack the scraps of paper in your hand so the circle section is on top, closest to your hand. As you drop the paper into the ashtray, keep the circle part in your palm, hidden from the spectator's view.

As you direct his attention to the burning scraps, pass your palm across your forehead or eyes, glancing surreptitiously at the words written on the paper.

For a spectacular finish, rather than announce the words you've read, on another sheet write a description or message conveying your success to the spectator and watch him gape as he reads it!

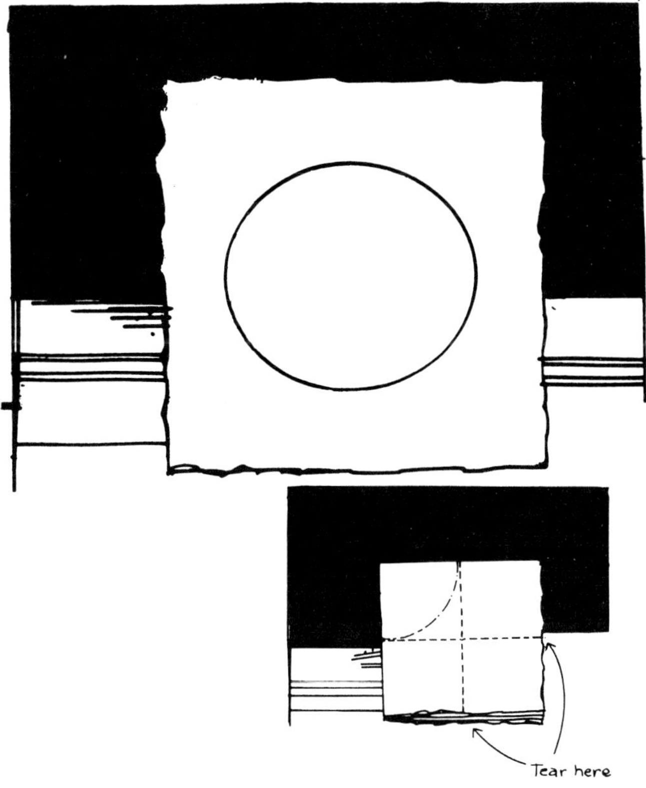

THE RESTORED STRING

This is a good impromptu trick for the living room or table, as long as you have prepared some simple props. It also may be done on a stage, but can be difficult for the audience to see if too far from the performer. Tell your audience you will insert a string through a straw, cut through both, and restore the string to its unbroken state.

Props: a paper soda straw
2 feet of string or thread
scissors

Advance Preparation: Cut a lengthwise slit about 3 inches long in the center of the straw. Make it a clean cut so that the straw does not appear to be doctored. Put the string and straw in your pocket.

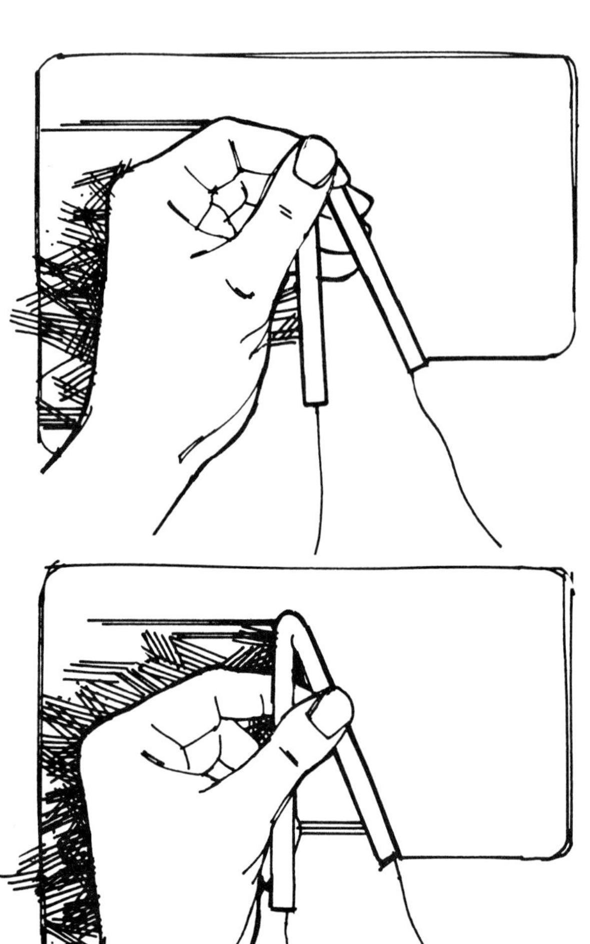

1. Insert the string into the straw, and suck on the other end of the straw to draw the string through. Now bend the straw in its center.

2. Tug subtly on the string ends to pull the string from the slit, concealing the action with thumb and finger.

3. Now snip the straw (and apparently the string) in half at the bend. Throw in magician's patter as you stick the straw together and "magically" pull the restored string through to show the audience.

THE SLAVE BRACELET

A classic that can be performed just about anywhere, this trick takes a bit of advance preparation, so it's not entirely spontaneous. Nonetheless, it probably has the greatest effect when done nonchalantly at the dinner table or in the living room. The basic idea is to have a spectator tie a rope between your wrists so you can magically string a bracelet on it without untying your hands. Since the trick is fairly simple and employs an obvious gimmick, it's important to do this trick quickly and with a lot of flourish.

Props: two identical bracelets (such as bangles)
a 2- to 3-foot length of rope, cord or twine

Advance Preparation: Start by wearing one of the identical bangles just below the elbow, where it will be hidden by your sleeve. The other bracelet can either be worn on your wrist in full view or can be pulled from a pocket and handed to the designated victim along with the piece of rope.

Have a spectator tie the rope between your hands and hand back the bangle.

Now turn your back and subtly shake the concealed bracelet down your arm and onto the rope as you slip the duplicate bracelet into a pocket.

Turn back to your expectant audience and display the results with finesse.

Should a heckler in your audience request that you repeat the trick without turning your back, reply with a snappy retort, such as, "A professional magician never repeats a trick for the same audience."

To reverse this trick, magically remove the bracelet from the rope by sliding the bracelet up your sleeve and substituting a duplicate taken from your pocket.

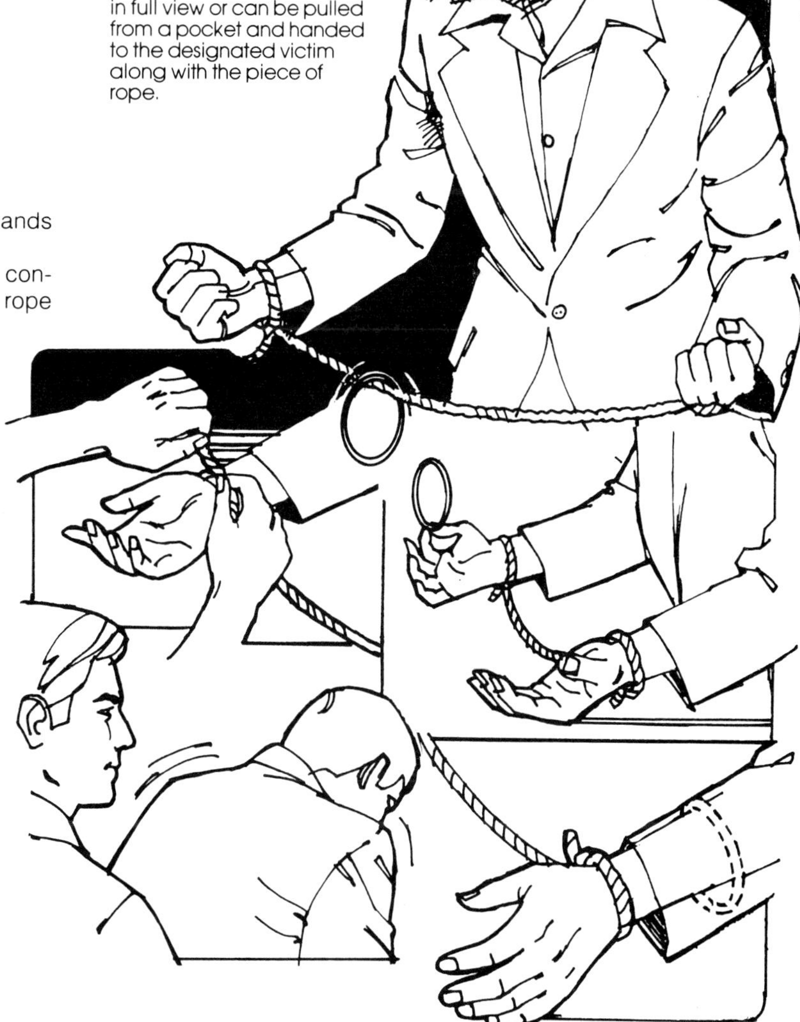

THE ROLL BOUNCE

You should practice this to get the timing. You see the whole escapade runs maybe ten seconds, in which time you will have done it twice and quit. Most times the laughter and the surprise last longer than the stunt itself.

Prop: a bread roll
Advance Preparation: Practice the timing.

The scene opens, you are seated at a restaurant table with a friend and there is a tray of dinner rolls in front of you. Offer one to your friend; take one yourself and mumble, "I wonder if these bounce." If you do the trick properly, your friend will see you toss the roll on the floor and it will bounce back like a tennis ball. You do it once more and put the roll on your bread plate next to the pad of butter.

Here's how it goes. With your right hand, start as though you were going to actually bounce the roll off the floor next to your chair. When your hand gets below the edge of the table where your friend's eyes can't see, you must do two things simul-

taneously. You must tap the floor with your foot and at the same time twist your wrist and flip the roll into the air so it "bounces" a few inches above the table top. Catch it. Do it once more and quit.

The second method is to have one hand below the edge of the table. With one hand you toss the roll into the other. Tap your foot and toss the roll back with the hand below the table edge.

The people behind you may wonder what the hell you are doing; but the people in front of you will be amazed, and that's what it's all about . . . I'm told.

THE TREASURE IN THE ROLL

Oriented strictly to the dinner table, this is a great and classic trick. The idea is to break open a roll or bun and, to your feigned surprise, find a coin inside.

Props: a coin
a roll or bun from the table
Advance Preparation: Slip a coin from your pocket (a dime is easiest to begin with) and hide it in your fingers by finger palming it.

To start the trick, hold the roll with thumbs on top and fingers on the bottom.

Bend the roll ends up just a little to crack it on the bottom and, in one motion, push the coin through as you bend the roll the other way.

Looking at the broken roll from the top, any spectator will think the coin was tucked into the middle of the roll.

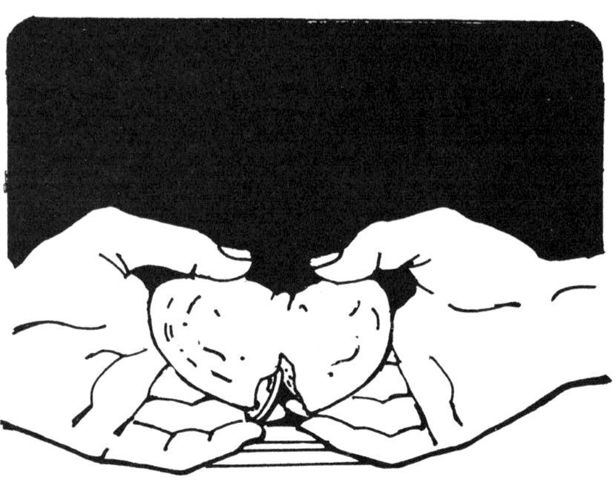

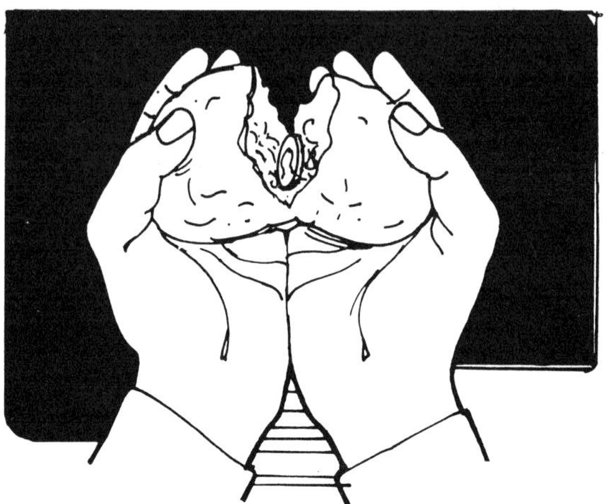

THE MYSTERIOUS MATCHSTICK

The basic concept involved closely resembles that of the Restored String, but the procedure is entirely different. Tell your chosen victim you will tear a match in half and make it reappear whole in his hand.

Prop: a book of paper matches
Advance Preparation: Conceal a torn match head between the second and third fingers of your left hand.

MAGICIAN'S LEFT HAND

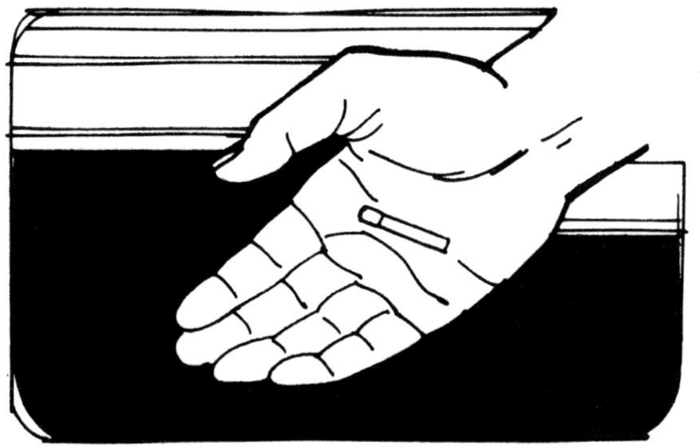

SPECTATOR'S RIGHT HAND

Instruct the spectator to hold out his right hand, palm up. Tear off a match and place it on the palm with the head pointing to your left. Keep the match head concealed in your left hand.

Tell the spectator to examine the match. Then pick it up by the end with your right hand and gesture with that hand as you tell the spectator to hold his left hand out, palm up. As you're gesturing, rotate the match in your hand to conceal the head between thumb and finger, immediately grasping the other end with your left hand. The spectator will think the head is in your left hand.

Now pretend to twist off the match head, pulling your left hand off the match and immediately showing the match head concealed there earlier.

Place the head in the spectator's right palm. Now place the whole match (which the victim thinks is the half without the head) on the left palm, holding onto the head until he has closed his fist around it.

Pick up the match head from the spectator's right hand with your right and pretend to transfer it to your left hand. But, rather, keep in in your right hand.

As your left hand makes a throwing motion toward the spectator's left fist, drop the match head on the floor. When your victim opens his left hand, he will find a whole match in his palm.

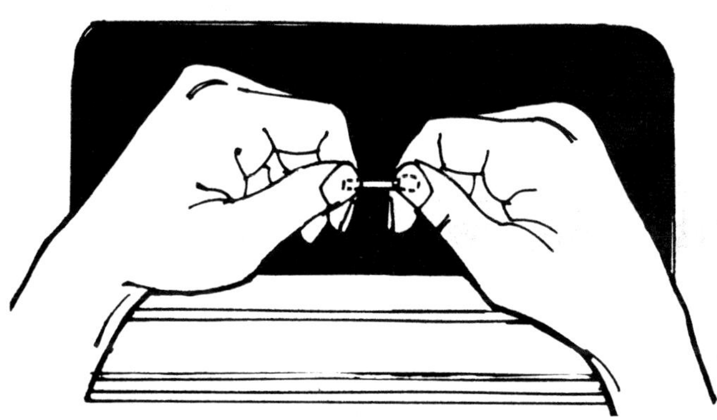

tricks with coins and cards

If you're going to do "Instant Magic," you'd better pick up on a few card and coin tricks.

Card tricks are popular because cards are readily available, inexpensive, and they don't take up much space. Coin tricks are popular because everyone has a few coins in a pocket or change purse and everyone knows what these things are. Anytime you do tricks with ordinary objects, the audience has to be impressed. They are also impressed when the lady floats on air on stage; but, they also know anything can happen on a stage because that's not really a part of the real world.

Some magicians know a lot of other tricks, but they do only card tricks. The late Billy O'Connor was billed in vaudeville as "Billy O'Connor and His 52 Assistants." Eddie Tullock has made a fortune with only a pack of cards.

We'll tell you how to do a few good card tricks and how to get started with cards, but we suggest you look elsewhere for further tutelage in this field. You see, there once was a fellow named Ellis Stanyon who ran a magic magazine from 1900 through 1920. He early began a series called the "Dictionary of Magic" and got through the letters A and B in less than a year, but he got hung up on "Card Tricks." When the magazine expired in 1920, he had published just over half of the card tricks he knew about at that time, and there have been more than plenty invented since then.

A concise selection of basic and impressive card tricks for the beginner follows. Before trying others, however, consider adding basic palming and card sleights to your bag of tricks.

THE CHARLIER CARD PASS

This basic move to cut the cards with one hand is also useful for secretly putting one half of the deck on top of the other when needed during a trick. While this is not a trick in and of itself, it is a useful move for several card tricks.

Prop: a deck of cards
Advance Preparation: none

1. Hold the deck in your left hand, with the card faces toward the audience, away from you. The ring finger and middle finger hold one side of the deck, while the tip of the thumb rests on the opposite side. The pinkie rests on one end of the deck and the forefinger on the other end.

2. Raise the thumb a little to let half the deck drop into your left palm.

3. Keeping the upper half of the deck in place with your thumb, lever the bottom half of the deck toward and against your thumb with your forefinger.

4. When the lower half clears the upper half, open your hand a little to let the upper half of the deck fall toward the palm of the hand. It now becomes the bottom half as the cards against your thumb fall on top. Square the deck with your fingers and thumb.

Now, so your practice will not be a total loss, here's a card trick to go with it. Have someone take a card out of the pack—look at it and remember it. Have him put the card back in the pack upside down. Next have him hand you the pack behind your back. Do the Charlier pass. (It was named after an old magician who lived in London around the end of the 19th century.)

Because most decks have a slight natural bend, the selected card winds up on either the top or the bottom of the deck. You bring it forward and confound the spectator. It takes a bit of a feel, but generally it is where the deck cuts most naturally. If the card is not there, don't blame me—blame Charlier.

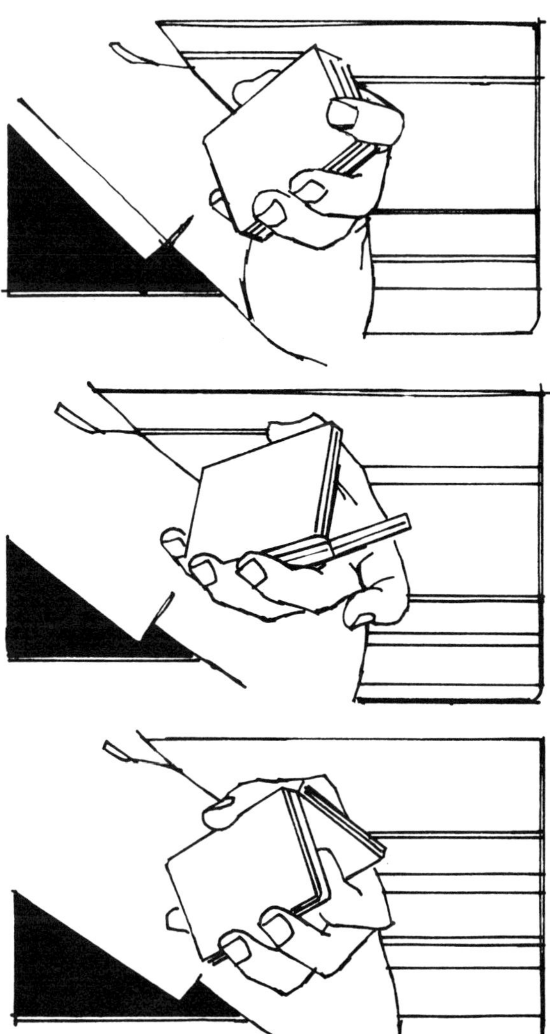

PALMING CARDS

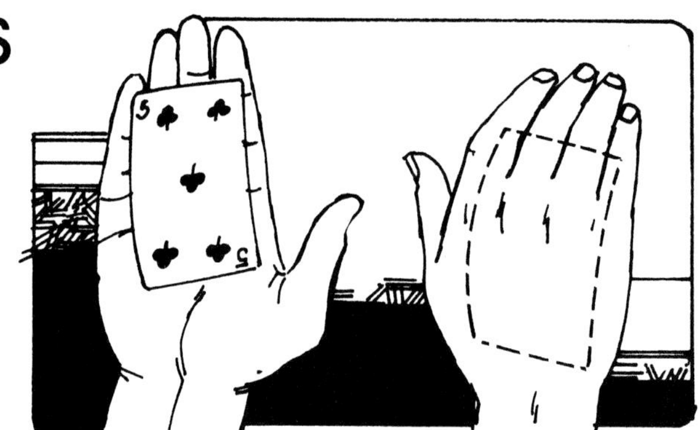

Palming cards is nothing more than holding cards in your hand so the audience doesn't see them. If your hands are not big enough to conceal a card or cards, find some way around it. Say, "I have to put the cards behind my back." When the cards are there, you can add a card or cards from your back pocket.

PICKING OUT PAIRS

This mathematical puzzle makes use of very simple mnemonics and is great for impressing a crowd. You can fool up to ten victims in a single sitting. Basically, each participant chooses a pair of cards behind your back and you use your amazing powers to deduce which pair belongs to which victim.

Prop: a deck of cards

Advance Preparation: Learn the following rules and moves and practice performing them smoothly. Memorize this sequence of words: ATLAS, BIBLE, THIGH, GOOSE. Imagine these laid out in a square of letters.

ATLAS
BIBLE
THIGH
GOOSE

During the trick, you will lay out cards so that each matches one letter in the above sequence. Note that in those words, every letter is used exactly twice and each word has a pair of identical letters. In the middle of the trick, you will deal pairs of identically numbered cards so that each card in the pair will fall on one of a pair of matching letters. Before doing the trick, pick ten pairs from the deck.

To start the trick, lay out the ten pairs on the table, face down. Leave the room or turn your back and have up to ten spectators choose a pair each, replacing them in pairs face down in any order whatsoever.

When all have been chosen, turn to the audience and put the paired cards in a stack in your hand.

Now lay the cards one at a time on the table by following your memorized pattern: Put the first card on the position for the first "A," the second in that pair on the second "A" in the pattern. For the next pair, put a card on the first "T," then the other card in that pair on the second T. Repeat for the ten pairs of letters, or for as many as the number of participating spectators. Make sure that both cards in each pair are resting in the positions indicated by pairs of letters.

To guess the pair chosen by the first spectator, have him tell you in which row his cards appear. He will not know that each pair can be in no more than two rows, and since no more than one pair of letters exists in each row, you will easily be able to name the pair of numbers he chose.

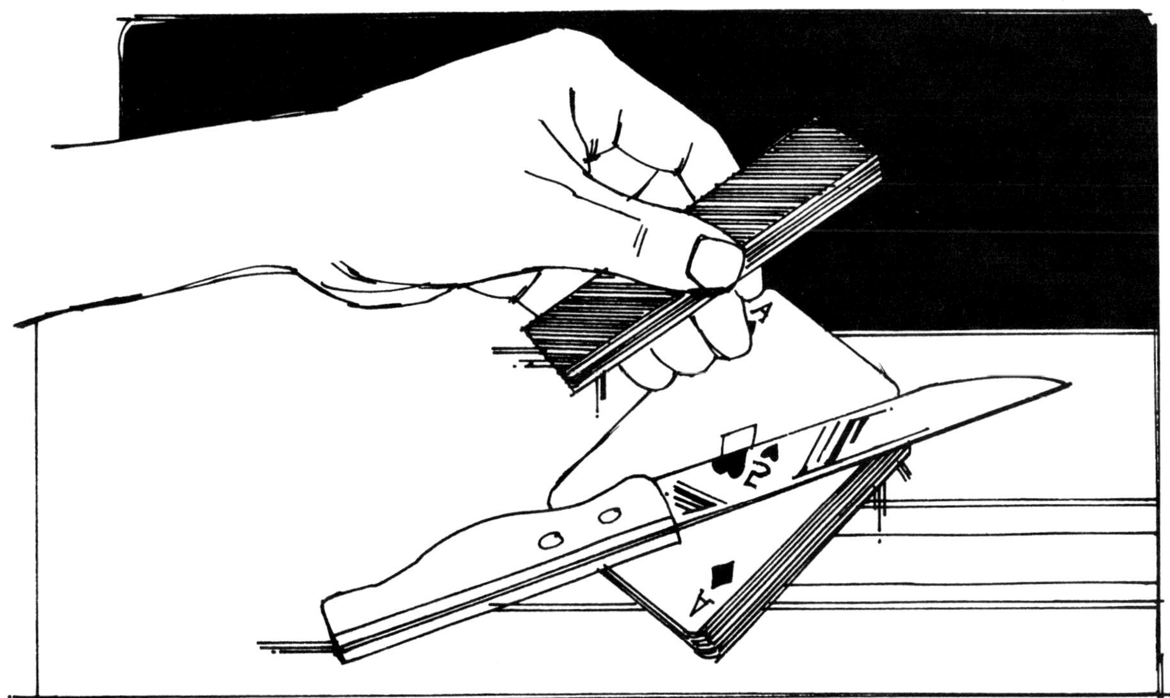

LOCATING CHOSEN CARDS

Many instant ways exist to locate a card chosen from a pack by a spectator.
These require no real sleight skills and can be done by beginners.

Prop: a shiny metal knife
Advance Preparation: none

To start, boast about your mind-reading powers. Have a spectator insert a knife blade anywhere in the deck to separate the cards into two piles. Instruct him to look at the card above the knife blade and replace the pile, leaving the knife between the cards at the same spot.

As you reach to pick up the deck and the knife, you twist the handle so you can read the reflection of the card in the knife blade. (It's reversed, of course.) Remove the knife and put it on the table. Concentrate before revealing the card.

THE STRAY CARD

This nifty little card trick takes some preparation of props. If done well, your gimmicks will not be noticed. Introduce the trick by saying you will identify a card chosen from the deck by a member of the audience, and it will be your last card trick of the evening.

Props: a deck of cards
a piece of thread about 2 feet long
a tiny dab of softened wax, blue tack, or chewing gum
a table
a pen or pencil

Advance Preparation: Choose a thread color close to that of your clothing to camouflage the thread. Tie one end to the bottom button of shirt, jacket, vest, or belt. Tie a knot in the other end and stick the dab of wax on the knot. Press the waxed knot into the button or belt to form a large loop that will hang from your stomach and just touch the table center when you bend the table surface toward you by tilting the edge.

Announce the trick and have a spectator from the audience choose a card from the deck without showing you which card it is and write his initials on its face. Hold half the deck above the other so the spectator can put his card in the middle.

You are holding one half of the pack in, say, your left hand and the spectator puts his selected card on top of this lot. As you move to put the other half on top of the selected card, bend a corner of the card which will go above it. Thus, you will have a bend on the bottom card of the half pack in your right hand. (This is called a crimp.)

Talk for a moment, then cut the cards. Be sure to cut the crimped card to the bottom of the deck and the selected card now will be at the top. As you turn to go behind the table, get the wax ball between your right thumb and forefinger and press it onto the back of the selected card. Come to think of it, you don't really need the thread at all if you have the right kind of table surface.

Turn the deck face up and place it in the middle of the table. Be sure to press the deck against the table, so the wax or blue tack will hold the new bottom card to the table surface.

Show one or two cards that are now on the face of the deck and ask the spectator if either is the right card. After negative answers, quickly tilt the table forward to send the cards cascading to the floor. The correct card will remain stuck to the table, showing the spectator's inscribed initials.

You must scrape the wax and the thread (if you use it) off the card with your thumbnail as you hand the card to the spectator and bow. Now, someone has to pick up 51 cards.

SLEIGHT OF FOOT

For another method to locate a card chosen by a spectator, brag that you can find the card without touching the deck since you can feel the vibrations of the chosen card.

Props: a deck of cards
a little salt
Advance Preparation: Secretly wet a forefinger tip with saliva and dip into a little salt. Do not let your victim or any other spectator see the salt on your fingertip.

Have a spectator cut the deck into two piles, turn over the top card where the cut occurs, and remember that card.

Then using your salted finger tap that card after it has been replaced, making sure you leave at least a few unnoticed grains on top of the card.

Now ask the spectator to replace the original top pile to make a full deck.

Casually transfer the deck to the floor (or have the spectator do this as he puts the deck back together). Kick the deck very lightly from the side to spread the cards. Due to the salt grains, a noticeable (to you only) break in the deck will appear just above the correct card. For extra finishing drama, push over the chosen card as well, to reveal its number and suit to the spectator.

The preceding tricks briefly introduce the world of card tricks. Once you have performed one or two, you will realize how simple it is to add to your card-trick repertoire. More often than not, one or more of your spectators will respond to your performance by showing you a card trick of his own.

The range of tricks you can do with coins is almost as broad as the wide variety of card tricks available to the instant magician. Below, a few of the traditional and outstanding routines are described.

THE FRENCH DROP

This, one of the oldest ways to vanish a coin, can stand on its own for spontaneous witchery, or as part of a more complicated coin trick.

Prop: any coin (or any other object that you can hold and conceal easily in your palm)

Advance Preparation: Practice until sure that the best of audiences cannot spot your lightning-quick moves.

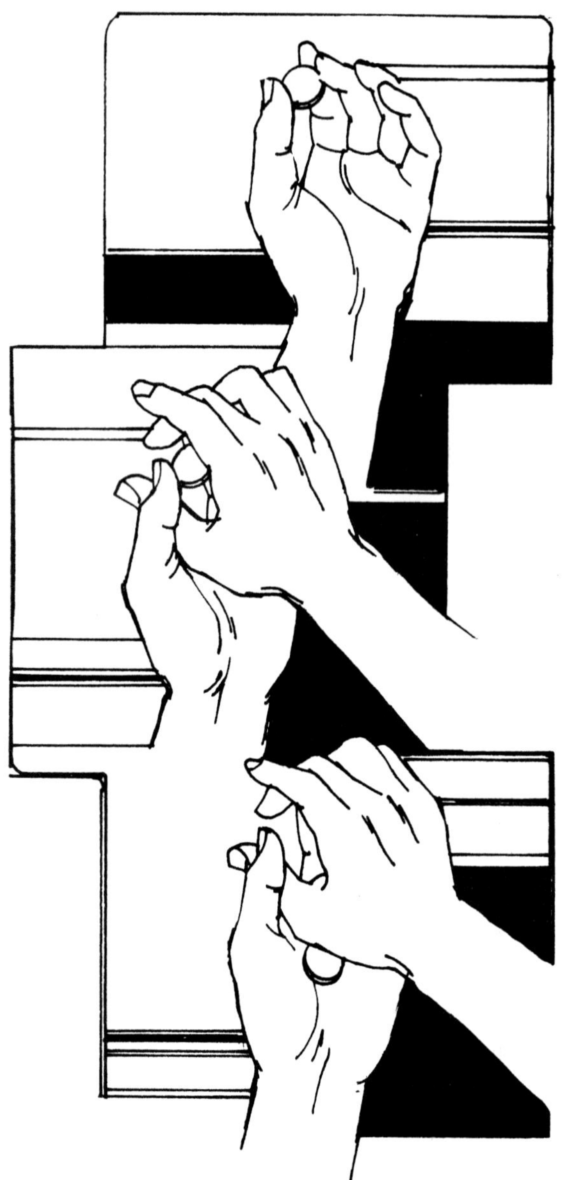

1. The best way to introduce a simple vanish is not at all. Borrow a coin from a spectator or provide your own; display it with your left fingers and thumb tip.

2. Shift your hand slightly so your fingers are between you and the audience, and bring your right hand over to the left as though you intend to take the coin between your right thumb and middle finger.

3. With left fingers hiding left palm, secretly drop the coin into your left palm as you pretend to grab it between your right fingers.

4. The way to practice the French Drop is to use a mirror. Hold the coin as described and actually take it in the right hand. Do this several times until you know what this move looks like. This move is what you must imitate in order to get a natural-looking vanish.

You must make it look as though you had actually taken the coin; but in fact, you drop it into the fingers of the left hand. Keep the left hand loose, casually turning it down as though it held nothing, and move the right hand up and away as though it did hold the coin.

5. To finish, open your right hand to show that the coin has vanished. Then reproduce it by pretending to pull it from some other site with your left hand.

COIN TRICKS

SNEAKY COIN VANISH

Purists may not approve of this trick because it does not allow spectators to examine the cloth from which the coin has disappeared. However, when done quickly it is convincing, and it provides a good opportunity for the beginner to become accustomed to the dramatics involved in a good vanish.

Props: a handkerchief, scarf or cloth napkin
a small rubber band
a coin

Advance Preparation: Before drawing attention to yourself, wrap the rubber band around the fingers and thumb of your left hand to make it tight but snap off easily in an instant. Drape a handkerchief over your hand and open your fingers as wide as possible.

To begin, borrow a coin and place it into the center of the handkerchief with your right hand, letting the fingers and cloth close around the coin.

Now, in a single quick motion, slip fingers from the rubber band, closing it around the cloth which holds the coin in a little pouch formed under the handkerchief. Immediately whip the cloth into the air to show the coin has gone, without showing the pouch and rubber band.

If you wipe your nose on the handkerchief before you put it in your pocket, very few spectators will ask to examine it.

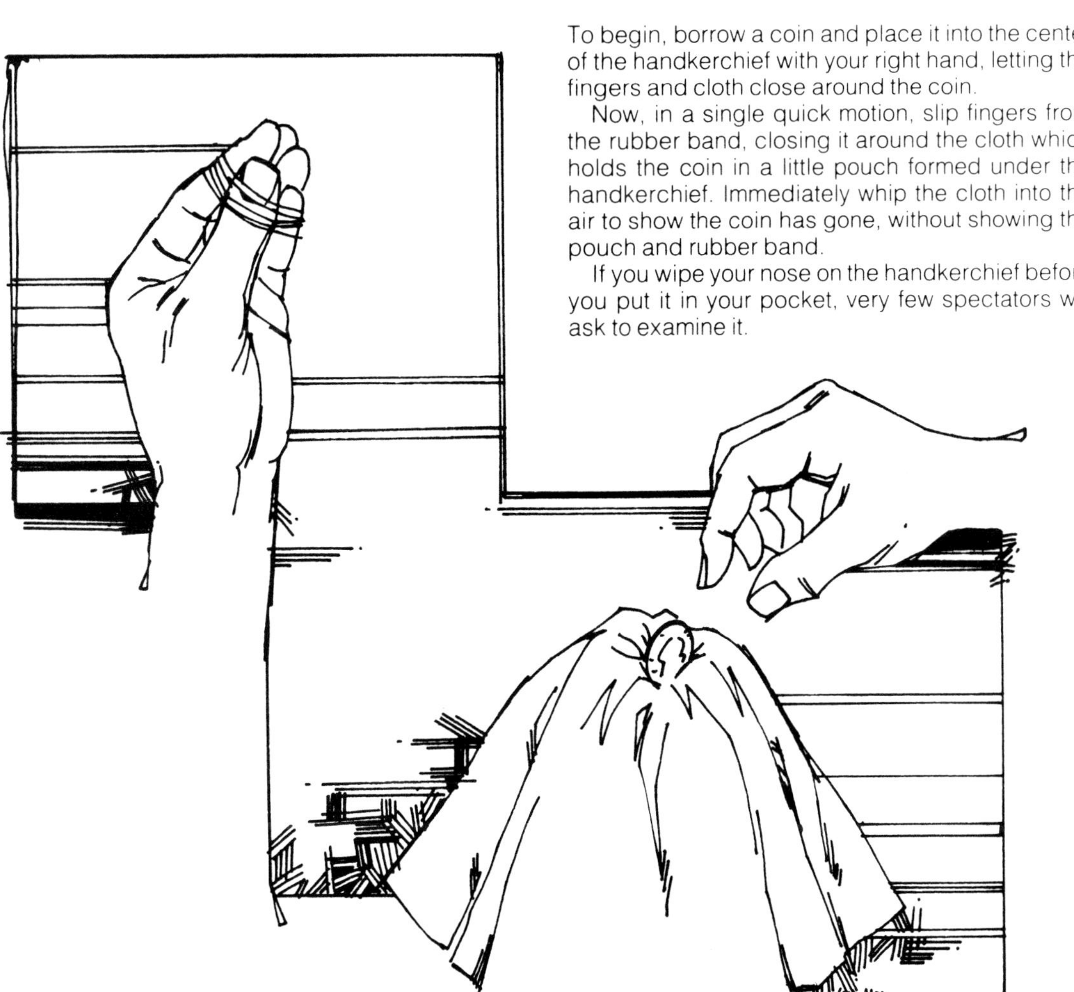

BASIC COIN PALM

If you had trouble with the French Drop, try this. Most coins are natural props to palm for vanishes, sleights, and other ruses. Here is one of the simplest ways to palm and vanish a coin.

Prop: a coin
Advance Preparation: Practice the sequence to assure your secret moves remain secret. A mirror or a critical friend can be helpful. Generally, if you goof it up, you audience will let you know.

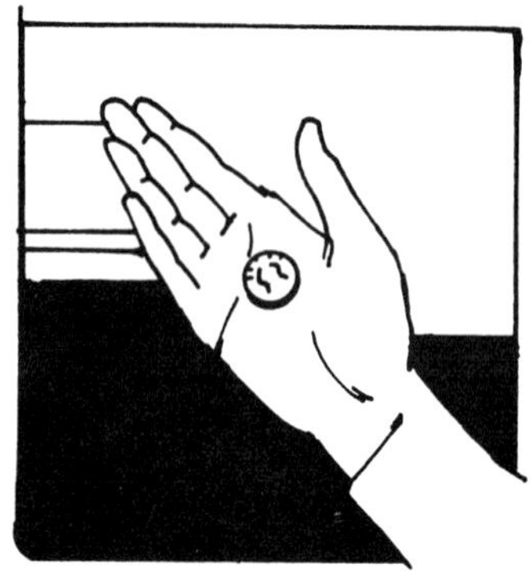

1. Borrow a coin or provide your own, showing it to your spectators by laying it in your right palm.

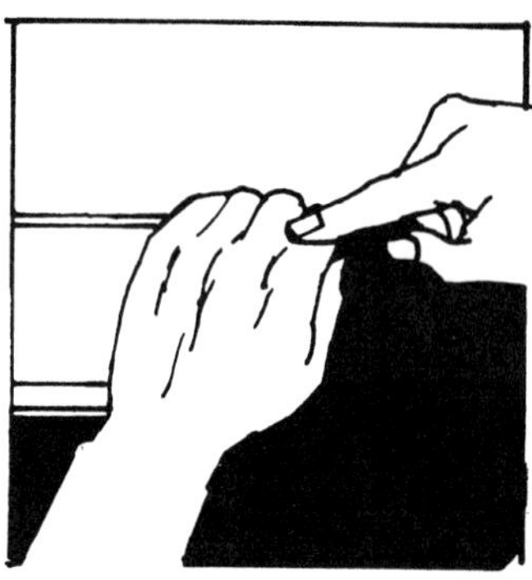

4. Your right hand keeps the fingers sufficiently bent to keep the coin palmed. You might even increase the suggestion that the coin is in your left fist by pointing to that hand with your right.

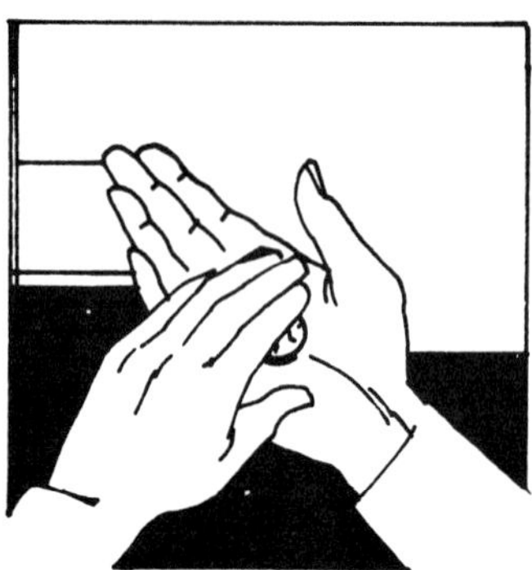

2. Reach for the coin with your left fingertips, subtly shifting your right hand so the palm is concealed from the audience.

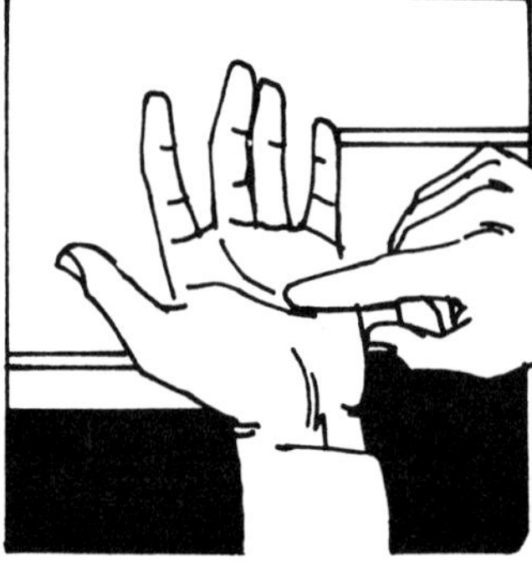

5. If you have provided your own coin, end the trick simply by opening your left hand and gaping as you find the palm empty.

3. Make your left hand, in the palm of your right, look as though you have taken the coin.

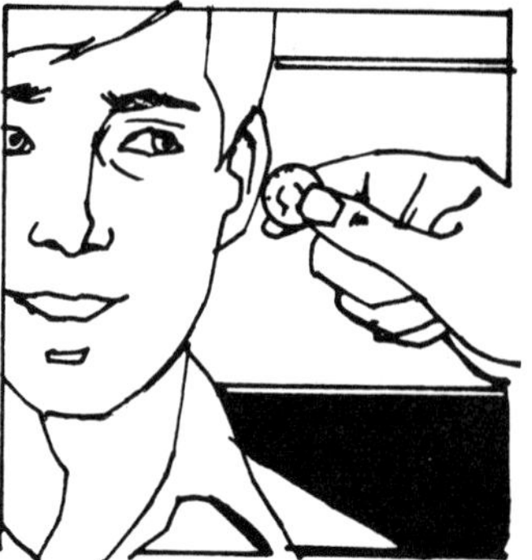

6. Or, reproduce the coin from your right hand, appearing to pull it from the owner's mouth, nose or ear.

HEADS UP COIN VANISH

This excellent and amusing coin vanish lends itself to performance almost anywhere.

Prop: a coin
Advance Preparation: none

Choose a spectator, or a diner opposite you. Have him hold one hand, palm up. Borrow or provide a coin and hold it between the fingers and thumb of your right hand. Your left hand holds the spectator's hand, palm up. Tell the spectator that he must close his fist around the coin on the count of three.

On the count of "One," lower the coin into his palm. Raise the coin to head level and then quickly lower it to the spectator's palm and count "Two."

Repeat this move quickly, leaving the coin on top of your head on the upswing. Without breaking the motion, and hitting the spectator's palm again with your empty fingers, count "Three." Immediately close both of your hands around his fist and ask him what he's going to do with the coin.

Now have him open his hand to show the coin has vanished.

To finish, ask the spectator to cup his hands. Tilt your head forward to let the coin slide off your head and into his hands, snapping your head back and up immediately, as if looking to the ceiling from whence came the coin.

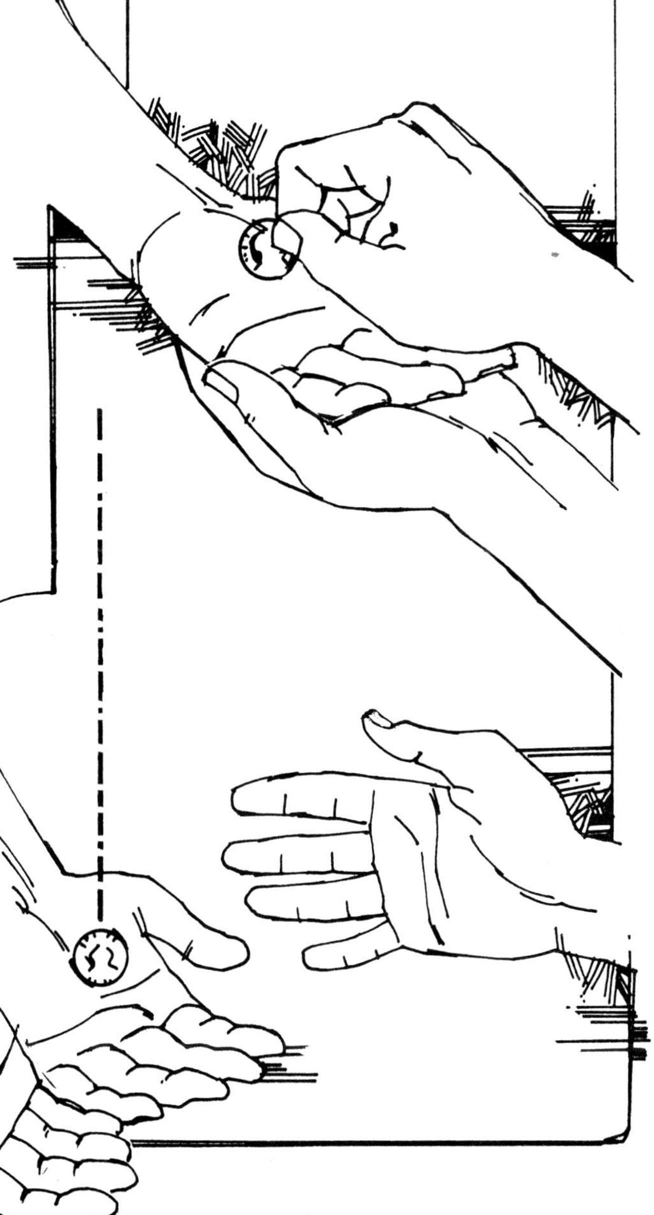

LEG PENETRATION

This quick and subtle stunt can be done spontaneously nearly everywhere.

Prop: a coin
Advance Preparation: Practice the moves to develop speed and smooth actions.

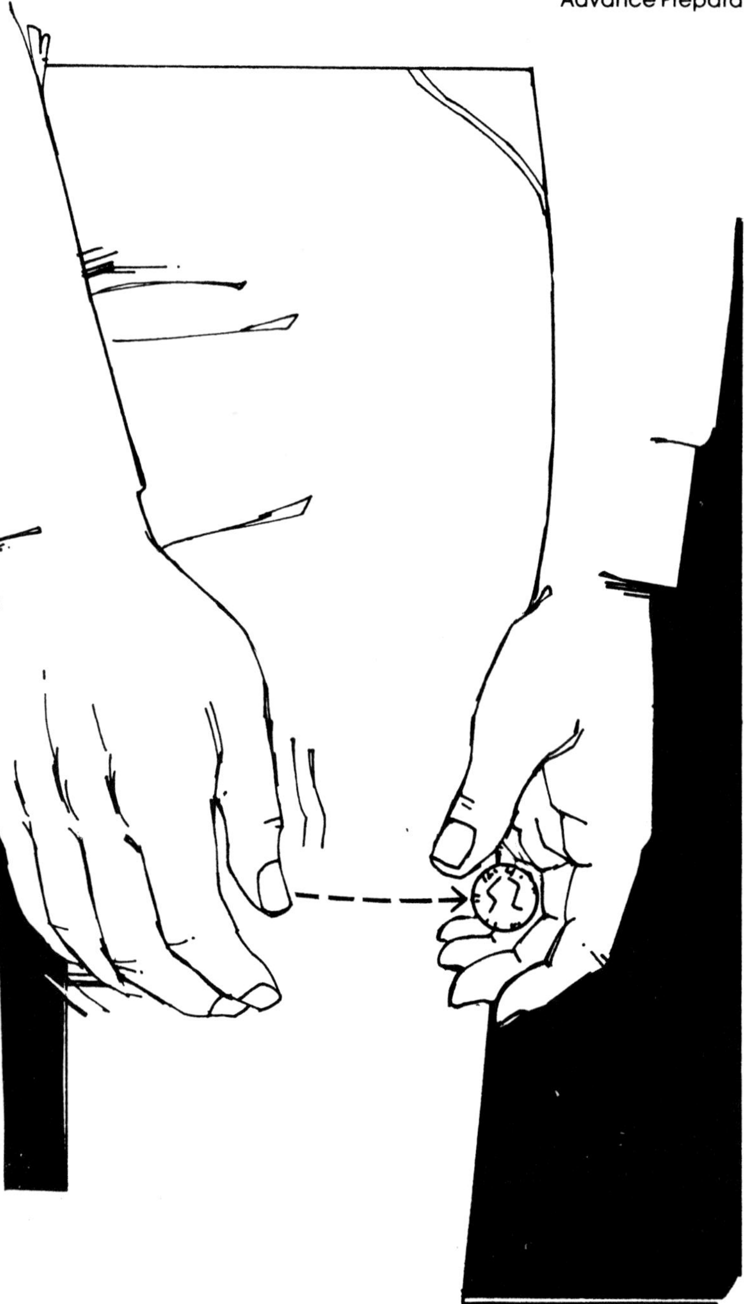

Explain as you borrow a coin that you intend to rub the coin through your leg front to back.

Flip the coin from your right hand several times during your introduction to focus spectators' eyes on the up-and-down motion.

You may not believe this, but after tossing the coin in the air several (two or three) times, you have set up the spectators' eyes to follow the coin up. Without warning you bend down and apparently slap the coin against your left thigh with your right fingers.

What you really do is to toss the coin into your waiting left hand which goes behind the left leg. The empty right fingers rub on the pants leg and slowly open showing the coin has gone. Jerk you left palm backward a fraction of an inch as if reacting to the impact of the penetrating coin. The left fingers now bring the coin forward and your trick is accomplished, almost before the spectators' eyes have refocused on your leg.

If you have laryngitis you can do this without pattern, chants, or explanation. You can even laconically say, "Watch!" and get the same reaction.

QUICK COIN TRANSPOSITION

To perform this startling effect at the dinner table, begin with what seems like one coin in each hand, but invisibly transfer so one hand is empty while the other holds two coins.

Props: 2 identical-denomination coins
a table
Advance Preparation: none

Place two coins on the table edge in front of you. Put the fingers of the left hand over the left coin and the fingers of the right hand over the right coin. As you say, "Watch!" the fingers of the right hand pick up the right coin, and at the same time the fingers of the left hand slide the left coin off into your lap.

Hold both hands up as though each held a coin. Show the coin in the right fingers as you move that hand below the table, where it picks up the coin from the lap.

The left hand is now slapped upon the table top and lifted to show the coin has vanished. The right hand slaps the underside of the table jingling both coins. Then bring both coins from under the table and slap them onto the table top. Voila!

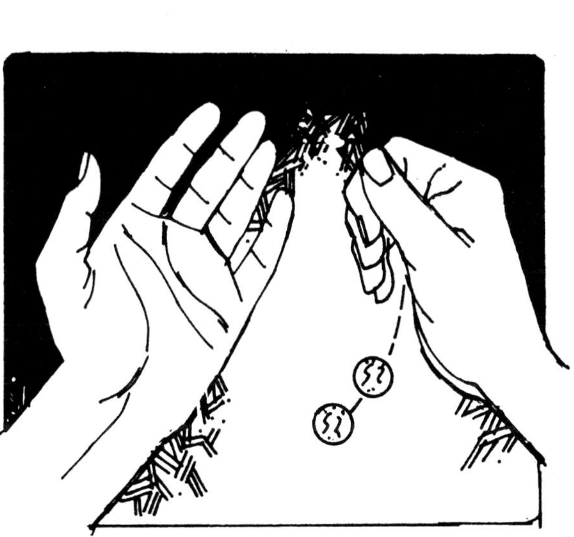

COIN TRANSPOSITION VIA MOUTH

When steps in this trick are done smoothly, it is really effective. Again, you begin with one coin in each hand and end magically with both in one.

Props: two dimes or pennies
Advance Preparation: none

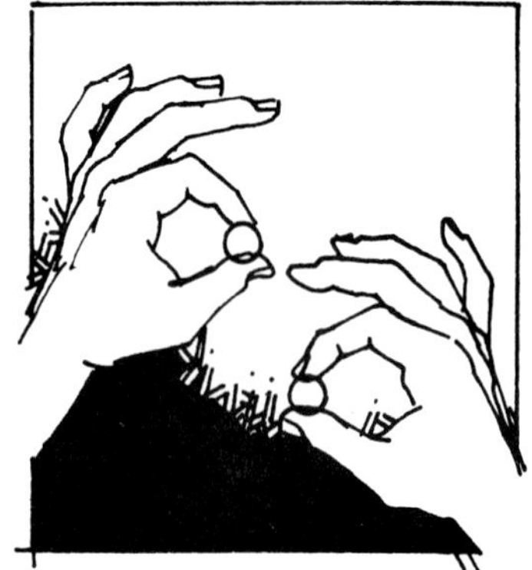

Borrow two coins or provide your own: show one between the thumb and forefinger of each hand.

Close your left hand into a fist as though holding a coin. Now openly take the coin from your lips into your right hand.

Now put the coin from your left hand between your lips and hold it there. Meanwhile, palm the coin in your right hand, pinching thumb and forefinger immediately afterward as though the coin were still there.

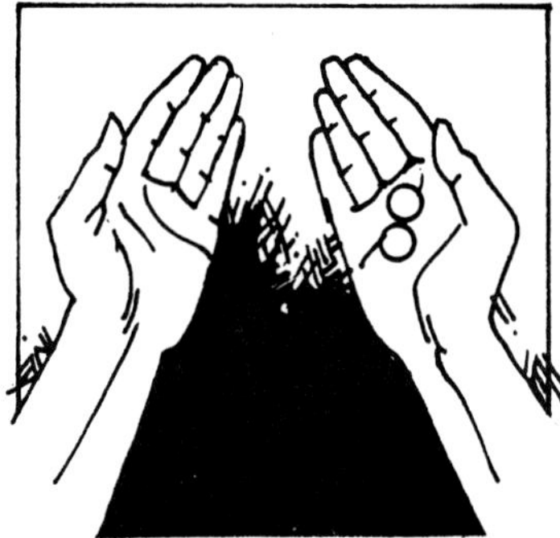

Pretend to toss the coin from the left hand into the right. Show the left hand empty and show both coins in the right. Marvelous!

Quickly move right hand to your left, pretend to drop the coin from your fingers into the palm but retain it in your right palm.

Thousands of variations on basic vanishes, transpositions and penetrations can be learned for coin magic. You can amaze your families and friends with a complete array of puzzles and challenges using numerous coins. Many audience members may have a few coin tricks, as card tricks, up their sleeves, which they probably will share with you.

mind reading acts

Tricks that call upon the baffling aspects of telepathy and psychic phenomenon have intrigued spectators for centuries. Through the tricks in this chapter, you can draw your audience into the world of the occult—read minds, transport objects inexplicably from place to place, and use your extrasensory perception to correctly identify things concealed from your view. You can perform these tricks on stage, though some are more suited to your living room.

Again, you need no special props. Memorize a few mathematical formulas and practice your arts of concealment and surreptitious glances at what you've hidden. Sometimes you may need an accomplice in the wings to help carry off your feat successfully.

Mind-reading and psychic tricks in particular call for you to perfect your spirit-conjuring routine. Invoke the spirits' aid as you perform your mind-reading marvels and convincingly call upon them to assist in transferring an object. Your incantations will set the proper mood for the mysteries of the occult—and, on the more practical side, help keep your viewers' minds off what you're really doing!

THE GHOST OF MA BELL

Purists might not consider this trick kosher, based as it is on a simple mathematical gimmick. However, the imaginative performer can turn this into real magic by pattering on the mysteries of mind-reading. Rather than emphasize the baffling aspect of the trick, turn it into a humorous challenge, focusing on telephone jokes. This tactic might dissuade your audience from asking for an encore, which would be deadly.

The object is to prove to the audience that you can recite a particular name listed on a particular page of a telephone directory, after a spectator has arrived at the allegedly random page number through a mathematical calculation.

Props: a pencil
a sheet of paper
a fairly thick telephone directory

Advance Preparation: The trick is not impromptu since preparations are needed, but it can be carried off spontaneously. If the trick is done onstage, you may invite the audience to examine the book to prove it is not marked in any way. If you have a chance to peek at the book for a moment in someone's home, you can make the trick appear truly instant.

To begin, find the tenth name from the top of the far-right column on page 89 of the phone book. Memorize that name and, at an opportune moment, casually offer to do the trick, using your impressive mind-reading powers.

Hand pencil, paper and phone book to the spectator chosen as your victim and have him write down any three different digits.

Now have the victim reverse the order of the digits and subtract the smaller number from the larger. There are only 10 possible combinations and 9 is the middle number in every one.

Ask the spectator if the resulting number has three digits; if not, have him put a zero in front of them.

Now have the victim reverse the digits in that number and add the two together.

Tell the spectator to turn to the page number indicated by the last two digits and check the name in the last column designated by the first two digits.

All you need at this point is to pretend you're receiving messages from the "ghost of Ma Bell" and call out the name you've memorized.

Since this simple gimmick works every time no matter which three digits the spectator chooses, the result of the calculations will be 1089. This is a dangerous trick to use often. In fact, if you repeat it for the same audience, they will catch on immediately when coming up with the number 1089 after beginning with different digits.

You might try to get away with the ninth name on page 108 or the top name on page 1089, although these last two versions don't work in small towns.

CALENDAR READING

Magicians may choose from many tricks that involve guessing the number or total of numbers chosen on a calendar by a spectator. The most complex involve advanced mnemonics, but a few simple versions exist for the beginner to try. The following is about the easiest calendar trick to perform. Claim that you can read the spectator's mind to derive the sum of numbers within a square drawn by a spectator on the calendar.

Props: a calendar
a writing implement

Advance Preparation: During the trick you will ask the spectator to name the lowest number within the square. Take that number, add eight, then multiply the sum by nine.

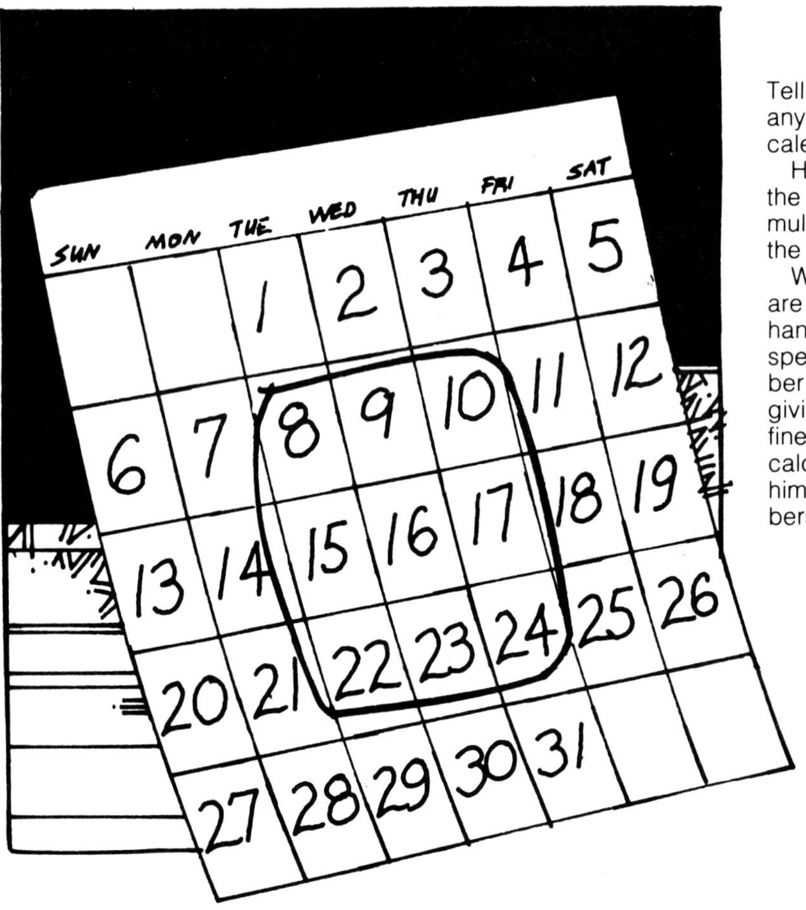

Tell the spectator to draw a square around any nine dates in any month of the calendar.

Have him name the lowest number in the square; apply the mathematical formula to arrive at the total of all numbers in the square.

With pocket calculators as small as they are these days you can have one in your hand as you turn your back. When the spectator tells you 8 is the smallest number in the group he has marked, you add 8 giving you 16. If you can do it in your head, fine. Otherwise, punch it into your pocket calculator and multiply by 9. You can tell him it's 144 before he can get all the numbers written down to total them.

THIRTEEN—THE SPIRIT NUMBER

The basis for this trick is a very simple mathematical formula. Claim you can tell whether or not a spectator has turned a die from one face to another thirteen times. Since you can focus on the traditional superstitions connected with the number thirteen, this trick is particularly suited to mind-reading patter. For instance, state that the number thirteen is so strong in the spirit world that those who inhabit the other world will send you a strong message when the die is turned a thirteenth time.

Props: a die
a sheet of paper
a pen or pencil

Advance Preparation: Memorize the following rule: If you look at any three die faces from one angle, the sum of their dots will be either odd or even. Then, when the die is turned a quarter-turn, the faces in that same position will change parity—odd will become even; even will become odd. Thus, if a thirteenth turn is made, a glance at the die from the same angle will give you an odd sum if the faces originally added up to an even number and vice versa.

Start by having the spectator place or roll the die on the paper. Then tell the victim to trace a square on the paper around the die, so that its position remains constant.

Now look at three of the faces and note whether the sum of the dots is odd or even.

Turn your back and ask the spectator to give the die twelve quarter-turns in any of the six possible directions, mixing the directions of the turns.

Then direct the victim either to give the die a thirteenth turn or not, without telling you which is done.

Turn to look at the die; being sure to look at the three faces you did originally, add their dots. If the parity is the same, a thirteenth turn was not made. If it is different, a thirteenth turn has been made.

Among hundreds of tricks performed with dice, a couple which allow you to read the mind of an astounded spectator amount to child's play for even the beginner. Both are good tricks with which to make your magic debut since they require no sleight-of-hand skills and no advance preparation.

THE DIE AND THE INVISIBLE EYE

This trick is especially suited to younger audiences in effect as well as technique. Merely claim that by reading your subject's mind, you can state how many dots are on the upper face of a die handed to you behind your back.

Prop: a die (it must have depression spots)
Advance Preparation: none

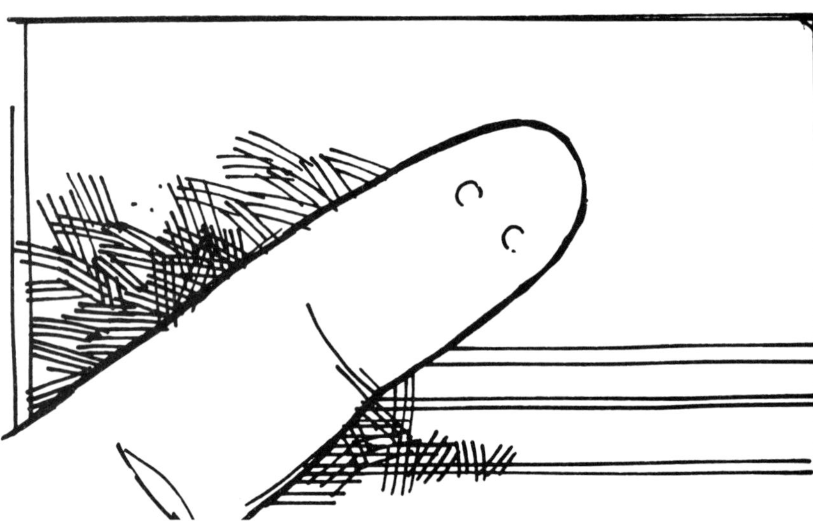

Put your hands behind your back and have a spectator (if you're onstage) or a friend put the die into them; tell him to memorize the number of dots on the upper face.

Instruct him to stand in front of you to verify you're unable to see the die as you "receive vibrations" telling you which die face is up. As you're concentrating, press the tip of your forefinger into the die's upper face, leaving an imprint of the dots on your finger.

Pass this hand over your forehead to "tune in the messages you're hearing," glancing at the imprint on your finger.

Now report which face the spectator turned upward.

You can also do this by pressing the finger into the bottom of the die. Subtract the impression on the finger from 7 and announce the difference.

DYNAMIC DICE

Quite similar to the preceding trick, this one uses a pair of ordinary dice. Announce that you can use your psychic powers to name the total of adjoining faces of a pair of dice handed to you behind your back. Suggest that merely holding them in your hands starts the flow of extrasensory vibrations allowing a correct "reading" of the total on the faces.

Props: a pair of dice
Advance Preparation: Memorize the mathematical rule stated in the trick's description.

Have a spectator put two dice together and silently note the sum of the dots on the adjoining faces before handing the dice to you behind your back.

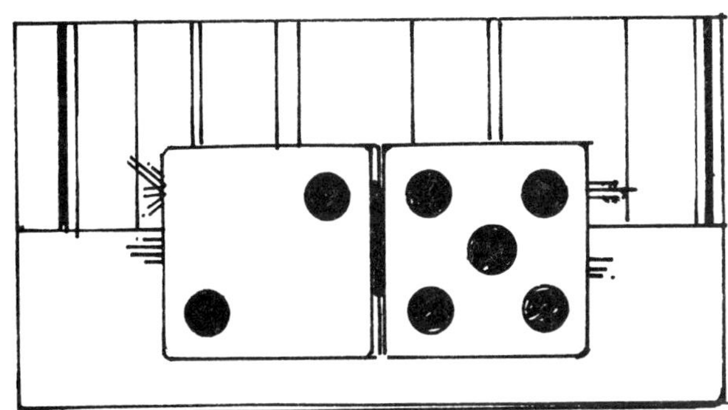

Take the dice from the spectator by holding them between thumb and forefinger of one hand; as you hold the audience's attention with witty patter, press thumb and finger firmly into the dice faces.

Return the dice to the spectator without looking at them and glance at the impressions left on thumb and finger.

Total the dots and subtract that figure from 14.

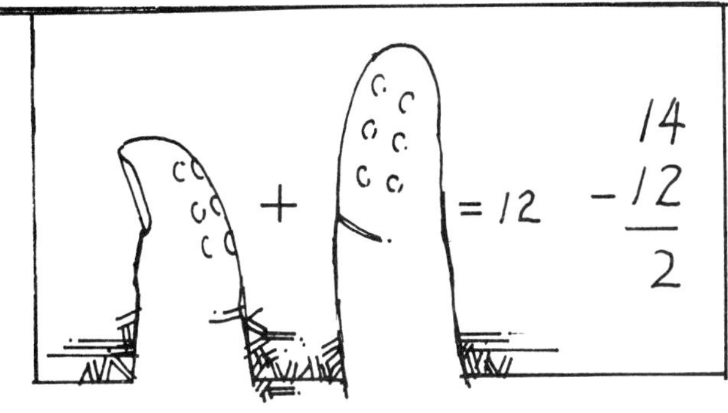

Wrap up your performance dramatically by correctly stating the spectator's total.

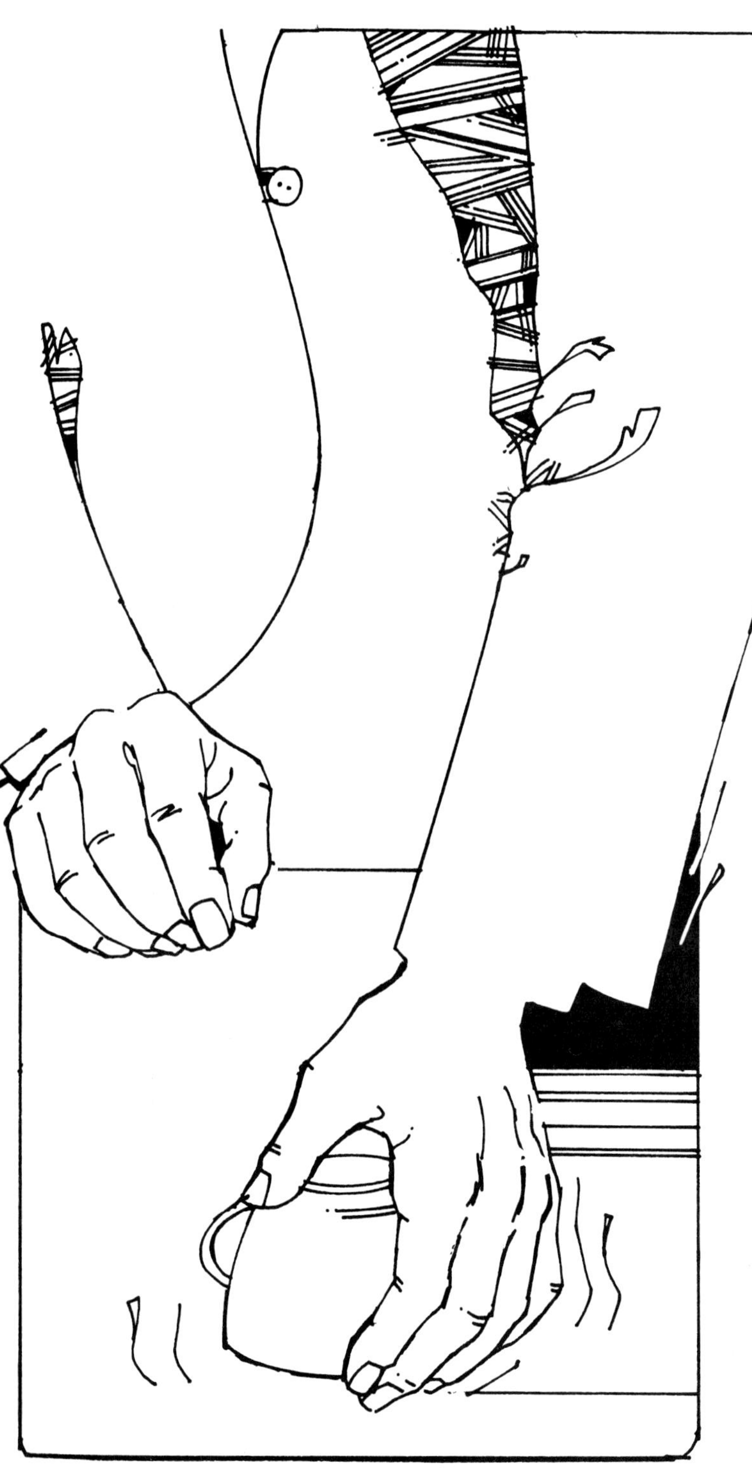

CUP AND DIE I

The concept of this trick is to guess the top die face; this version is impressive because you cover the die with an opaque cup, leaving the audience no doubt that you cannot see the die.

Props: a die
a die cup or a coffee cup
a table

Advance Preparation: Moisten one die side with saliva or water, memorizing the number of the wet face, before announcing the trick. Also, be sure you know which die faces oppose each other —one and six, two and five, three and four (opposite sides add up to 7).

Begin by throwing the moistened die into the cup and handing it to a spectator. Have the spectator shake the cup and invert it over the die on the table.

Now start to move the cup around as you evoke the spirits to give you the information you need. Shake it occasionally to flip over the die and watch the table surface carefully.

When a wet streak appears on the table next to the cup, you will know the moistened face is down and you can name the upper face. For instance, if you moistened the two, the upper face will be the five.

Lift the cup to show the correct face, but when the trick is done be sure to pick up the die and cup yourself. Otherwise, the spectator who picks it up may notice that one side of the die has been moistened.

CUP AND DIE II

Easier to perform than the preceding trick, this one allows you to peek at the die under the cup.

Props: a die
a paper cup (thin enough to let some light through)
Advance Preparation: Make a small hole in the side of the cup large enough to see a die inside.

Tell the spectator you are going to use the paper cup like a dice cup. Hold it up about eye level so he can't see your thumb through the hole you've got in the side. Have him roll the die around in his hands and then drop it in the cup.

You shake the cup and turn it mouth down on the table, and tell him, "Neither one of us can know which number is uppermost and the odds are that I could guess it correctly one time out of six. If I get three correct guesses out of six will you admit it is a pretty good trick?"

Do the thing three times, look through the hole and tell the number. Then crumple the cup. Tell him you don't want to press your luck.

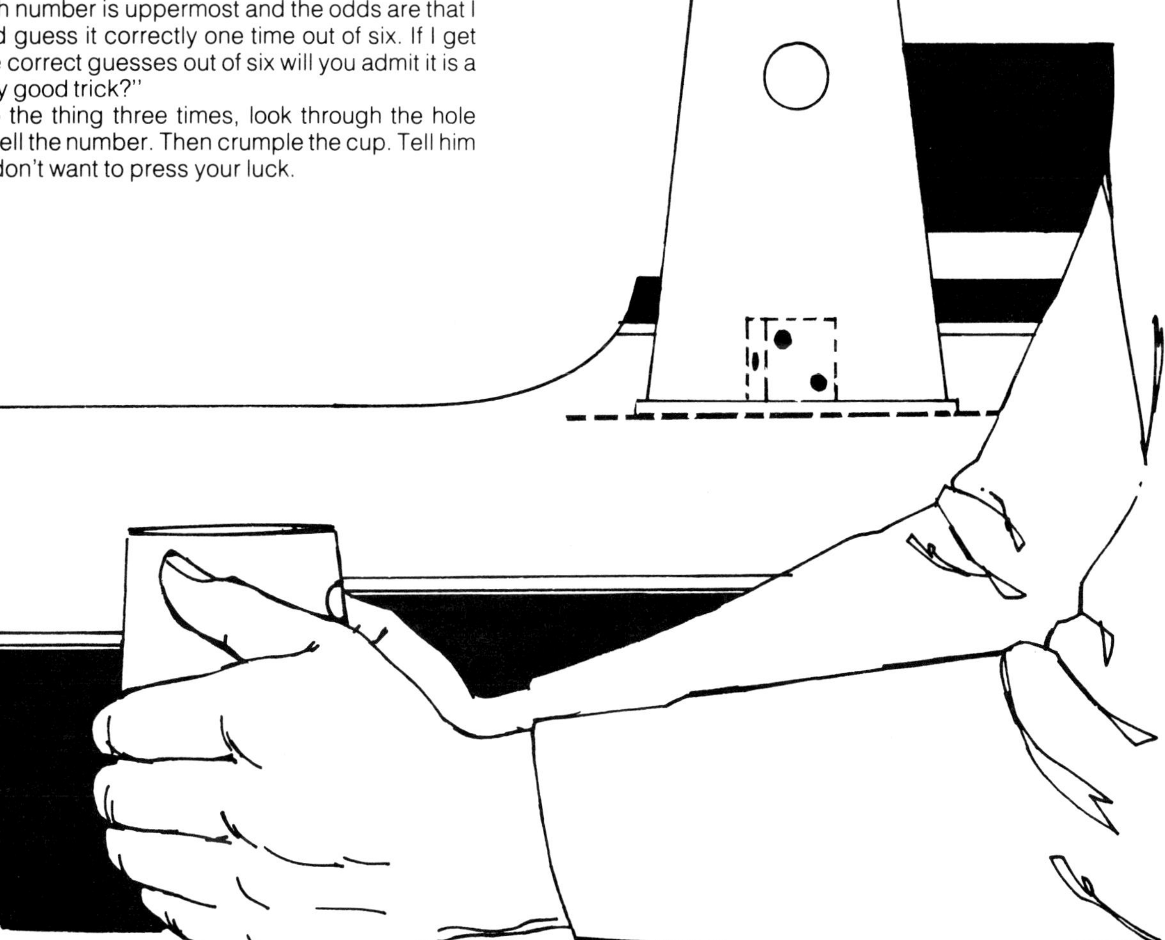

THE DIE AND MENTAL VIBRATIONS

This version of the routine whereby you miraculously name the upper face of a die without seeing it claims that you can wrap the die in a hankie or napkin after it is rolled by a spectator and guess the upper face by feeling the vibrations through the cloth.

Props: a die
a white or pastel-colored handkerchief or napkin

Advance Preparation: Merely make sure that when the hankie or napkin is wrapped tightly around the die, the dots can be seen.

Behind your back, have the spectator roll the die on a table and cover the die with the cloth.

Turn around and pick up both die and hankie or napkin. As you lift the die to press it against your forehead, pull the cloth tightly around the die so you can glance at the dots.

Go through mind-reading patter and then name the correct die face.

A favorite trick of magicians past and present is to guess an object's color without appearing to look at it. Top performers from all corners of the magic world have devised scores of ways to sneak a glimpse at an object and create the illusion that it has never come within their field of vision. The following two tricks use two of these methods. The first is designed for guessing the color of a larger object, while the second is intended for small objects that can be easily palmed.

THE PSYCHIC EASTER BUNNY (OR JUGGLER)

This trick can be done impromptu in the living room by a smooth performer or for a young audience.

Props: a selection of balls, blocks, or Easter eggs of varying colors

Advance Preparation: Wear a jacket or coat since you will "read" the color of the chosen object by slipping it up a sleeve and glancing surreptitiously at it.

Put your hands behind your back and have a spectator choose one colored ball or egg and place it in your hands. Have the spectator return to a seat in front of you, concentrate on the color of the object chosen, and proceed to read his mind. Meanwhile, behind your back slip the egg up one sleeve. Leaving the other hand behind you as if holding the egg, nonchalantly hold you hand to your forehead as though suffering the pangs of intensive concentration and glance into your sleeve.

After identifying the color, return your hand behind your back and let the egg slip into it. Announce the color and then victoriously display the egg.

THE MIRACLE MARBLE

This trick, more difficult than the preceding, employs the same basic concept—guessing the color of an object handed to you behind your back. A little practice to back you up makes this an extremely impressive impromptu trick.

Props: several marbles or other small objects of different colors
a few coins

Advance Preparation: Wear a coat or jacket with pockets and slacks or a skirt with side pockets. To prepare for the trick, stand with coat unbuttoned and your hand in your right pants pocket. This pushes the right side of your coat (with pocket) to the back. You should have a coin or two in your right coat pocket. Stand in this position before approaching your audience, so no one will take particular notice of this pose.

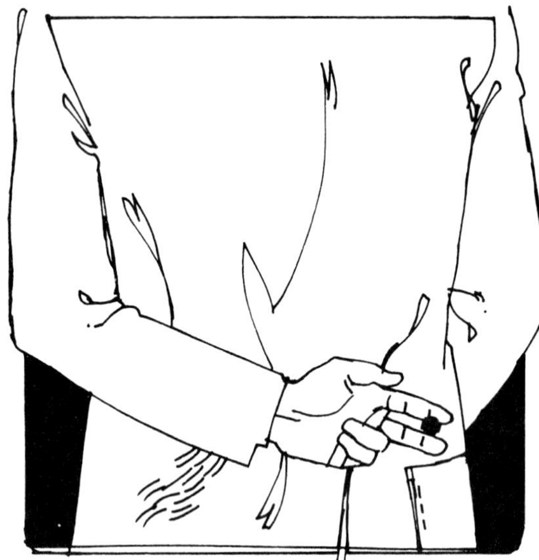

Choose a spectator, hand him the marbles and turn your back. Put your left hand behind your back and have the victim place one marble in it. Now turn to face the audience.

Clip the marble between the first and second fingers and drop it into your right coat pocket behind your back.

Now comes the subtlest part of the trick: Remove your right hand from your pants pocket and pass it over your forehead as you concentrate on reading the spectator's mind. If your audience has seen this trick before, they may think you have palmed the marble and are glancing at it under cover of this act. Further confound them at this point by casually making it obvious you have nothing in that hand. This detracts attention from the next step when you *do* palm the marble with that hand.

Express such confidence in your success that you are willing to bet a quarter (or a dime, or so on) on it. Reach into your coat pocket to pull out a coin, simultaneously finger-palming the marble.

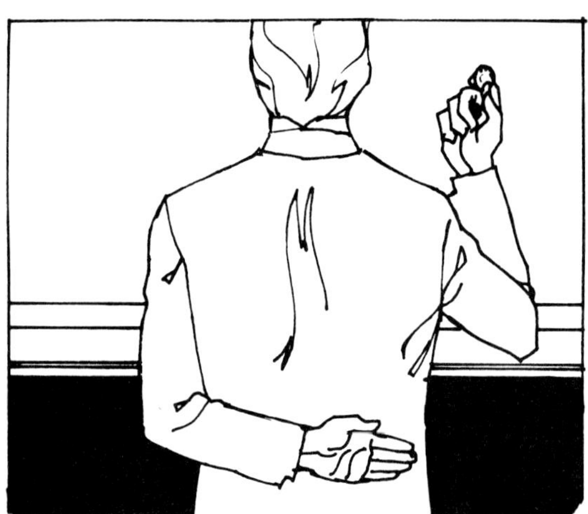

Hold the coin up between thumb and forefinger, the back of your hand to the audience to conceal the marble in your palm. If the wager is accepted, put the coin on a table, retaining the marble; if not, drop the coin back into your pocket, holding on to the marble.

Now put your right hand with your left behind your back. Turn your back to the audience for a moment to display the object still in your hands, out of your line of vision; then name the color and display the marble.

READING CRAYON COLORS

Similar to preceding tricks, this one is perfect for the novice. You claim to read a spectator's mind to identify the color of a crayon he has placed in a box.

Props: a selection of colored crayons
a small box or other container that closes completely
a nail file to clean your fingernails, afterwards

Advance Preparation: none

Turn your back to the audience and have a spectator choose a crayon of any color. After the victim has placed the crayon in the box, have him hand it to you behind your back.

Face the audience and as you pretend to receive messages by feeling the box behind your back, surreptitiously open it and scratch the crayon with a fingernail.

Hiding that fingernail from the audience, bring the closed box to the front and pretend to get further vibes by holding it against your forehead, tapping and shaking it, making jokes to amuse the audience.

In the meantime, maneuver the box so you can glance at the color under your fingernail. Proceed to guess the correct color, to your audience's delight.

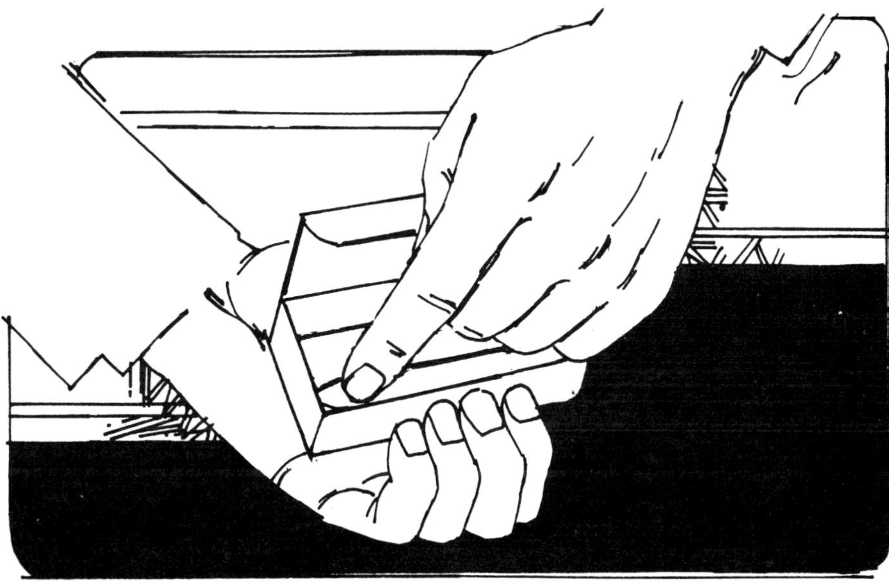

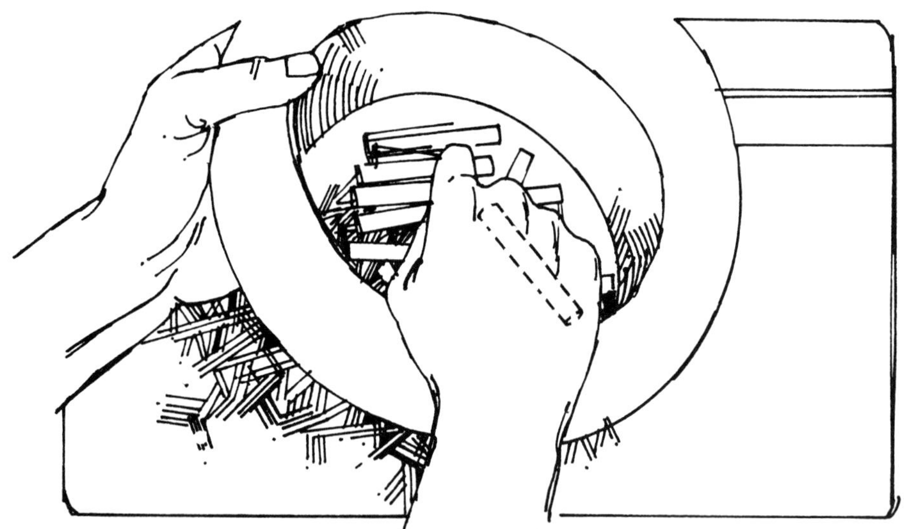

THE MARKED CIGARETTE I

This mind-reading act is a real cheater since it depends on the nature of tobacco rather than on sleight of hand or misdirection by the performer. Thus it is ideal for the beginner who has not acquired these skills. Claim that, with the aid of certain spirits, you can pick out a cigarette marked by a spectator and placed in a hatful of cigarettes—without looking, of course.

Props: a stale cigarette
a package of the same brand of cigarettes
a hat or box
a pen or marker

Advance Preparation: The stale cigarette (exposed to air for several days), plus an unopened package of the same brand of cigarettes, must be placed in your pocket.

To start the trick, pull the new pack from your pocket and hand it to a spectator for examination. Once he is convinced it has never been opened or tampered with, open the package and dump the cigarettes into a hat or box. Shake the cigarettes around as you explain your powers of ESP to the audience.

Then, reach into the hat, with your stale cigarette palmed in your hand, and pull the cigarette out as though from the hat. (To palm the stale cigarette, casually return your hand to your pocket as you shake the hat of cigarettes, taking out the palmed cigarette as you announce that you're going to hand a cigarette to the spectator.)

Have the spectator initial the cigarette with a pen, then put it back into the hat.

With the hat held above your eyes, feel around the hat until you find the one cigarette that is noticeably harder than the others. This will be the marked cigarette—your powers have proved themselves again.

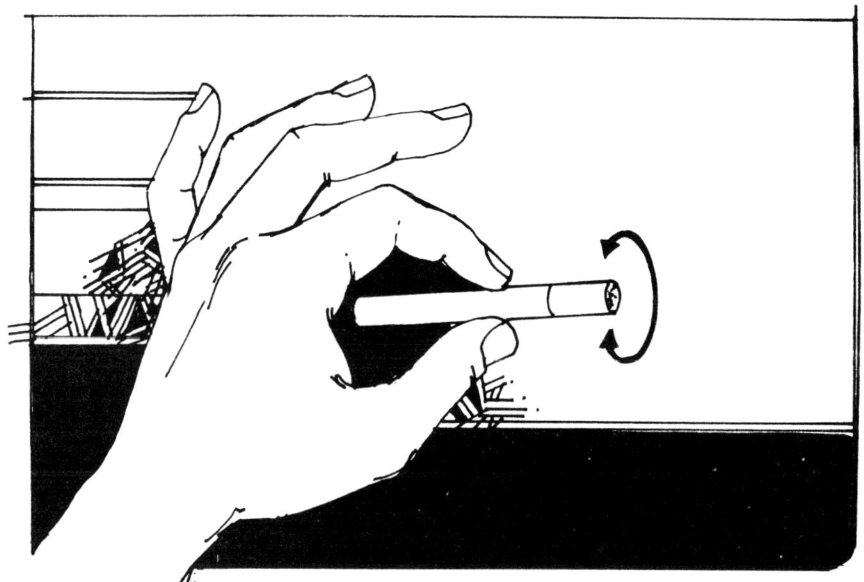

THE MARKED CIGARETTE II

This trick also depends on the characteristics of tobacco in a cigarette paper, but since it requires no advance preparation or skills, it is a great impromptu trick for tyro magicians. You will need a hat, box, or other container and a pack of cigarettes. This time, however, any pack of cigarettes will do, so you can dissolve any suspicion about your props by borrowing a pack from a spectator.

Props: a package of cigarettes (may be borrowed from a spectator)
a hat or box
a pen

Advance Preparation: none

Follow a routine identical to that of the previous trick, except identify the initialed cigarette by marking it with a subtle pinch. As you pull a cigarette from the hat, roll and pinch it a bit in one spot. This will compress the tobacco without compressing the paper, and you need only feel the dent in the cigarette to identify it.

For a nice variation on this theme, impress the audience with quantity mind-reading and use three cigarettes. Make sure you have a package of filter cigarettes for the trick, and as you pull them from the hat one by one, pinch one near the filter, one near the center, and one near the tip, keeping the location of the pinch connected in your mind with the person who picked that cigarette.

End this trick with a flourish as you draw each cigarette out of the hat and toss it to the correct spectator.

THE WIZARD IN THE WINGS

Magic experts may scorn this trick as more of a gag than a demonstration of skill, but it is worth adding to your repertoire for emergency situations. The trick not only requires advance preparation, but also the cooperation of a friend and his telephone. The object is to tell a crowd of friends of an astounding person whose extrasensory perception is so strong he can deduce over the phone which card a spectator has chosen from a deck. This is a good trick and there are some wild variations.

Props: a deck of cards
a telephone
an accomplice

Advance Preparation: A willing friend must be briefed ahead of time according to the description below.

Have someone in the room choose a card from a deck and show it to you so that you may assist in sending silent messages to the distant mind reader. You might even suggest that everyone in the room look at the card and concentrate on its suit and number.

You now call your telepathic friend. If he doesn't answer the phone, you're out of luck. But if the wizard is at home, proceed as follows.

When your accomplice answers, say, "Hello, is this the Amazing Albert (or some other name)?" On this cue, your partner begins to recite the suits. When he reaches the correct suit, interrupt and ask, "Will you bring him to the phone, please?" (or other prearranged phrase).

The wizard then starts to name the cards in a deck (1, 2, 3, and so on), and when the correct one comes up, you say, "Here he (she) is," and hand the phone to your patsy. Your talented friend then astounds the victim by naming the correct card.

Every magician's trick bag includes a few routines that solicit the aid of spirits but which do not fall exactly into the category of mind-reading. For instance, many tricks involve the use of invisible or spirit writing, no-hands movement of objects from one place to another, and similar techniques. Of course, most of these actually are accomplished through sleight of hand, misdirection, gimmick props and other nonoccult factors. But the overall effect is focused on sending and receiving messages between our world and that of the spirits. Following are interesting effects you can attribute to psychic phenomena.

THE SPIRIT INK TRICK

Observant spectators are likely to catch on to this old and simple trick, but children will usually be awed. Tell your audience that you will engage the spirits around you to move an ink line from your palm to the back of your hand.

Prop: a ballpoint pen that writes smoothly (you may have to experiment to find a pen with the right ink for this transfer)

Advance Preparation: none

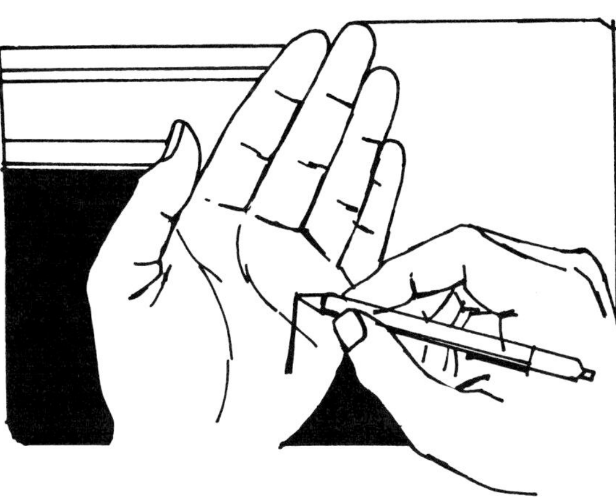

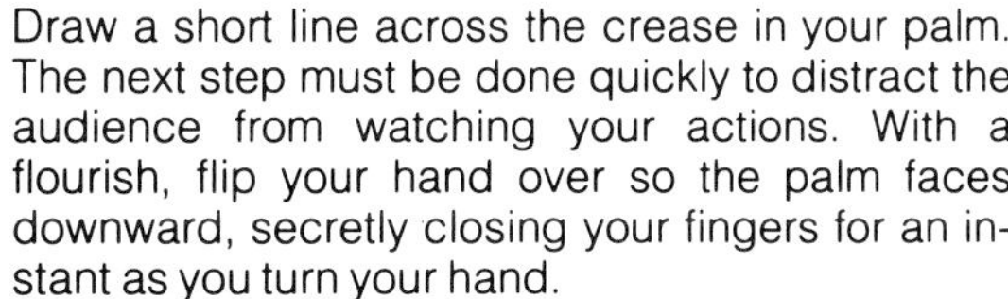

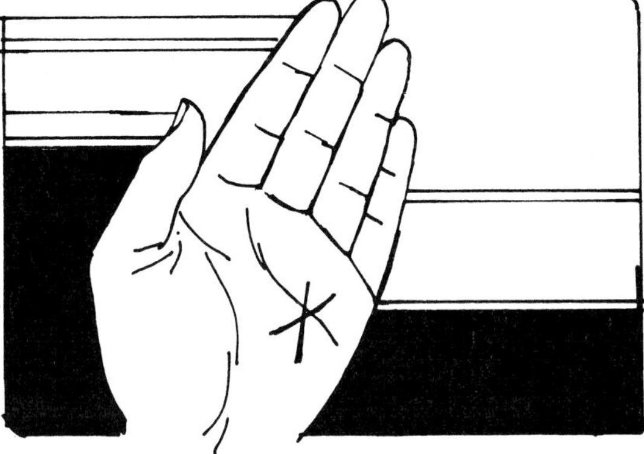

Draw a short line across the crease in your palm. The next step must be done quickly to distract the audience from watching your actions. With a flourish, flip your hand over so the palm faces downward, secretly closing your fingers for an instant as you turn your hand.

With patter, draw another short line on the back of your hand. Show it to your audience and then erase it by rubbing with your other hand, which you've wetted, saying that the spirits will transfer the mark to your palm.

Now turn your hand over, and show the audience where the second mark has crossed the first on your palm. (Obviously, when you closed your finger momentarily, the ink spread in a cross-hatch pattern caused by the crease in your palm.)

THE SPIRIT CHALK TRICK

Similar to the preceding trick, this one is also quite simple to perform. The idea is the same—you transfer a chalk mark from one place to another with the help of psychic forces.

Props: chalk
a table

Advance Preparation: Make two small crosses in chalk on the nails of the first two fingers on the left hand.

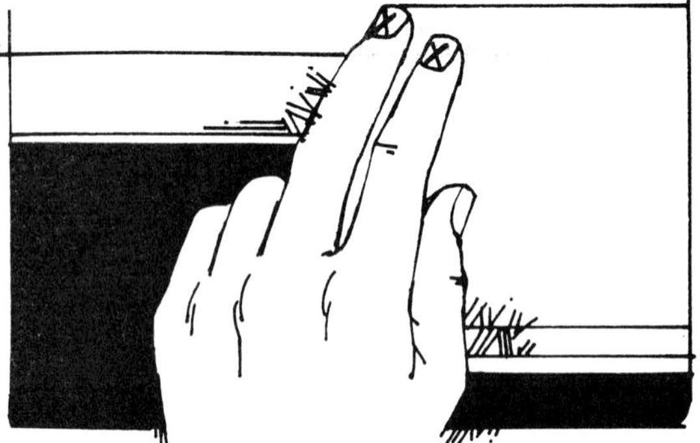

Show your left palm to the audience as you announce the trick, obscuring the fingernails with the chalk marks. Claim that you can draw a cross on the table and transfer it to your hand.

Put your left hand under the table and make a fist secretly, which transfers the chalk marks to the palm near the base of your thumb. Keeping the hand under the table, use the chalk to draw a cross on the table with your right hand.

Erase the mark with your hand, calling on the spirits to transfer it.

Now display the chalk crosses on your left palm.

The X marks in the pictures are black; but you're supposed to use white blackboard chalk if you want this to work.

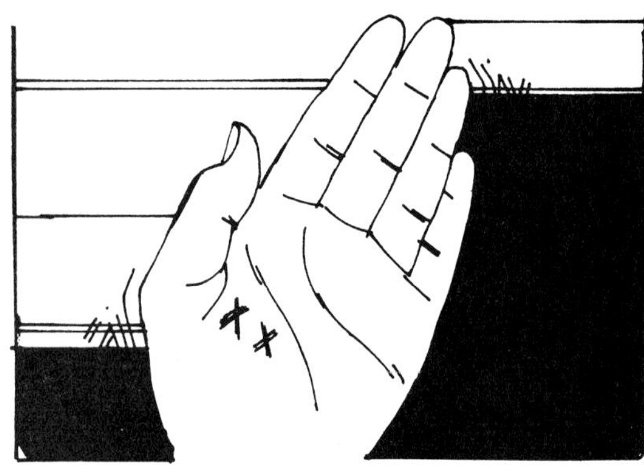

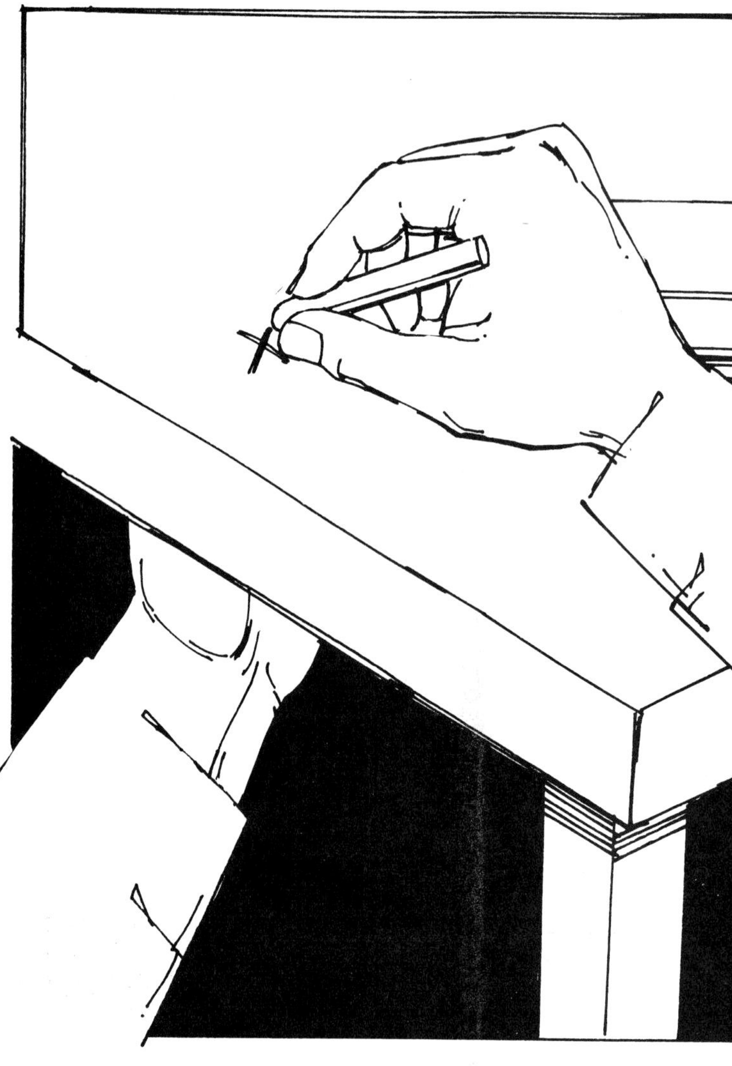

READING THE HAND

This psychic phenomenon trick may be attributed either to telepathic powers or other psychic force. The idea is to claim that you can determine in which hand a spectator held an object while you were out of the room. This good impromptu trick can be done anywhere.

Prop: any small object that can be hidden inside a fist (such as a coin, matchbook, or ring)

Advance Preparation: none

Begin by handing the object to a spectator. Announce that after your departure from the room a spectator should put the object in one closed fist and raise it above his head.

You can change the trick's effect from humorous to mysterious by having the spectator read or recite either a funny song or poem or an eerie call to the spirits as he holds up his hand.

When the recitation is finished, the spectator should close both fists. Return to the room and immediately point to the fist holding the object.

You can make a big deal of examining the spectator's hands when you return to the room or stage, but actually you can determine the correct answer in an instant. A quick look at both hands will tell you which is whiter (from holding the hand in the air for several minutes); this is the hand with the object. If you can't tell by looking at the hand, make a guess. You've got a 50-50 chance of being right.

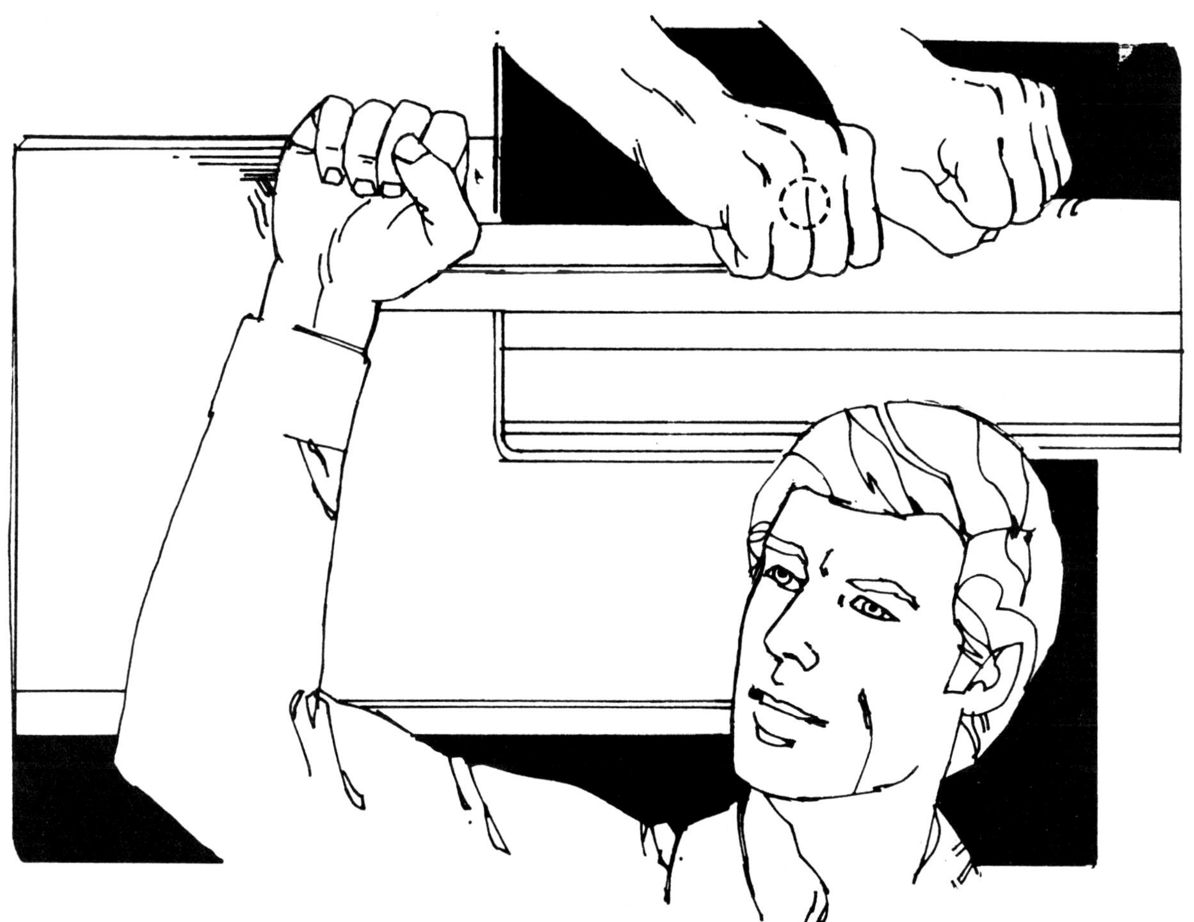

A slew of tricks are available in which you allow or direct the spirits to move an object at your will and nearly all are simple enough for the novice conjurer to perform. These are good tricks for the dinner table and are apt to be most convincing to children. The following are classic variations on this theme.

THE MOVING PAWN

Obviously, this trick is particularly suited to performance after a game of chess. Or, you might try offering to do it in the middle of a game to rattle your opponent.

Props: a chess board
chess pawns
a hat

Advance Preparation: None is necessary, but you might want to try this a time or two before performing it.

Claim that you will contact the spirits and, focusing your attention on your hat, have the spirits move a pawn in the same direction as you move the hat.

Put a pawn *on its side* on the chess board and start moving the hat in a circle above the pawn. Make sure that the hat is in a position to block the spectator's view of your mouth.

Under cover of the hat, gently blow on the pawn to rotate it in a circle on the board. It's hard to make this work, but maybe with a weighted pawn you can.

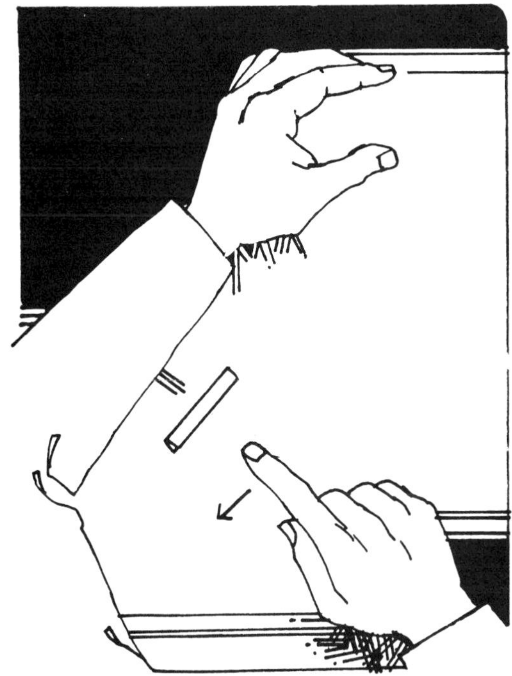

MOVING CIGARETTE I

The principle of this trick is the same as the preceding.

Props: a cigarette
a table
Advance Preparation: none

Claim you can call on the spirits to move a cigarette toward your moving finger, a statement that makes it seem impossible you're accomplishing this result by blowing on the cigarette.

Lay your left arm on the table, elbow bent a little, with the cigarette between your arm and your body.

Tell the audience to concentrate on your right forefinger, which you pull toward you. As they are distracted by helping the spirits in this way, subtly blow against your left arm. The air will bounce off your arm and blow the cigarette toward your finger.

MOVING CIGARETTE II

Here is another version of the same trick

Props: a cigarette
a match
a table
Advance Preparation: none

Lay the cigarette crosswise over a match on the table. Put one finger near either end of the match and claim to be able to pull the cigarette toward it. Merely blow it gently and subtly.

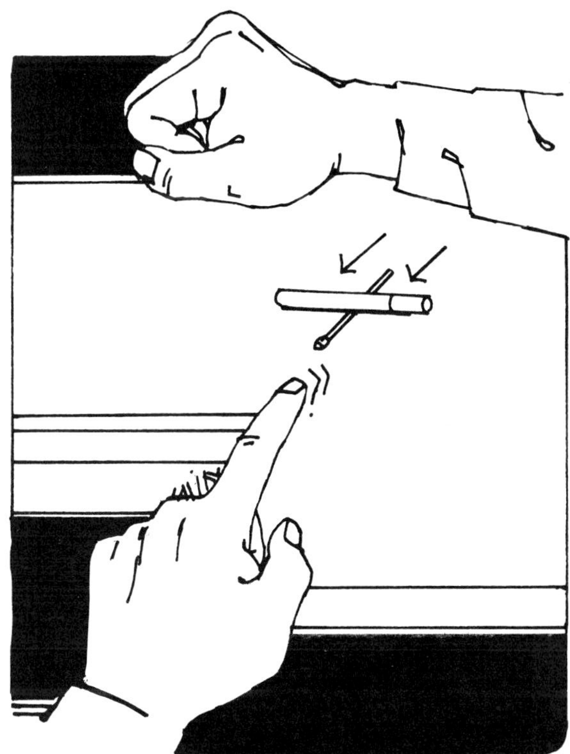

MOVING CIGARETTE III

This slightly different trick employs the same principle as those above.

Props: 2 cigarettes
a table
Advance Preparation: none

Place the cigarettes parallel to each other and a few inches apart on the table. Pretend to force them apart by contacting the spirits through your finger, which you move in a circle on the table around the cigarettes. Instead, blow gently between the cigarettes.

THE LOYAL PAWNS

This impromptu trick is based on a simple physical property, the transference of heat, and is designed for spontaneous performance following a chess game; it is an especially gratifying way to show up an opponent who has just checkmated you in four moves. Basically, you claim that you can unfailingly choose the correct color pawn chosen by your opponent when all chess pieces are placed in a hat and held out of your line of vision.

Props: chess pieces
a hat or box (or other receptacle)
Advance Preparation: none

You must decide to do this trick at some point during the game. So, if you know you're going to lose, start preparing by nonchalantly or absentmindedly handling the pawns you capture from your opponent. Your hands will warm the pawns as you hold them, and your opponent will probably be so busy gloating over his superior chess skill that he will not think much of your behavior.

When the game is over, suggest that your opponent test your ESP prowess. Have him put the pawns into a hat or box and name the color pawn he wants you to remove. You might suggest that though you lost the game, the chess pieces have taken on your vibrations and those of your color will be drawn to you.

Now reach into the hat and remove a pawn of the specified color. Your opponent's pawns will be warm from the heat of your hands, while yours will be cool.

You can also do this with coins and you will find the metal retains the warmth a bit longer than wooden or plastic chessmen. Even so, don't wait too long or you'll just be guessing. Tell the spectators you will find the coin with the date 1979 amongst a dozen or so of different dates tossed into a hat. You can also do a reverse method by holding your coin against an ice cube or a cold drink so the coin you find is the cold one instead of the warm one. Be sure to take your mittens off.

Following are two of many mind-reading tricks performed using books. Using either routine, you can locate and recite the word(s) at the top of a page chosen by a spectator. These tricks are suited for stage use or for thrilling your family and friends on a dull Saturday night.

THE SPIRIT CARD

Props: a book
a standard index card
a soft (number one) pencil

Advance Preparation: Hand all the props to a spectator and have him flip to any page in the book without showing you the page. Ask the spectator to write the first word, or the whole top line if you choose, in the middle of the card and stick the card into the book facing the page he has chosen. Make sure the card is projecting enough to allow you to pull it out.

Take the book from the spectator. Press the covers together firmly with one hand as you withdraw the "magic" card with the other hand. The soft lead will smear on the correct page as you pull out the card.

As you remove the card, close your eyes or turn your head away so the spectator cannot think you peeked at the card. Hand it to the spectator and say that you're going to try to receive the message the card left in the book.

Now flip through the pages, making a big deal of it to distract the audience as you glance at the book to locate the lead smudge. When you have found it, recite the word(s) on the top of the page chosen by the spectator.

You may also do this trick with the aid of an assistant who stays offstage, receives the book from the magician, and looks for the smudge mark.

TRICKS WITH BOOKS

BOOK-TO-BOOK TELEPATHY

This trick may appeal to you more than the preceding since there is no dependence on a physical gimmick like a lead smudge.

Props: 2 books

Advance Preparation: Before you perform, choose a few pages randomly from one book, preferably one each from the front, back, and middle. Memorize the page number and the first word or phrase on each page.

Hand the book from which you've memorized pages and words to your victim and riffle the pages of the other book. Instruct the spectator to tell you when to stop. When he does so, call out one of the page numbers you've memorized, and have the spectator turn to that page in his book. Now astound him by reciting the correct word or phrase at the top of the page!

Obviously, the trick is that the victim will believe you're telling the truth when you call out the page you've stopped at in the book. Dr. Faust makes a miracle of this. I have seen him select a single word or phrase and the page number at a glance as he asks you to pick out two books from a newsstand book rack. As he tells you what he wants you to do he steals his peek. The book is then selected by the "Conjuror's choice."

In Conjuror's Choice, you already know which of four different objects (such as coins of different denominations) you want your victim to choose. Tell him to point to two of the four. If your chosen item is one of the two he selects, you remove the other two. If he didn't choose it, remove the two he selected. Then tell him to pick one of the remaining. If he selects your chosen item, remove the other—or vice versa. You always end up with the item you want.

THE BIG H

This simple trick takes advance preparation but no skill on the part of the magician. The idea is to place nine playing cards face up on a table in an H pattern and to guess which of the nine a spectator has pointed to while you were out of the room.

Props: a deck of cards
an accomplice

Advance Preparation: You need only nine of the 52 cards in a deck, and it doesn't matter which they are as long as at least one, and preferably two, is a nine. You also must brief an accomplice on the trick.

To prevent your audience from guessing the gimmick, prepare the deck beforehand by placing at least one nine among the top nine cards of the deck. Note that the pips on a nine are arranged in an H pattern.

Start by announcing the trick and laying out the cards face up in an H pattern on a table. You may justify the H pattern by choosing a victim whose name begins with H, or by calling this the Horseplay trick and as you deal the cards call out a letter for each card:

H-O-R-S-E-P-L-A-Y

or making up some reason why the spirits will help you receive messages through the H figure.

Instruct your victim to point to one of the cards when you leave the room, making sure the rest of the spectators see his choice so there will be no doubt about your success.

When you return to the room, have your assistant begin pointing to and tapping the cards, asking you, "Is this the correct card?" for each one. Watch your assistant carefully so you can catch the cue on the nine.

Now astound your audience by replying, "Yes," when your assistant taps the correct card.

Part of your advance preparation involves briefing your accomplice. Inform the chosen assistant that when you return to the room he will point to each card laid out in the H pattern, asking you which is the correct card. When the assistant comes to one of the nines, he will specifically tap on the pip corresponding to the position in the H of the victim's chosen card. For instance, if the victim has selected the top left card, the assistant will tap the top left pip in the nine.

You can repeat this trick by having a third party point to the cards asking, "Is this the correct card?" each time he points to a card. You still use your accomplice; but on the second time he remains absolutely motionless until the correct card is indicated, at which time he moves a finger or turns his head every so slightly. The magician then knows to say, "Yes, that is the correct card."

In the illustration the accomplice is pointing to the pip which would indicate the 2 of hearts was the designated card.

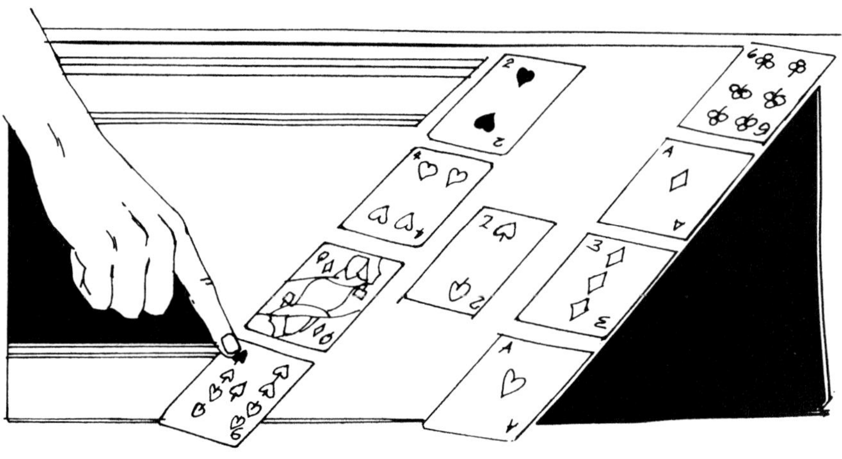

CARD DETECTIVE

This classic routine is a simple way for a beginner to identify cards cut by several spectators.

Prop: an unopened pack of cards
Advance Preparation: Make sure you use an unopened pack of cards.

A brand new, unopened pack of cards with the seal unbroken is the clue to this miracle. It has even been done by mail. The spectator seems to do everything. His instructions are to break the seal, open the pack of cards, and spread them to make sure all the cards are there. His steps are as follows:

1. Remove all the advertising cards, scoring cards and jokers, so there are just 52 cards.

2. Give the cards a single cut and complete it, so the magician doesn't know what card is on the top or bottom.

3. Give the cards a riffle shuffle.

4. Give the cards another riffle shuffle.

5. Cut the pack in two piles and remove a card from the middle of one of the piles and look at it—remember it.

6. Put the card into the middle of the other pile.

7. Give the magician either half of the deck.

The magician studies the cards for a few moments and then announces the name of the selected card.

Here's how. As you look at a new pack of U.S. playing cards, there is generally a Joker on each end of the pack and an advertising card which has contract bridge scoring points on the back. Sometimes there is a sample card from another pack as well. The face card is the ace of spades and all the rest of the spades follow in order. Next are all the diamonds from ace to king, followed by the king of clubs in reverse order down to the ace and finally the king of hearts down to the ace of hearts.

To learn this trick, set up any old pack in this order and follow what happens when you follow the instructions as given. While you are learning, leave out Step 2 where you give the cards a cut.

Two riffle shuffles will mix up the pack a good bit, but you can still pick out the four suits and find a sequence of cards.

Here is an example: AH 10D JS 9D 2H 10S 6C 3H 4H 7C 8C 7D 5H 6H 7H 6D 9S 9C 5D 8H 9H.

I was handed this part of the pack and I determined the 8 of diamonds was the selected card. I determined this by following the sequence of the spades. There were only three of them and there were no gaps. Next, I went to the diamonds and found there were a 5, 6, 7, and the next card was 9. How smart do you have to be to figure out the missing card is the 8 of diamonds?

On the other hand, I might have been handed the other half of the pack and I would have found the 8 of diamonds was between the ace and the 2 of diamonds, so again it doesn't take too many smarts to figure.

If you include Step 2 and have the cards cut before the two riffle shuffles, you have to look at the top and bottom cards of the half-pack you get to determine the order of the deck before the shuffles, and compensate for that.

One note of caution: If you use a pack of cards manufactured in Great Britain, be aware that the British arrangement in an unopened pack of cards is not the same as the American.

stage magic

Like some tricks in chapter 1, the stage routines that follow are based on magically transforming one prop into a completely different object. This can be done through various means, but whatever the technique, your audience is likely to react with astounded oohs and aahs. Most of the wonder-working described below requires some preparation of props, but no purchased gimmicks are necessary. All the equipment you need is available in most households.

Remember that advance preparation is one key to success. To make props appear or disappear, you must be able to conceal an extra prop nearby. And on stage this isn't always easy!

But most important of all is perfecting your ability to distract your audience by talking about something totally dissociated, to seem absentmindedly to draw your listeners away from the actions of your hands as you prepare your next move. Chatter along and lead your audience toward the faking hand to hide your actions with the other. And learn to pepper your somber acts with lighthearted tricks to give contrast to the overall effects of your show.

Like some in chapter 1, the routines that follow are based on magically transforming one prop into a completely different object. Whatever the technique, your audience is likely to react with astounded oohs and aahs. The wonderworking described below generally requires preparation of props, but no purchased gimmicks are necessary. All equipment needed is available in most households.

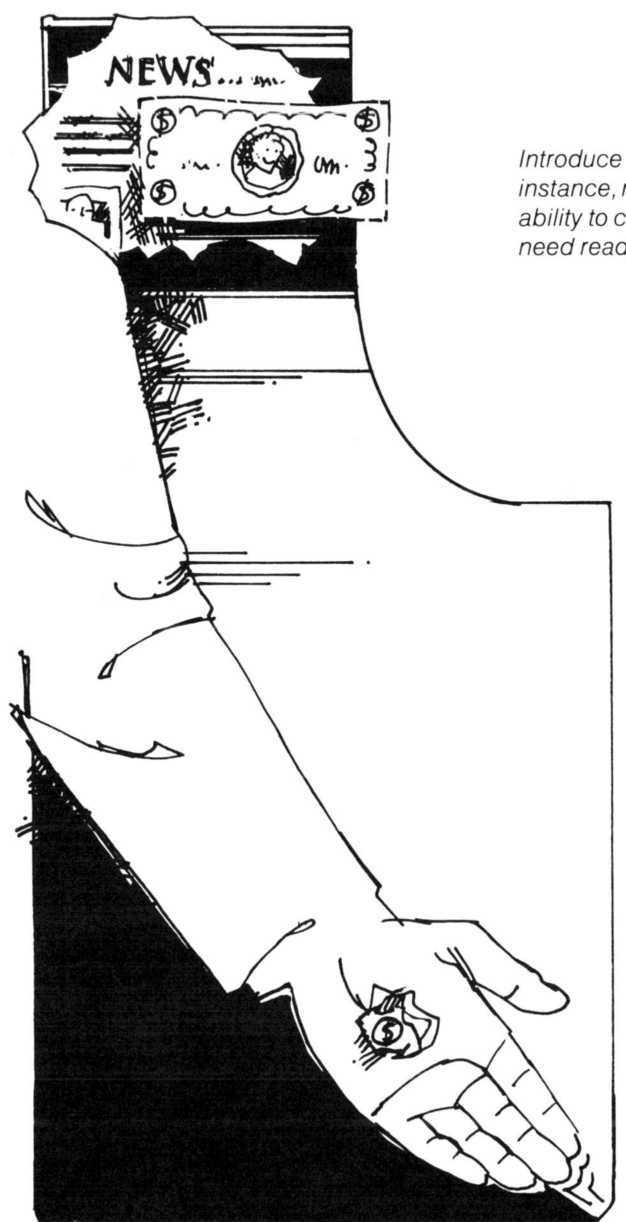

FROM NEWSPRINT TO GREENBACKS

Introduce this trick with reference to the high cost of living. For instance, mention the peculiar advantage of being a magician: the ability to create money from a simple wad of newspaper when you need ready cash.

Props: 2 small balls of crumpled newspaper
a bill of any denomination crumpled into a ball of the same size as the newspaper

Advance Preparation: Finger palm the currency ball in your right hand before announcing the trick.

To begin, lay the newspaper balls on a table. You may wish to start with two small pieces of newspaper, rolling them into balls as you introduce the trick.

Choose a victim from the audience and have him point to one of the two newspaper balls. With your right hand, lift the designated ball and pretend to drop it into your left hand. Instead, drop the palmed currency ball into your left hand, palming the newspaper ball in a sneaky switch.

At this point, the audience thinks your right hand is empty, so you may pick up the second newspaper ball from the table and drop it, with the first palmed ball, into a pocket or other receptacle onstage into which the audience cannot see.

Perform mumbo jumbo over your left hand, opening it to show your success in transforming cheap newsprint into expensive money.

Note that when you have passed the bill to your left hand you may allow the audience a glimpse before closing your hand around it, because it will appear identical to the newspaper.

BLACK MARKET CIGARETTES

In this trick, a prepared cigarette is transformed into a rolled dollar bill. You might introduce the trick with a story about the high cost of cigarettes in distant ports or during a certain era.

Props: a pack of cigarettes (preferably the long, or 100 ml variety)
a dollar bill
a glass of water

Advance Preparation: When offstage, prepare a cigarette from the pack as follows: Remove all tobacco from the cigarette and insert the rolled bill inside the paper. Stuff a little tobacco into the cigarette end to disguise your prop. Place the cigarette in the pack where it can be pulled out easily.

Start the trick by pulling the prepared cigarette from the package, letting this remind you of an anecdote about black market cigarettes, or some similar tale. Carried away by your enthusiasm for the story, "accidentally" drop the cigarette into a nearby glass of water. (A bit of saliva will do it. You don't need to soak the cigarette in water.)

Remove it and finger it as though deciding what to do with it, but actually rub it between your palms. The wet cigarette paper will dissolve into minute shreds to reveal the bill rolled beneath. Make an appropriate reference to your introductory anecdote, showing the dollar-bill cigarette in your hand:

1. "And that's how I smuggled the money out of Slobovia."

2. "You can light a dollar bill with a cigarette, which is some sort of switch."

3. "Just goes to show there is still money in tobacco."

4. "Smoking is bad for you. The Surgeon General says so."

5. "You've seen people roll cigarettes, haven't you?"

6. "I'm gonna smoke the water and drink the cigarette."

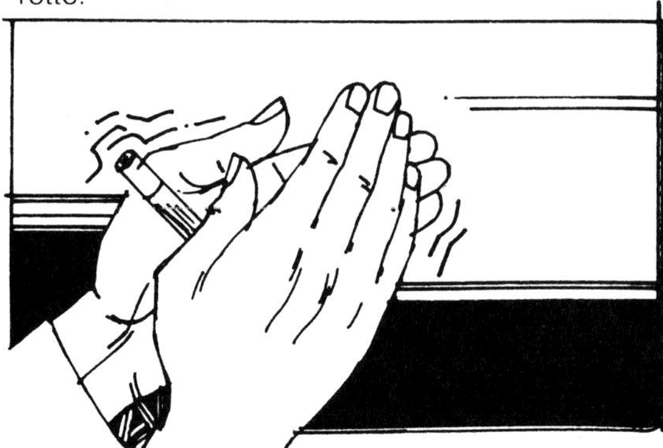

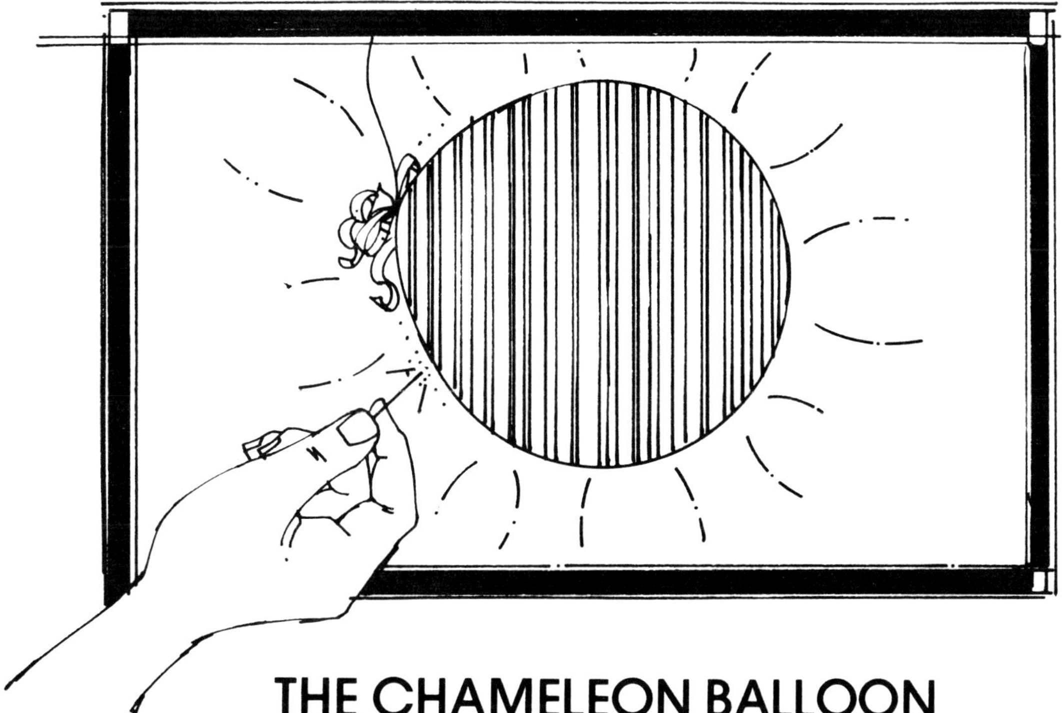

THE CHAMELEON BALLOON

This trick is appropriate for performance at a children's party, or onstage as a filler amusement between more complex tricks.

Props: 2 balloons of different colors
a pin, or any other sharply pointed object
Advance Preparation: Prepare balloons as described below.

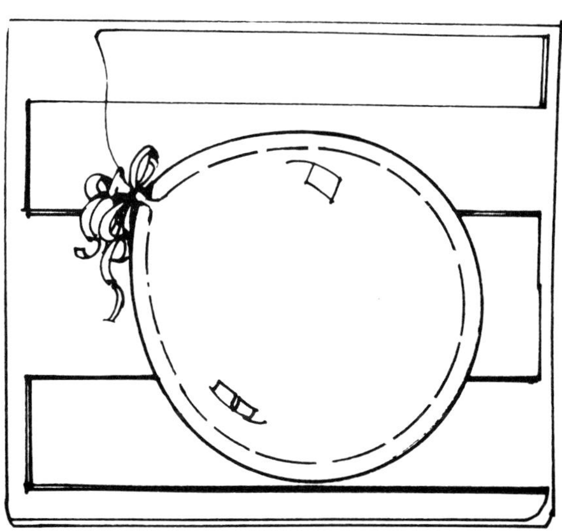

Stick one balloon inside the other. Blow into the inner balloon to inflate both. Tie the inner balloon, then blow into the outer balloon to create a small air space between the two; tie the outer balloon. Decorate the stage or party room with one or more double balloons before starting your act so you will be ready to perform the trick as the spirit moves you. Be sure a dark colored balloon is outside a light colored balloon.

Whenever you sense flagging audience interest, carefully touch the balloon with a pointed object to burst the outer balloon, only. The audience, jumping from the popping noise, will expect to see the balloon disappear. They will be delighted by its apparently changing color when you come in contact with it.

If you accidentally burst both balloons, say, "Nobody sleeps in my act."

The tricks in this section could be considered conceptual opposites of the vanishes. Rather than make a prop disappear, you conjure an extra object from thin air.

CASH ON HAND

Most audiences find tricks especially intriguing when the extra object produced turns out to be cash.

Props: 2 identical-denomination coins
a table
a dab of sticky substance such as chewing gum, softened wax or rubber cement

Advance Preparation: Using a dab of wax, gum or cement, conceal one coin under the table edge near you. The second coin should be on top of the table.

This trick, so quick and simple that it is best used as a part of another, may end a routine in which you have made a wager with a spectator. Surprise the bet winner by doubling the stakes.

The simple move comprising the trick must be done quickly to avoid discovery. Pretending to hand the coin to the spectator, slide the top coin off the table, and when your hand reaches the edge secretly pull the other coin from the underside with your thumb.

You may feign surprise when you hand the spectator both coins.

INCREASING THE ODDS

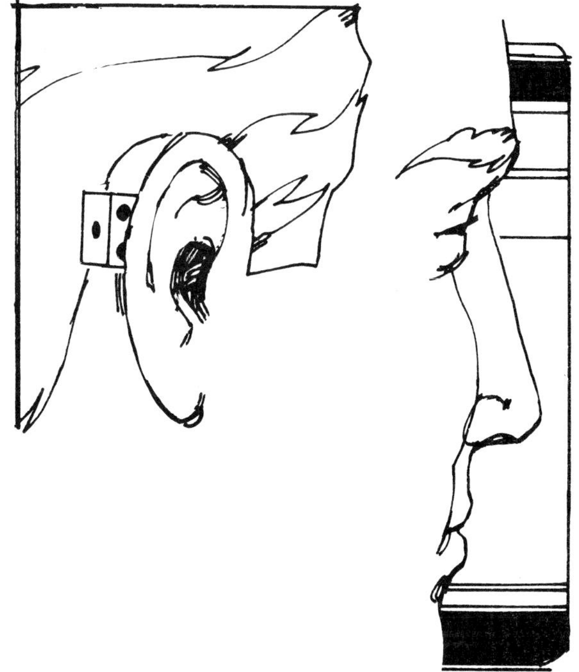

This old trick may not fool those who have seen many magic shows. However, this nifty move can be performed during a game that involves dice. You produce an extra die, saying you wished to increase the odds in your favor. If you do this while playing for serious money you may be rewarded with a broken hand or head.

Props: 3 identical dice

Advance Preparation: Practice the following moves in front of a mirror to be sure your legerdemain is unnoticeable. Before doing the trick, conceal one die behind the ear on the same side as the hand with which you intend rolling the dice.

Roll two dice across a table several times, each time raising your hand to your ear to shake them. On the third or fourth roll, quickly palm the die hidden behind your ear, rolling it out with the other two. You can say, "Fourteen's my point," or whatever total the three dice show.

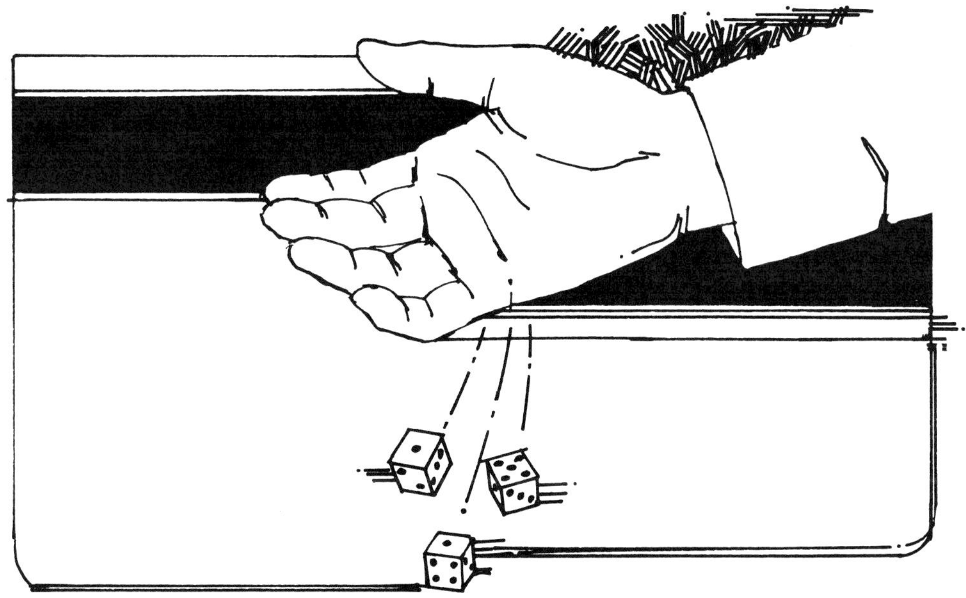

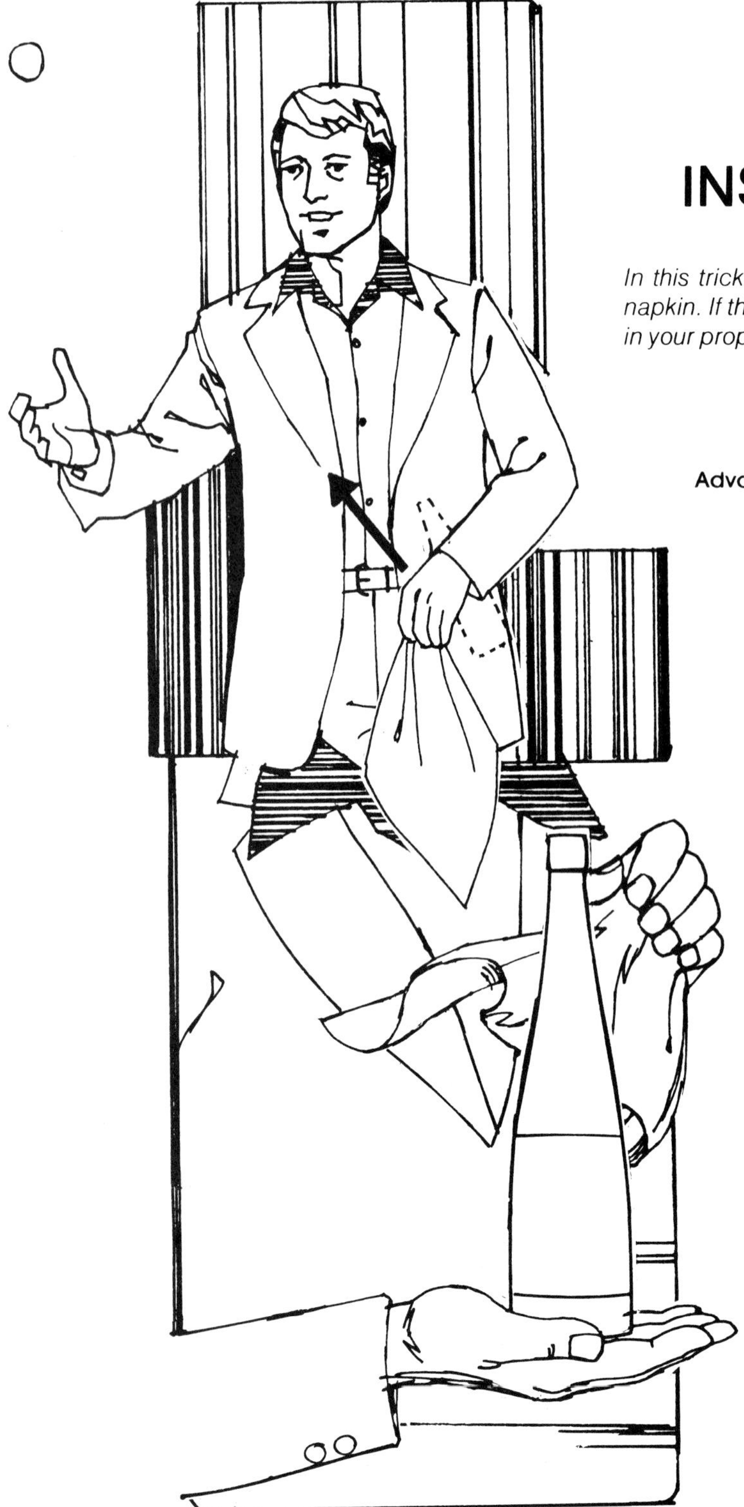

INSTANT REFRESHMENT

In this trick the magician produces a bottle under a large table napkin. If the bottle contains wine, be sure to include a corkscrew in your prop list.

Props: a large handkerchief or dinner table napkin
a tall thin opaque wine bottle

Advance Preparation: For this one you wear a loose fitting jacket and slacks or skirt with a belt. Shove the bottle under your belt toward the left side and button your jacket.

You can walk around all evening until someone asks, "Do you know where I can get a drink?" This is your cue to reach into your right coat pocket and pull out a ball and into your left coat pocket to pull out the large handkerchief. Hold the handkerchief by one corner and unbutton your coat. Toss the ball in the air and catch it all with the right hand, as the left hand is stealing the bottle by the neck under cover of the napkin or handkerchief. About the third time you've tossed the ball in the air you should be able to catch the ball and move it to the lower corner of the napkin, grasp the bottom of the bottle, and with the left hand pull away the cloth with a flourish, the ball being held under the bottle. Someday you might get to see an English magician named Bob Read. He does basically this trick; but he will fool you even when you know, because he has worked out the misdirection so perfectly.

DOUBLE COMBUSTIBLES

This non-instant but amusing effect should be incorporated into any trick in which you need to light a match. To your feigned surprise, the match lights twice.

Props: 2 matches (preferably one with a wider shaft than the other)
Advance Preparation: Prepare matches as described below.

Make a minute bend just below the head of the wider match. Place the head of the other match halfway down the first one.

The corner of the match formed by the bend should be toward you so that your audience cannot see it. Hold the matches in your hand so your fingers obscure the head of the narrower match.

Whenever you need a flame for a trick, light the upper match and let it burn a few seconds, making sure the head is a glowing red ember before blowing it out.

Immediately slide your thumb halfway down the hidden match, holding it still with pressure from your fingers, then quickly slide it up so that the heads of the two matches touch. The second match head will combust seemingly spontaneously, and from the audience's view it will appear a single match is lighting a second time.

RETURN OF THE PRODIGAL MATCH

This and the following trick serve as nice follow-ups to the one preceding. After watching the match apparently light twice, act concerned and pick up a matchbook to examine it for strange defects. In this trick, a burned match apparently torn from the book returns to the book.

Props: a full book of matches
a single match torn from an identical book
Advance Preparation: Have the single match available on a table. Before starting the trick, burn one of the matches in the full book without tearing it out. Then bend it backward and hold the matchbook with the burned match hidden under your thumb.

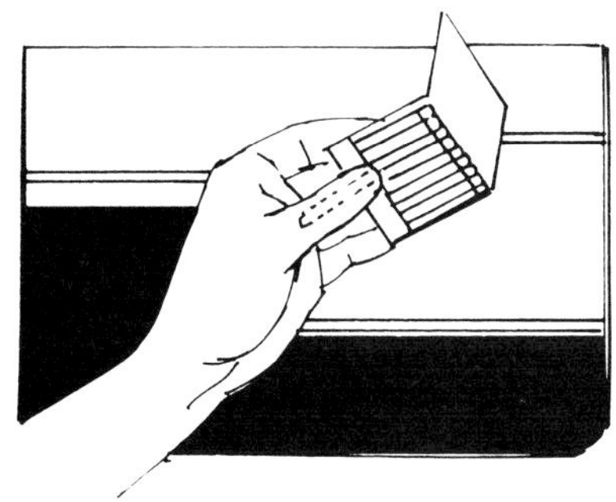

To start, hold the matchbook toward your chosen victim in the audience, without letting go or changing the matchbook's position.

Ask the victim to count the matches in the book, then close the book, quickly and secretly pushing the burnt match back into it during this action.

Put the matchbook down and pick up the single match. Light it and blow out the flame; then vanish the match by pretending to toss it in the air, but dropping it on the floor on the down-swing.

Now casually pick up the matchbook again and open it to discover the burned match has returned to the book from whence it came.

THE ETERNAL FLAME

This similar trick requires no sleight of hand, but it is less convincing, so make your moves quickly and patter throughout the trick to distract the audience from questioning.

Prop: a full matchbook
Advance Preparation: Have the matchbook on hand with the cover inserted between the front and back rows of matches.

To begin, hold up the matchbook to show it to the audience, but do not dwell on this step. Otherwise, your audience may guess that the back row of matches is concealed behind the cover, rather than assume the book is only half full, as you intend.

In front of the audience, tear out the first row of matches. If this trick is a follow-up to the Double Combustibles, you may explain that you are destroying the "faulty" matches.

Dispose of the torn matches so there can be no doubt about palming them, either by handing them to an assistant or dropping them into a pocket or wastebasket.

Now recite a hex or spell over the matchbook. Open the book to show the matches have magically returned to the book. Finish the trick by sighing that at least you know you will never be short of matches.

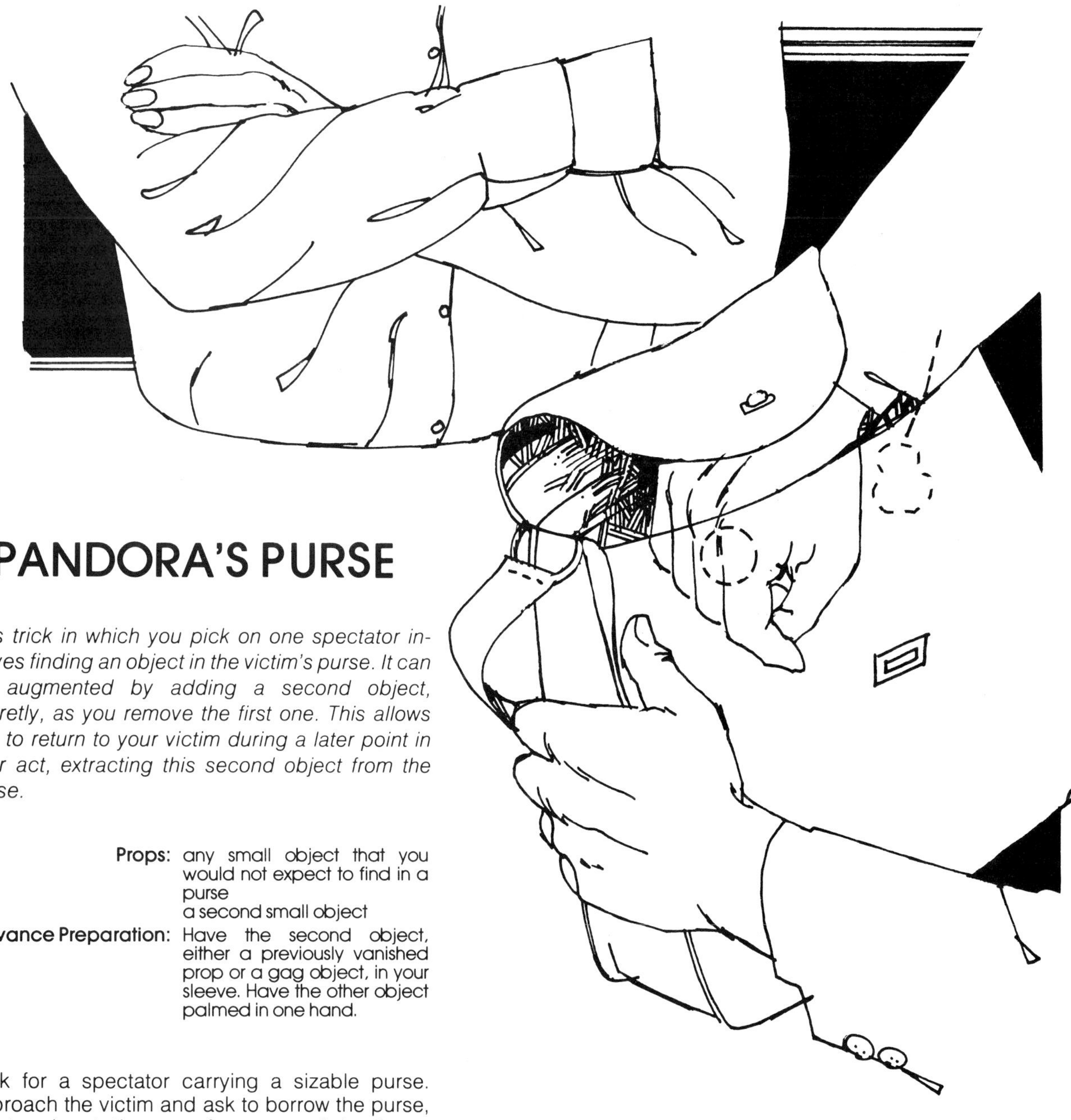

PANDORA'S PURSE

This trick in which you pick on one spectator involves finding an object in the victim's purse. It can be augmented by adding a second object, secretly, as you remove the first one. This allows you to return to your victim during a later point in your act, extracting this second object from the purse.

Props:	any small object that you would not expect to find in a purse a second small object
Advance Preparation:	Have the second object, either a previously vanished prop or a gag object, in your sleeve. Have the other object palmed in one hand.

Look for a spectator carrying a sizable purse. Approach the victim and ask to borrow the purse, but stay close to the owner for a more subtle effect.

As you lift the purse and reach into it, let the sleeved object drop into the purse, making sure no one sees this. As you withdraw your hand, pretend to pull out the first object, merely displaying the palmed prop as though it came from the purse. (You must realize it is possible to drop a third article into the purse as you retrieve the second one, and so on ad nauseum.)

BEWITCHING BONUSES

MORE WATER

This Oriental classic is best done with two shallow rice bowls or sauce dishes, outdoors.

Props: 2 cups or sauce dishes half filled with water

Advance Preparation: Practice this well before trying it on an audience. Be sure you can hold water in your mouth without swallowing, gulping simultaneously to make it look as though you have swallowed it.

Hold the two bowls shoulder high (they are half filled with water). Pick up one cup or sauce dish in each hand and shake with a circular motion so centrifugal force causes a little of the water to slosh over the edge, showing there is water inside.

Pretend to drink from the righthand sauce dish, pouring the water into your mouth and gulping, but returning the water surreptitiously to the dish as you lower it from your lips. Do the same with the other sauce dish, so spectators believe both are empty. Say, "More water."

Slosh water out of the righthand sauce dish again, and stare at it in surprise. The vessel has been magically refilled! Repeat with the lefthand dish.

Continue this routine, pretending to drink from one then the other, each time sloshing a little water to verify they have been refilled. However, actually swallow a little water each time so that toward the end of the trick, only a small amount is left in each.

On the last series of sips, leave the water from the righthand sauce dish in your mouth and as you raise the lefthand dish to drink, expel the water into that dish. Now show the audience that the lefthand dish is again full.

Look confused by all this, and glance quickly into the righthand dish as though intending to catch it in the act of refilling. Turn it upside down to show that somehow this one has finally emptied: look disgusted and toss that dish aside, drinking water from the lefthand sauce dish and patting your stomach, now full as possible.

The following tricks resemble the penetrations described in chapter 1.

CIGARETTE PENETRATION

This trick is quite similar to the Penetrating Pick described on p. 39.

Prop: a cigarette (no cork tips or filters)
Advance Preparation: none

Begin this simple routine by pulling a cigarette from a pack as though you intend to smoke.

Absentmindedly draw the cigarette horizontally across your upper lip until one end hits your nostril.

Move your hand to a vertical position, with fingers pointing upward and holding the cigarette.

Pretend to shove the cigarette up your nostril by pushing your fingertips toward the nostril, letting the cigarette slide back along your fingers. The cigarette will appear to go up one nostril into your nose.

Immediately move your fingertips to your lips seeming to catch the cigarette as it comes from your mouth. Reverse the previous step by gripping the cigarette end with your lips and sliding your hand off the cigarette.

End by releasing the cigarette from your lips, or leave it there and proceed to light it as though nothing happened. This should be done with a plain cigarette. Cork tips and filters give it away.

PLATFORM PENETRATIONS

BUTTONS, BANGLES, BEANS OR BEADS

This is the old classic bean trick from Sach's Sleight of Hand. *This impressive sleight of hand trick can be carried off well by the beginner, but don't dismiss this as something you can pick up and do without practice.*

You pretend to place several buttons, beans or beads in various facial features (nose, ears, etc.), then show that they have somehow penetrated your body to appear in your mouth. The series of moves is more amusing than most single penetrations or sleights, since amazement builds while you proceed through the trick.

Props: 5 small identical buttons, or beads or beans

Advance Preparation: Practice in front of a mirror or a friend until your sleights are undetectable.

Do not introduce the trick. Merely show five buttons in your left hand, and nothing in your right.

Pretend to take one button from the hand with your right thumb and forefinger, but actually take two buttons. Conceal the second button by sliding your thumb back along your forefinger so that the first button projects but the second is hidden completely between your thumb and forefinger.

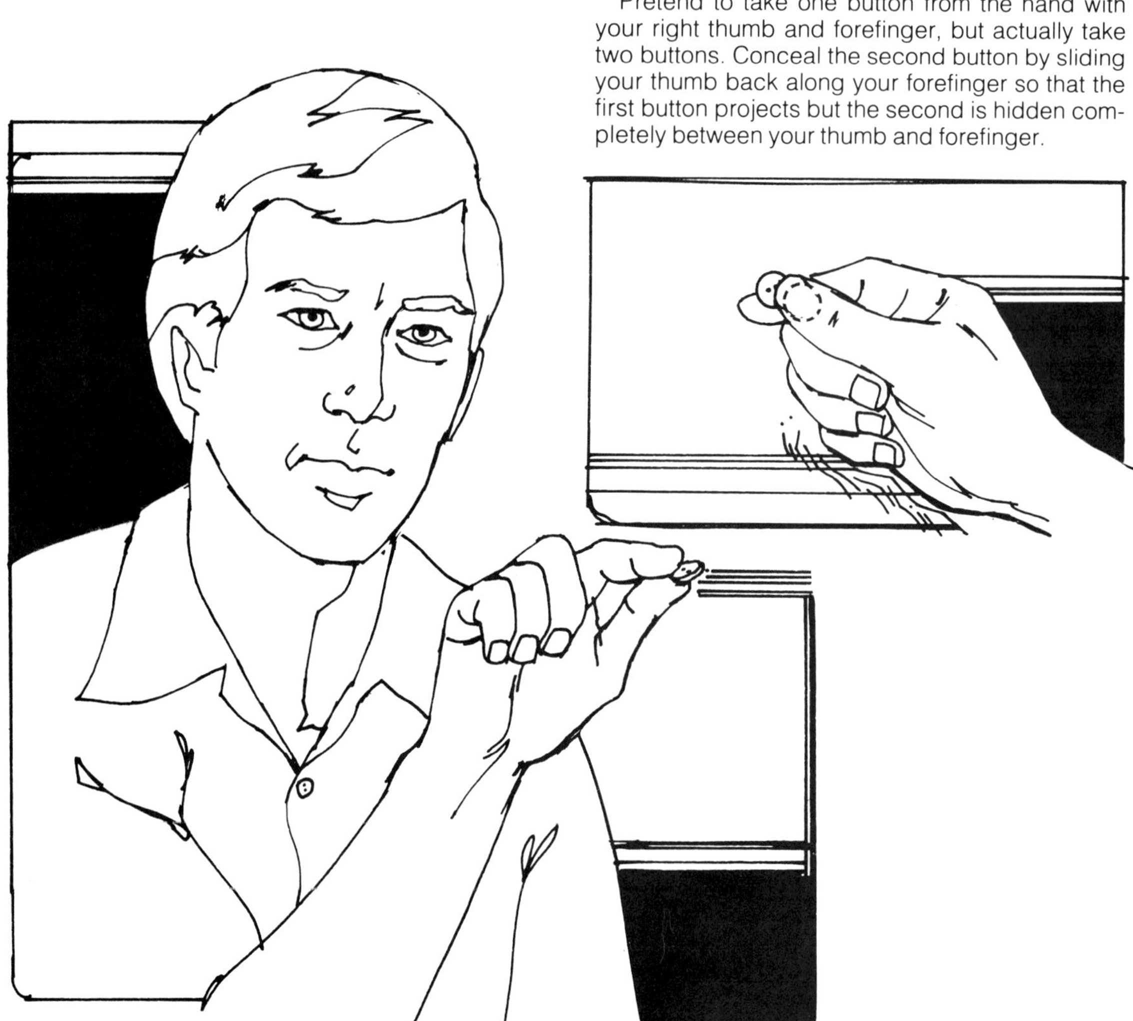

If Demosthenes could talk with a mouth full of marbles, you can probably say a few words with some buttons or beans in your mouth. Each time say, "I have to moisten them," using this excuse to push the first, the visible button the audience has seen into your mouth. Quickly slip the second button forward in your fingers so it looks like the first button and place it on top of your left fist. Show the wet button and say, "This goes in the right ear," Pretend to take the button for your right ear but actually let it drop into your left fist, and you put empty fingers to the ear.

The audience now thinks you have a button in your right ear. Casually show both sides of your right hand to prove you have gotten rid of the button.

Now open your left hand, where you will find four buttons.

Repeat the moves for three buttons, pretending to insert one each in the other ear and each nostril. Say, "The last button goes in the mouth . . . and attracts all the others . . . lookee, lookee."

Open the left hand and take the last button and place it in your mouth with the four concealed buttons. Show both hands empty. Now slap some part of your head and let one button fall out of your mouth.

Do the same for the remaining buttons, counting them with fingers as they fall. The hindus used to spit the beans on the ground, so this is not the best of dinner table wizardry. Note that for maximum effect the moves in this trick should be done quickly and smoothly. The buttons should appear to travel from one part of your head through another in quick succession.

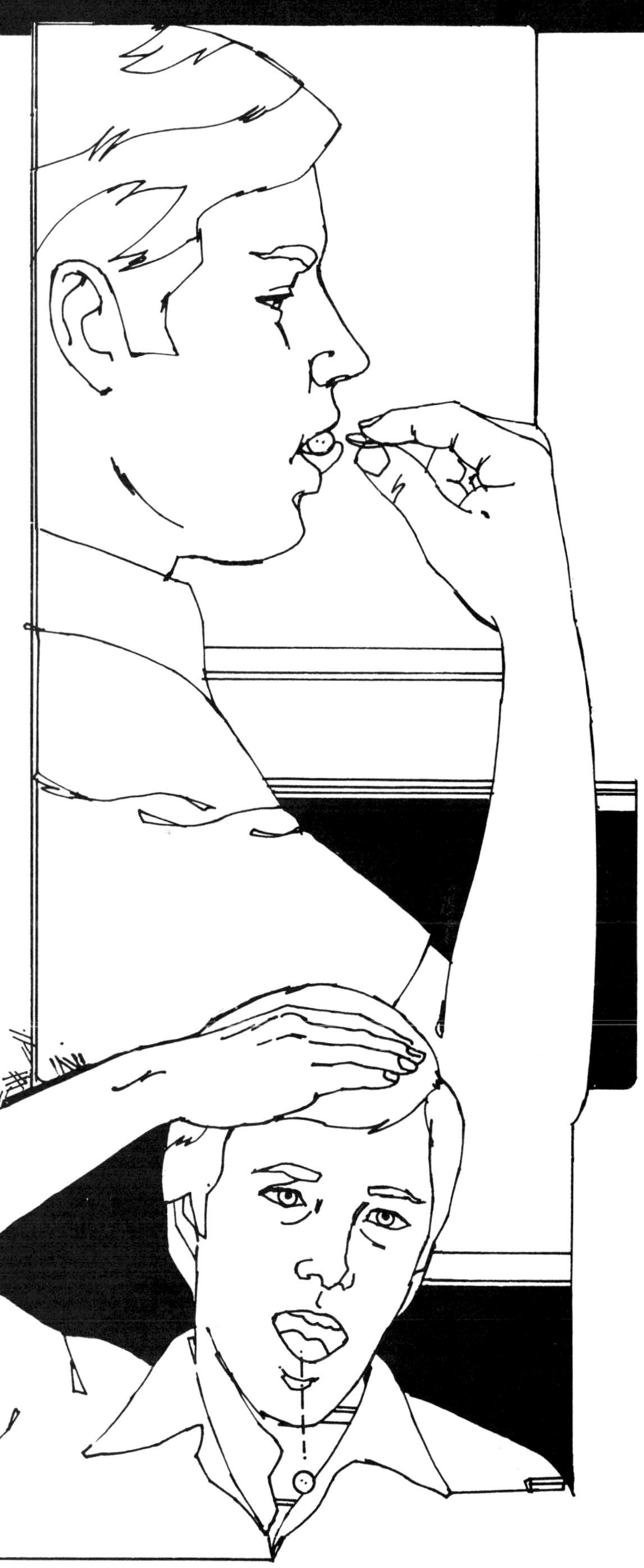

BOTTOMLESS CUPS

This slightly difficult sleight creates the illusion that one cup when dropped into another penetrates the bottom.

Props: 2 metal cups (do not use glass)

Advance Preparation: Experiment with various types of cups before performing for an audience. It is a good idea to stay away from cups made of glass, to avoid dangerous accidents. Try various sizes and shapes; many magicians find that short, wide cups give the best effect. The sound of one hitting the other is important in creating the illusion. Be sure you can do this trick several times in a row without failure, because it takes delicate movement to produce success.

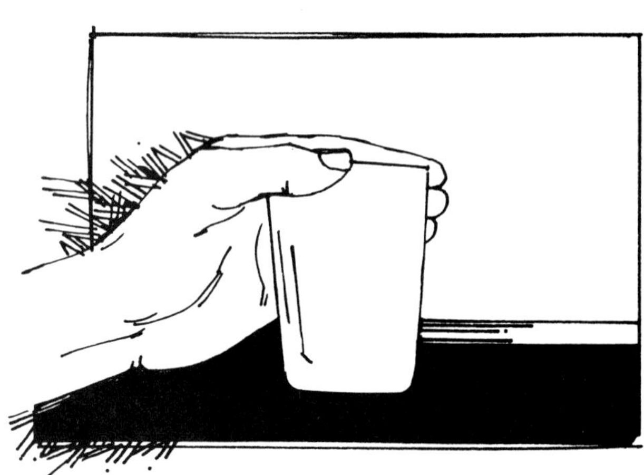

Announce the trick and then hold the first cup between the thumb and forefinger of your left hand very loosely at the very edge of the cup.

Pick up the second cup in any fashion and hold it directly above the first. Lower the top cup to about three inches before dropping it.

Let the cup fall from your right hand into the cup held in your left hand. Try to catch the bottom cup with your right hand before it hits the table. Your left thumb and forefinger quickly grasp the very edge of the top cup in its place. If the left fingers are held loosely and they regrip the top cup "faster than the eye can see," the top cup will appear to penetrate the bottom cup as it falls toward the table.

Note: the cups must also fit together loosely for an effective illusion. Straight sides won't work.

RUBBER BAND PENETRATION

This simple and somewhat obvious trick is nearly identical to the Slave Brace-let trick on p. 63. It is most likely to impress children.

Props: 2-3 feet of cord or string
a rubber band
Advance Preparation: none

To start, have a spectator tie the cord between your wrists, then hand you the rubber band.

   To put the rubber band around the cord between your wrists, first turn your back. Slip it over one hand and all the way under the cord loop on either wrist. With the other hand pull the rubber band over your hand and over the cord loop and onto the cord between your wrists. Turn to face your audience and bow.

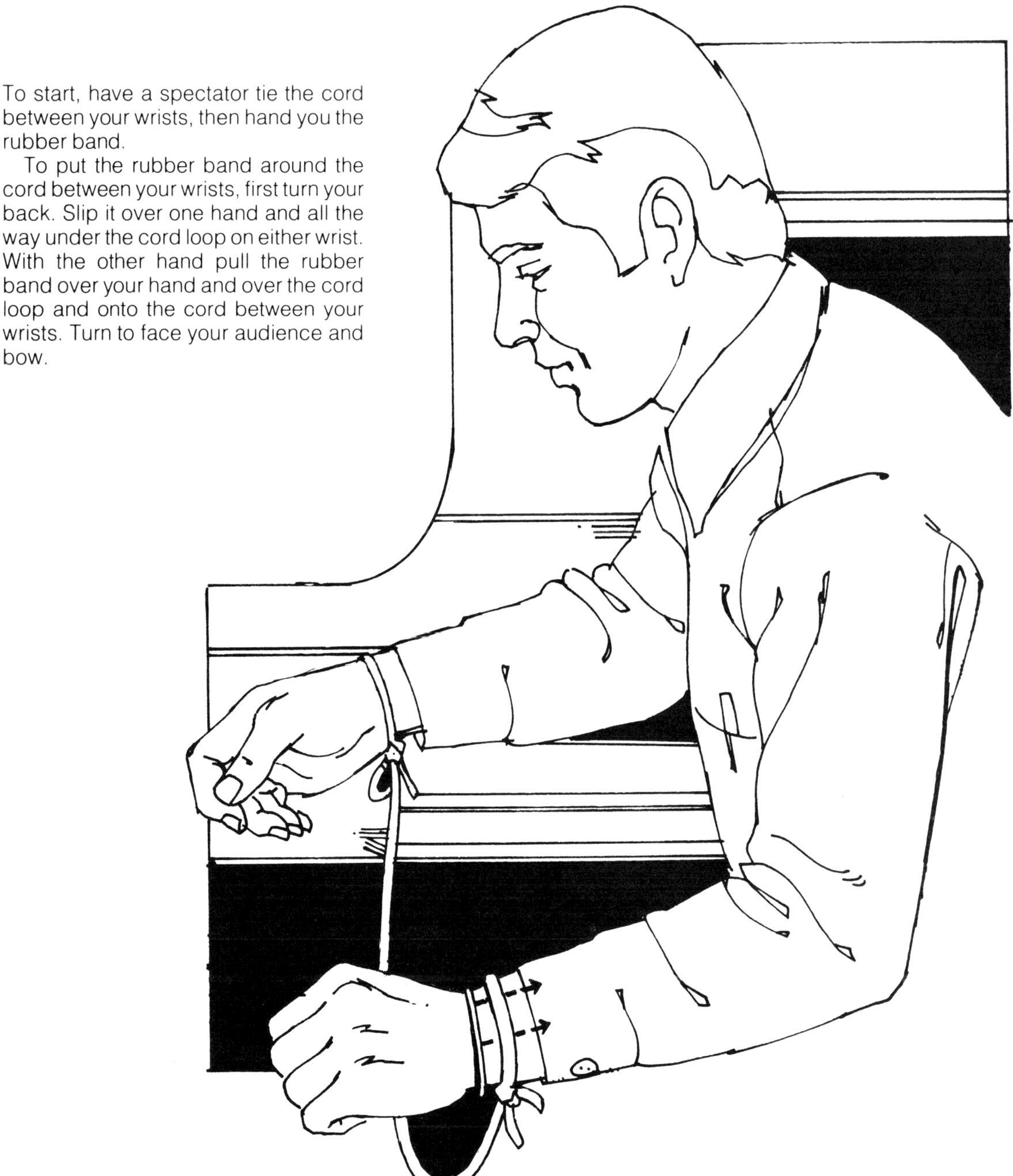

THE ELASTIC RING

This simple penetration is suitable for stage performance because it allows you to borrow a wedding band or other simple ring from a member of the audience. In choosing your victim, look for someone with fingers a good deal larger than your own, since the ring must sit loosely on the tip of your middle finger. The idea of the trick is to slip the ring under a twisted rubber band around your fingers.

Props: a rubber band
a borrowed ring
Advance Preparation: Provide your own ring and offer it to a victim from the audience for inspection, or borrow a ring as described below.

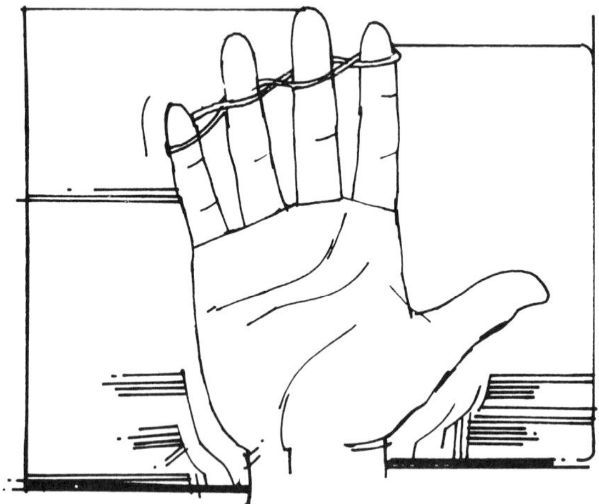 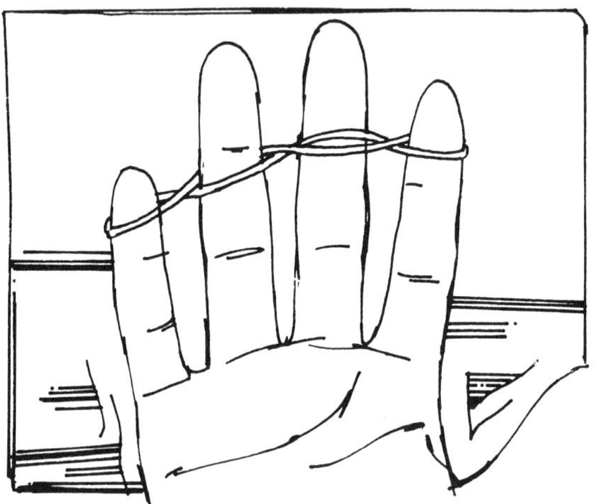

As you announce the trick, wrap the rubber band around the fingertips of the right hand and put the ring into your left hand.

As you hold up the ring to show the audience, casually lower your right hand to the side and secretly slip your middle finger out of the band, letting two strands of rubber rest on the inside of your hand.

If you have quick fingers, you may show both sides of the hand to the audience without giving away the trick. But you must switch your finger from one side of the rubber band to the other as you flip your hand. If you are not dexterous enough to carry this off, try adjusting the band when your hand is at your side so that one layer of rubber rests completely underneath the other and out of sight.

The ending must be done quickly. Shake your hand around or wave it in a frenzy to effect the penetration: actually slip the ring down your finger with ease.

Reverse the moves, remove the ring quickly and hand it back to its owner.

ENVELOPE PENETRATION

This is a simple sleight-of-hand penetration.

Props: an envelope
2 identical postage stamps
Advance Preparation: Lightly moisten one stamp and finger palm it with the right hand before you announce the trick.

To start, hold up the envelope with your left hand and show both sides of it to your chosen spectator and your audience.

Pass it to the right hand, gripping it so that you can stick the stamp palmed in your right fingers into the appropriate corner of the envelope, on the side away from the audience.

When the envelope is in your right hand, pick up the other stamp (from the table or a pocket) with your left to lick it, but actually tongue it and hide it in your mouth.

Put the envelope on the table and press your left fingers against the corner above the first stamp as if to glue the second stamp in place.

Now lift your hand and act puzzled to find that the stamp is nowhere to be found—on your hand or on the top side of the envelope.

End the trick on a humorous note by searching for the stamp in ludicrous places before finally turning the envelope over as a last resort. With this approach, it is better not to announce the trick at all.

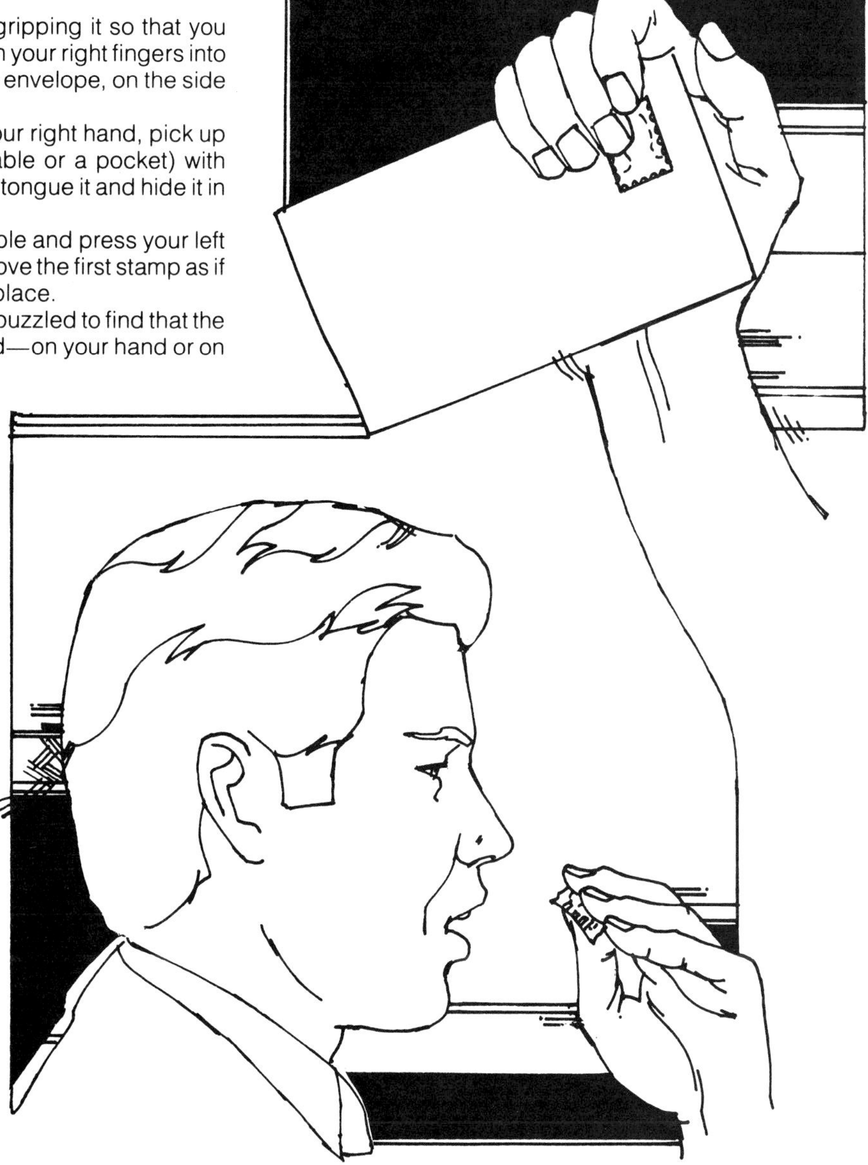

SHARPENING A BUTTER KNIFE

This simple impromptu trick can be done at the table, but extra distance between you and the audience may make it more convincing. Say that you can take a knife with a blunt blade and sharpen it to the extent that it will penetrate a glass without shattering it.

Props: a butter knife
a transparent glass
Advance Preparation: none

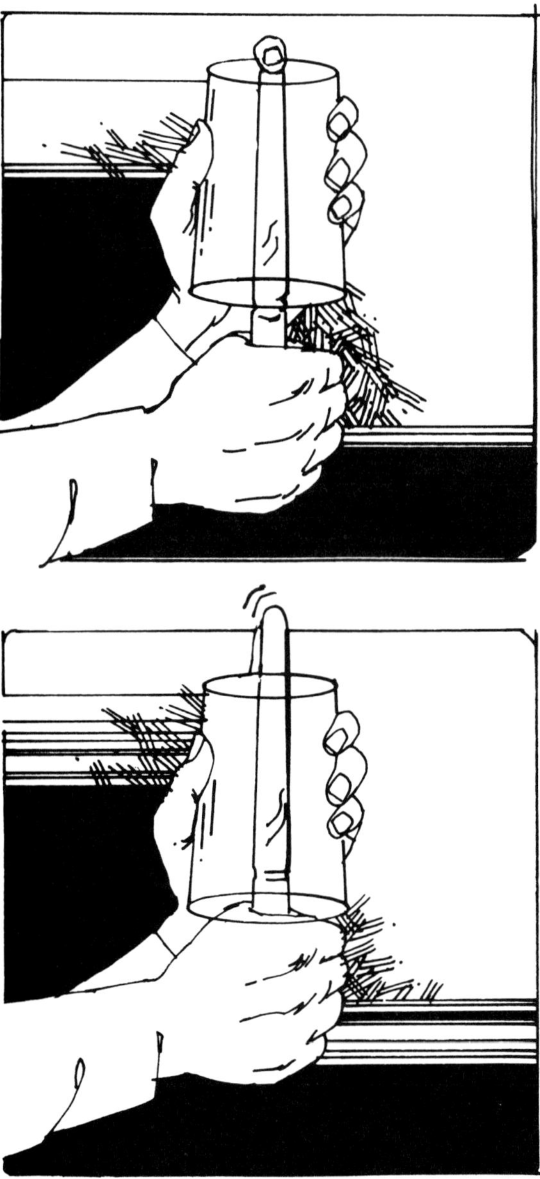

Announce the trick, then in your right hand hold the knife by its handle. With your left hand, invert the glass, apparently over the knife blade. Actually the knife blade goes behind the glass with your left forefinger resting on the inverted glass bottom, and the tip of the blade touches the base of the left forefinger.

To "weaken" the glass and "sharpen" the knife, pretend to thrust the knife upward inside the glass so the blade strikes the bottom. Actually let the knife hit the underside of your left forefinger, moving that finger subtly toward the side of the glass to tap the knife against it, producing the convincing sound that will lead your audience to believe the knife is striking the glass bottom from the inside.

After you have tapped the knife in this way several times, suddenly push the knife vigorously upward, straightening your left forefinger to point upward behind the knife. The audience will think the knife actually has penetrated the glass bottom. Pull the blade down, turn the glass mouth up and fill with some satisfying beverage. Skol!

THE PHANTOM TEAR

This fairly old trick is still quite effective. You appear to draw a closed safety pin through a handkerchief without damaging the cloth.

Props: a large safety pin (2 inches or more)
a handkerchief or scarf (you can borrow the handkerchief)

Advance Preparation: none

To start, ask two spectators to assist you. Fold the cloth in half lengthwise and have each victim hold an end at the crease. Put the pin through the two layers of cloth near the fold.

Grab the loop end of the pin and pull it so the point of the pin slides along the cloth without tearing as you pull the pin along the edge of the cloth.

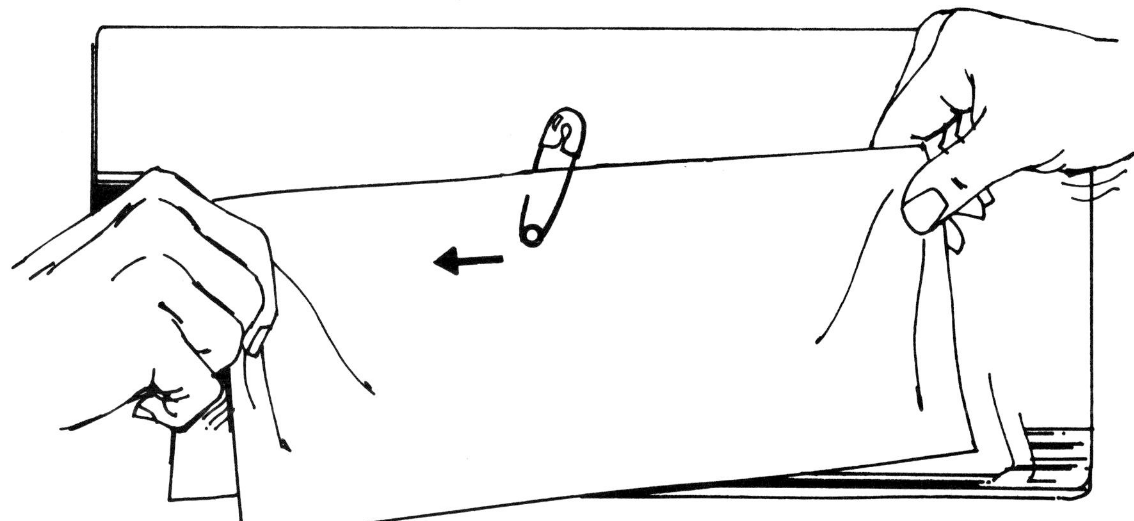

When you reach one end of the cloth, quickly turn the pin again so that the pin appears to penetrate the handkerchief.

Unclasp the pin and have the two spectators show both sides of the cloth to the rest of the audience. Magically, it has remained undamaged!

The way to learn this is to take a handkerchief and a safety pin that is at least two inches long. Have some friend hold two adjoining corners of the handkerchief taut and stick the pin through near the top edge and fasten it.

Twist the loop end 90° and pull the pin a couple of inches along the top edge of the handkerchief. If there is a two-inch tear, you pulled the pin in the wrong direction. If there is no tear, you've found the right direction but you have a pin on its side with the cloth trapped between the point of the pin and the cap. To correct this, push the pin as you turn back that 90° so the pin is straight up but two inches further along the hanky edge.

You can go back and forth several times before you unfasten the pin and give the handkerchief back to its worried owner. Do make sure you have learned the right direction and how to twist the pin.

The following stunts employ all sorts of techniques to come up with an amusing result. These are the light tricks used to get a laugh rather than to elicit a spirit of mystery. As such, they are most effective through contrast.

INSTANT FLAMES

Use this simple one-step gag absentmindedly for a quick laugh. You light a cigarette or cigar without opening the matchbook.

Props: a cigarette or cigar
a matchbook
a single wood match

Advance Preparation: Before going onstage, insert the wooden match into the tobacco of a cigar or cigarette, letting the tip protrude.

For a fast double-take effect, pick up the cigarette or cigar with one hand and the matchbook with the other. Simply and casually strike the tip of the cigarette against the matchbook to light it. Beware of smoking the whole thing, however, because of the wood inside. The Surgeon General says wood smoke is dangerous to the health.

WIRE FACES

Truly instant only as a parlor trick, where you can simply borrow some wire hangers, this trick is great for amusing a young audience, or for use with a gag story or humorous puppet show.

Props: wire coat hangers
pliers

Advance Preparation: If your fingers are strong you might enjoy making these wire puppets without the aid of pliers. For the rest of us, however, pliers are essential. Experiment with your own props to create imaginative profiles, and add other props such as scarves and handkerchiefs (for headgear), string and yarn (for head and facial hair), and so on to embellish the puppets.

If your audience is very young, simply creating and displaying the puppets may be sufficient. For a more sophisticated audience, introduce this routine by beginning some humorous tale, adding characters to your scenarios as you bend the wire into profiles with the pliers.

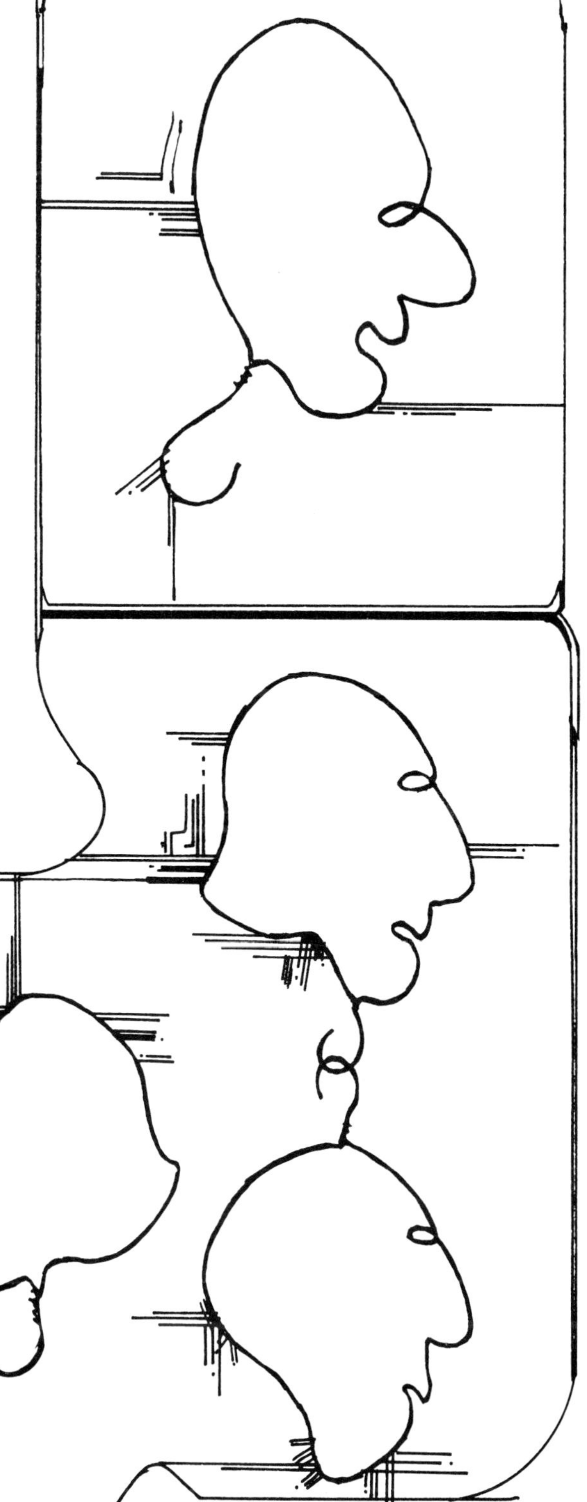

THE FLYING FLAME

Preparation for this trick must be done discreetly.

Props: a cigarette
a book or box of matches

Advance Preparation: This must be done immediately prior to the performance of the trick, so make sure your audience does not notice. While your back is turned, light a cigarette on one side just below the end.

Turn so the audience is to your side, with the lit side of the cigarette facing away from them. Casually light another match, then hold it as far away from your mouth as you can. Draw on the cigarette.

As the burning tobacco spreads to the tip, it will appear as though the distant flame has leaped three feet through the air.

DUMBO EARS

This silly sight gag requires some comedic acting. Use discriminately.

Props: cellophane tape
flesh-colored thread

Advance Preparation: If you have very short hair, your audience may be able to spot your gimmick once you turn your back. String a piece of thread between the backs of your ears, securing it with small pieces of tape. Tie another length of thread to the middle of the first piece and let it hang down your back under a jacket or loose shirt. It must be long enough to hang from the bottom of the jacket or shirt.

Whenever you feel this gag would be appropriate, subtly grasp the end of the string with one hand behind your back and pull on the string to wiggle your ears backward for a laugh.

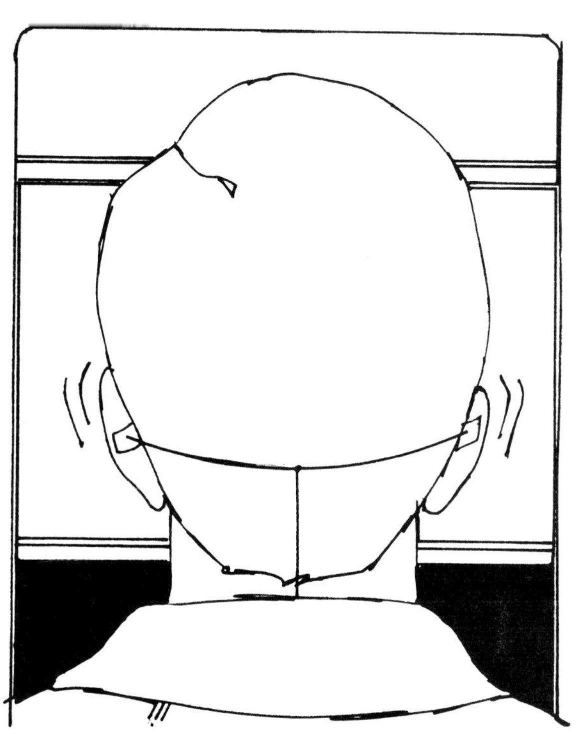

THE HEAD ON THE LOOSE

This is another sight gag effective only when timed well. Have an assistant do this trick, while you play the straight man, or vice versa.

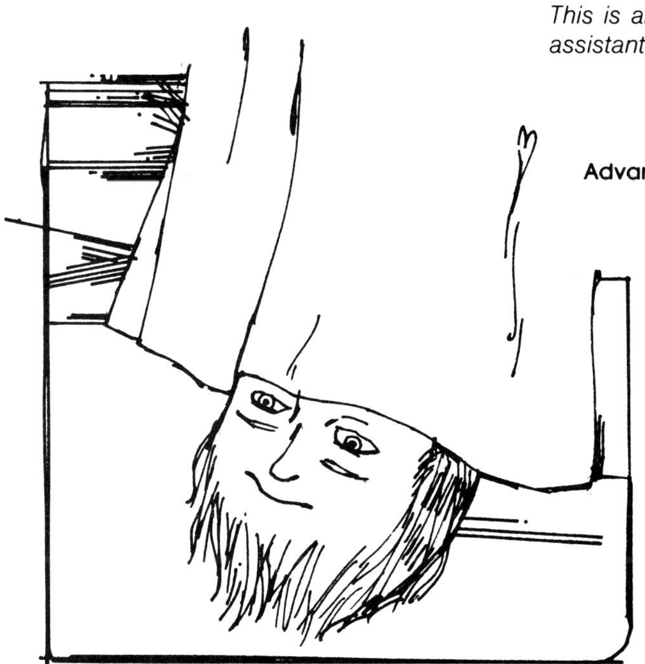

Props: a table with a floor-length tablecloth
greasepaint or lipstick (or other cosmetics)

Advance Preparation: The person who performs this trick should have relatively short hair since his head hair will look like a beard. For the best effect, the person should be waiting in ready under the table before the show begins to surprise the audience at the proper time.

Have the assistant lie on his back under the table, with only the top part of his head protruding so that his nose and mouth are covered by the tablecloth. Spread his hair over the floor to simulate a beard and, using greasepaint or cosmetics, draw a nose and mouth on his forehead. Note that if the person has heavy eyebrows, the hair under the eyes will add a bizarre effect. Now have him hide completely under the table again.

Whenever you feel that your assistant's appearance will draw the biggest laughs, have him pop out his head from the table, keeping nose and mouth covered, as in the preparation for the trick.

THE PHANTOM RUBBER BALL

This amusing pantomime can be quite convincing if performed well and without introduction. You catch coins out of the air, ending the mime with a really convincing touch.

Prop: a brown paper bag (lunch bag size or a small grocery bag)
Advance Preparation: Turn about an inch or two of the bag edge to the outside.

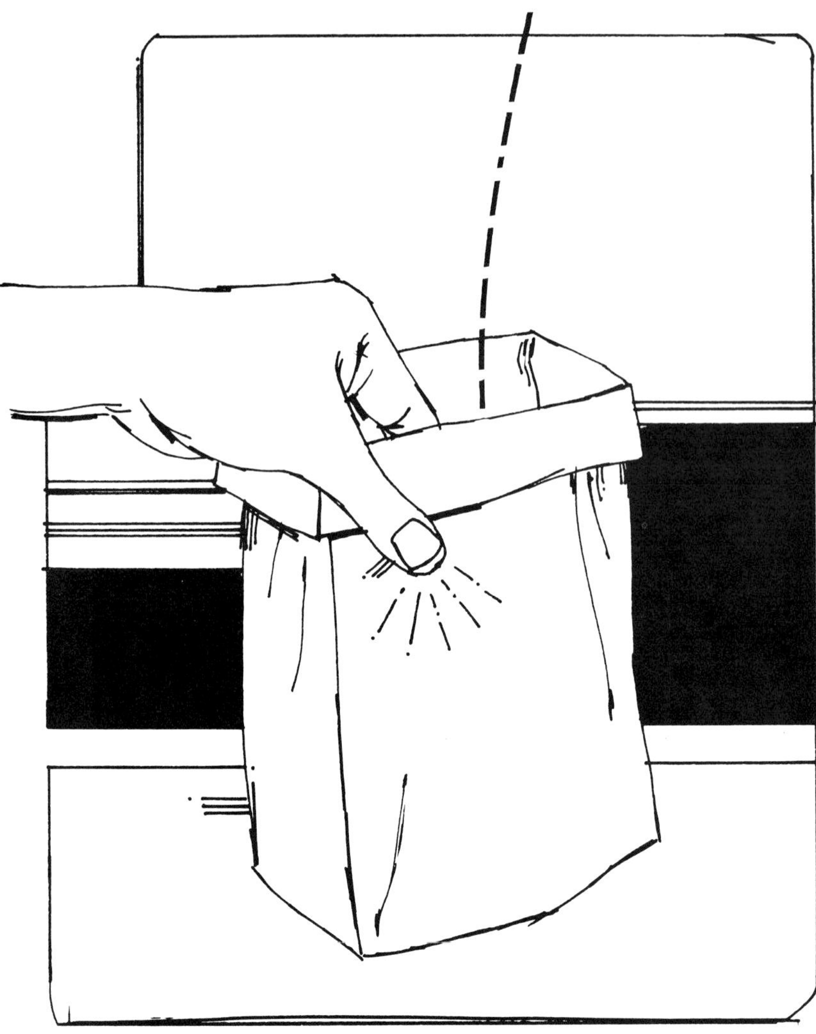

The theme of this exercise is something from nothing. You catch an imaginary object in a paper bag. What it involves is snapping your fingers while you are holding the bag in your hand. There now, that's not too tough is it? The rest of it is acting, and since you don't have much to go on, OVERACT.

You can pretend to take up a collection and gather the coins from the crowd in the paper bag. Except there are no coins and every time you catch an imaginary coin you snap your fingers in the bag. For a laugh on the skeptics, reach into the bag at the finish and take out four or five dollar bills.

REMOTE-CONTROL LIGHT BULB

This can be used either as a sight gag or as part of another trick. It is adaptable to the living room for truly instant performance, as well as to the stage.

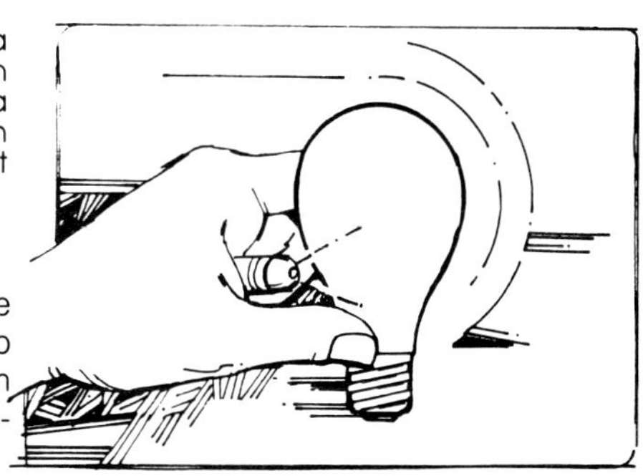

Props: a frosted (or soft-glow) light bulb
a pen-type flashlight

Advance Preparation: If done in the living room, merely unscrew a light bulb from the host's lamp to make this an impromptu trick. If done onstage, have either a loose light bulb on hand or a lamp from which you can unscrew the bulb. Also, the penlight should be sleeved before doing the trick.

Do not introduce the trick. Merely take the bulb in the hand on the side in which the penlight is sleeved, and slip the penlight out into your palm. Turning the light on and off behind the light bulb with your last three fingers makes it appear the bulb has a self-contained, invisible switch.

TELESCOPIC NECK

This sight gag can be used as part of a stage trick or amusement for the living room.

Props: a hat with a brim
a coat

Advance Preparation: Put the hat on your head and drape the overcoat over your shoulders. Lift the coat collar up and tuck the back of it into the back hat brim. Bend your elbows and hold onto the side of the hat brim with your hands, making sure your hands are not visible from behind.

To start this trick, announce it by introducing your assistant as a person with an amazing, adjustable neck; or incorporate it into another trick. For example, if you need someone to examine several items hanging at different heights on a wall or stage curtain, call in your assistant.

The person to perform this trick must enter the stage or room sideways so the audience never sees him from the front. When the person pretends to look at an object high on the wall or curtain, he slowly and carefully raises the hat and coat collar with his hands to simulate growth in height. The move is reversed to look at a lower object. This ploy can be quite convincing when done well and punctuated by humorous comments by the magician and/or assistant.

THE SELF-TIPPING HAT

This sight gag is best when done by a male magician and may be used when greeting a spectator you have called to the stage.

Props: a brimmed hat
2 safety pins
a good-sized rubber band

Advance Preparation: Fasten safety pins to the hat's sweat band, one above each ear. Then stretch the rubber band around the inside of the hat, looping it over the pins to hold it in place. Wear the hat pulled down tight on your head.

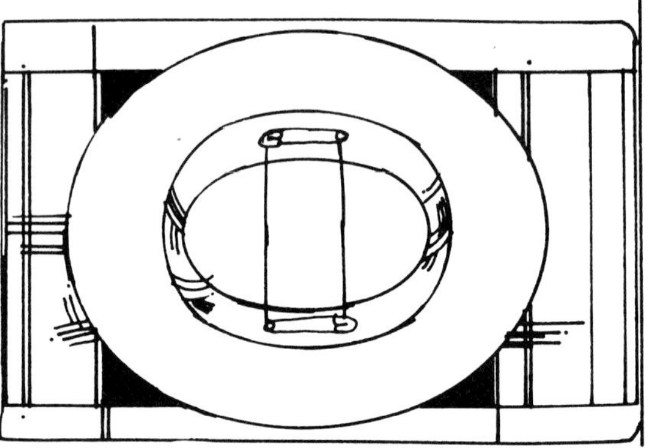

After calling on a spectator, introduce yourself courteously and raise your eyebrows a few times while you are shaking hands. This will wrinkle your forehead, thus loosening the hat, which will rise mysteriously from your crown and rock back and forth ludicrously.

HAPPY HANK

This is an impromptu puppet you can make from a small ball, a handkerchief, and three rubber bands. You can put the ball on top rather than underneath the handkerchief.

Props: one white rubber ball with a hole for the right index finger and with eyes painted on
three rubber bands
a borrowed handkerchief (or one you supply)

Advance Preparation: Put the rubber bands into the hole in the ball and place in a pocket.

Remove the ball from your pocket and take the rubber bands from the hole and place them on a table. Borrow a handkerchief, and shake it open.

Insert your right forefinger into the hole in the ball, with eyes facing away from your palm. Fold your ring finger and pinkie against your palm and extend your thumb and middle fingers upward. Drape the handkerchief over your right hand, being sure to cover the thumb and middle finger entirely.

Now place a rubber band over the ball on your index finger to create Hank's neck; tug on it so it fits tightly and Hank's eyes will show through in ghost-like shadows. Position the remaining rubber bands over your thumb and middle finger to create Hank's hands. Position the rubber bands near the first joints to give you freedom to move the "hands."

Now Hank is ready to help you perform card tricks or other routines in your repertoire.

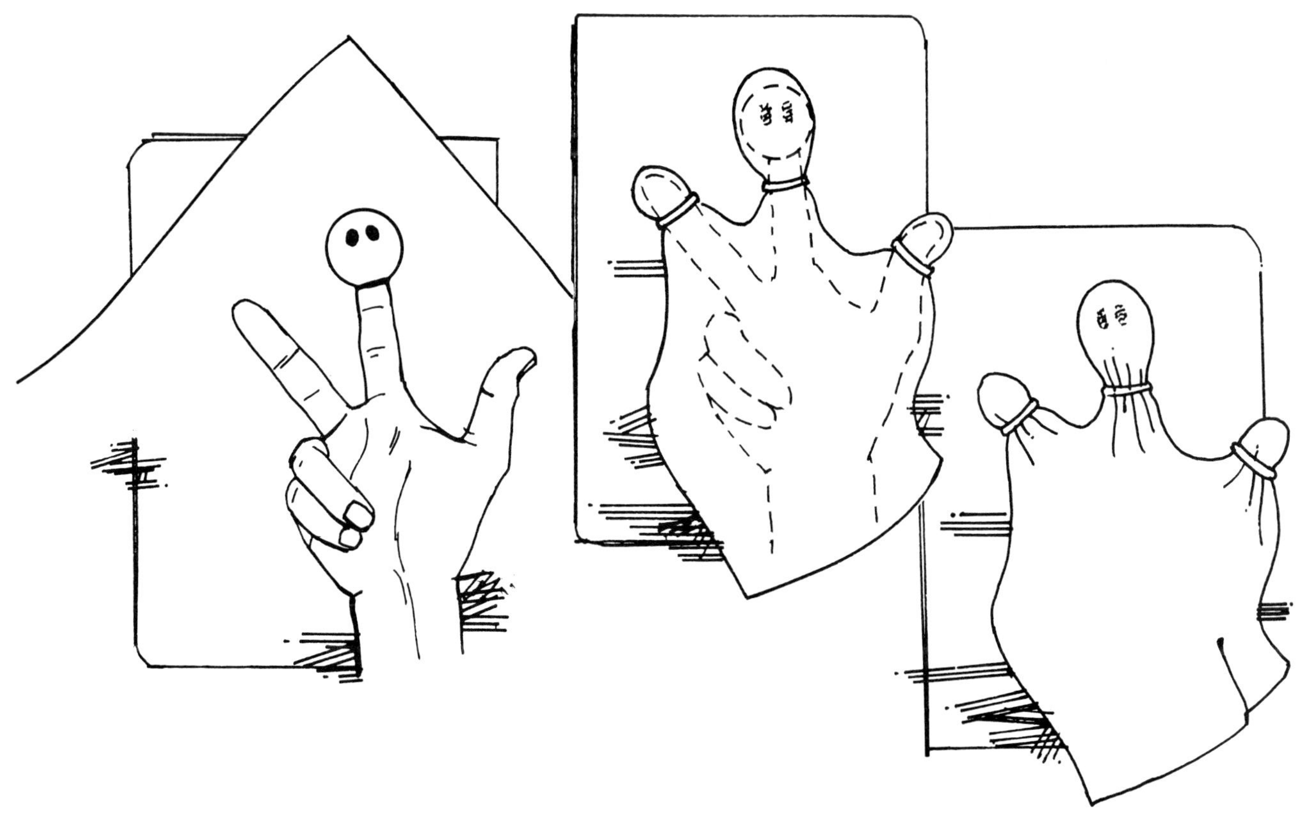

MISCELLANEOUS HUMOR FOR THE STAGE

THUMBS UP!

This gag should be performed only for certain audiences. Unless you invent one, there is no magical finale; the joke is in the lack of trickery at the end.

Prop: a handkerchief or scarf
Advance Preparation: none

Do not announce the trick. Merely toss the cloth over your left hand—palm outstretched or closed into a fist—as though to see what will happen.

Now pick up the center of the handkerchief with your right hand and slowly lift it upward, raising your left hand with it to remain covered by the cloth. Slowly begin to point your thumb upward until it meets the center of the cloth.

To end the trick, you may remove your right hand, showing that the point of the cloth stands up on its own. Then whip off the cloth to see what is happening, looking embarrassed as you realize it is only your thumb. Or, as you raise your thumb and feel it through the cloth with your right hand, grab it with your right hand and pretend to wrestle it through the cloth as it continues to rise higher and higher, forcing you to stand on your toes. Then manage to yank your left hand down, and whisk away the cloth with a sigh of relief. Wait for the laughs as you stare in puzzlement at your thumb. (Don't wait too long.)

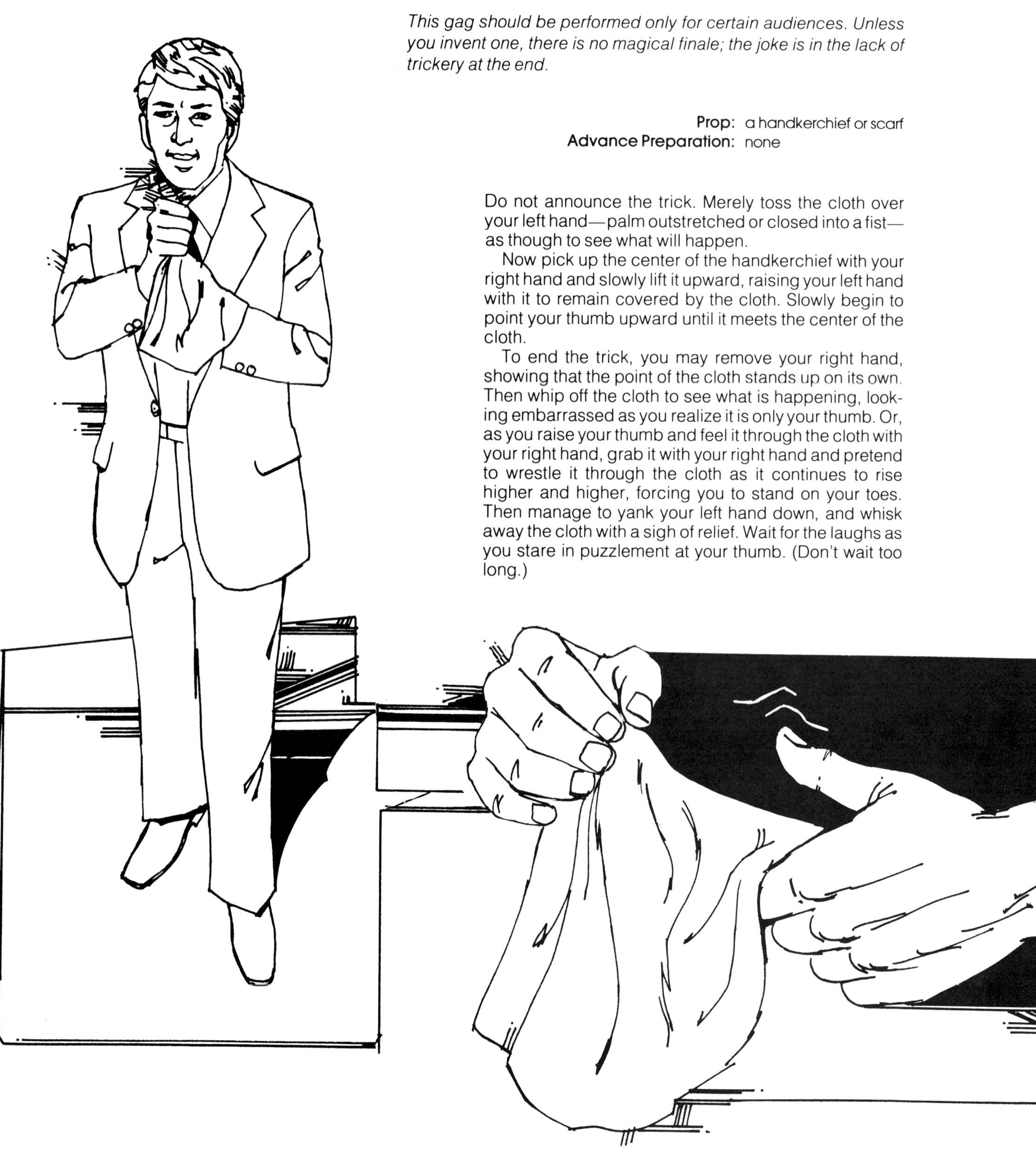

TICKETS TO HEAVEN

This old club or stage routine can be varied at will. The stock story is that two contemporary figures—one considered virtuous and one not so virtuous—are named as candidates for everlasting life in heaven, but only one has a ticket. The single ticket is torn and the shreds divided between the two; the unfolded pieces tell each his fate.

Props: a sheet of paper
scissors

Advance Preparation: Memorize a joke-filled version of the above narrative, using any two characters your audience is likely to appreciate.

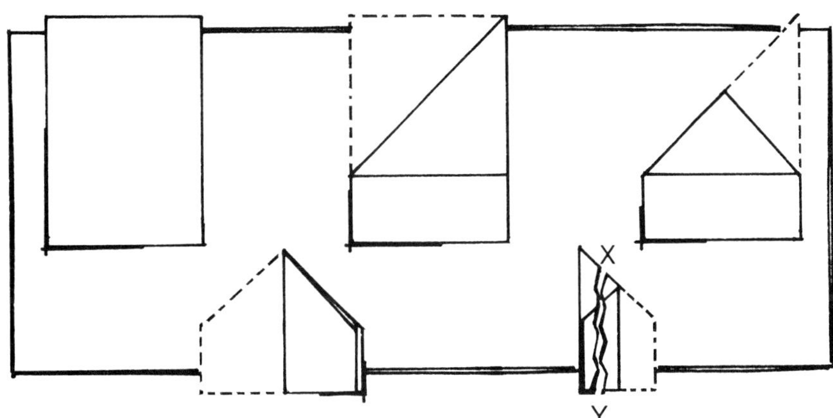

Begin your story. As you describe the scenario, fold the paper as shown. Tear the paper along line XY.

Say that your hero hands over one pile of paper pieces, and point to the pile of smaller pieces.

Unwrap all pieces in each pile. The one large piece assigned to your "good guy" will open as a cross, indicating a heavenly afterlife. The loser in your story receives pieces that can be arranged to spell the word "hell" in capital letters. Note that if you use an ordinary sheet of typing paper, the "h" in hell will be shorter than the other letters.

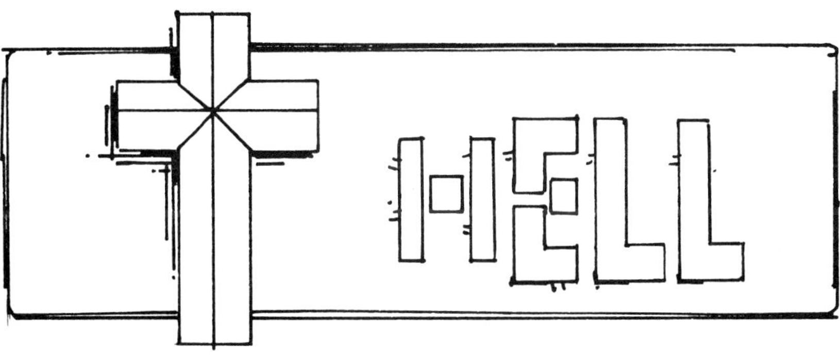

Vanishes are standard fare in a magician's repertoire, whether used as the trick's main point or the means to another end. Those included below are among the most popular and easiest to perform for the beginner in stage witchery.

VANISHING SILVER

This simple but impressive coin vanish can be performed nearly anywhere.

Props: a coin (a half-dollar or dollar is easy to see)
a handkerchief
Advance Preparation: Be sure to wear a jacket, vest or shirt with a breast pocket on the left side.

Hold the handkerchief by a corner between the index and middle fingers of the right hand. As you apparently cover the coin held by the thumb and fingers of the left hand, the coin is picked off by the thumb and index finger of the right hand and dropped in the upper left hand breast pocket. This should be done in one continuous smooth sweep without any hesitation as you pick up and deposit the coin.

The right fingers let go of the corner of the handkerchief and after the coin is dropped in the pocket they come forward to pick up the center of the handkerchief. (The spectators think this is the coin but it is only the middle fingers of the left hand.)

Right hand holds the handkerchief by the center and the left hand is shown empty. Left hand takes a corner of the handkerchief and empty right hand drops the center. The coin is gone and both hands are empty! Show the handkerchief on both sides.

THE SLIPPERY KNOT

This trick should be used in conjunction with or as part of another trick since it is a single move. You simply make an ordinary knot tied in cloth disappear.

Prop: a scarf made of silk or another slippery fabric
Advance Preparation: Practice this trick well, because it is a sleight that takes a little skill to perform. Smoothness is essential, but when the simple move is perfected, the result is disporportionately impressive.

Use this for a laugh in any trick requiring a knot in a scarf. Simply tie an ordinary knot in the middle of a silk scarf. Keep the knot loose, but not conspicuously so.

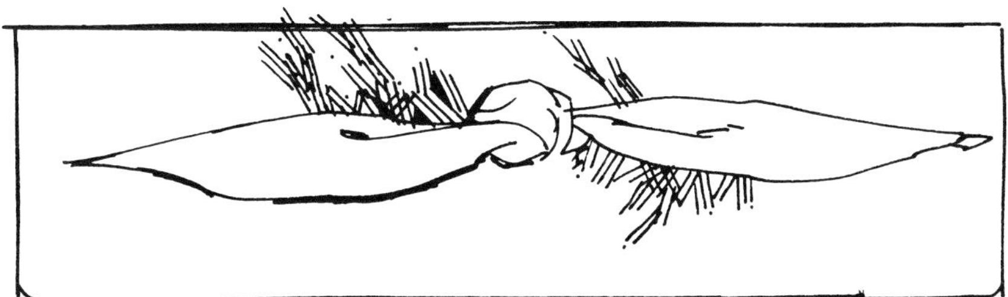

Holding one end of the scarf in your left hand, stroke your right palm downward over the knot toward the other end. As you stroke, secretly stick the tip of your right middle finger over and into the knot to keep it loose as you pull it toward the end.

If you do this quickly and smoothly, the knot will seem to magically disappear as you pull it off the end of the scarf on the final stroke.

COIN VANISH WITH A HANDKERCHIEF

An oldie but goodie, this trick is more difficult than others described and requires practice to carry off, but the classic effect is well worth the effort. Obviously, the point of the trick is to vanish a coin under cover of a handkerchief.

Props: a square handkerchief
a half-dollar (or other small object)
Advance Preparation: Practice thoroughly to avoid embarrassing mishaps.

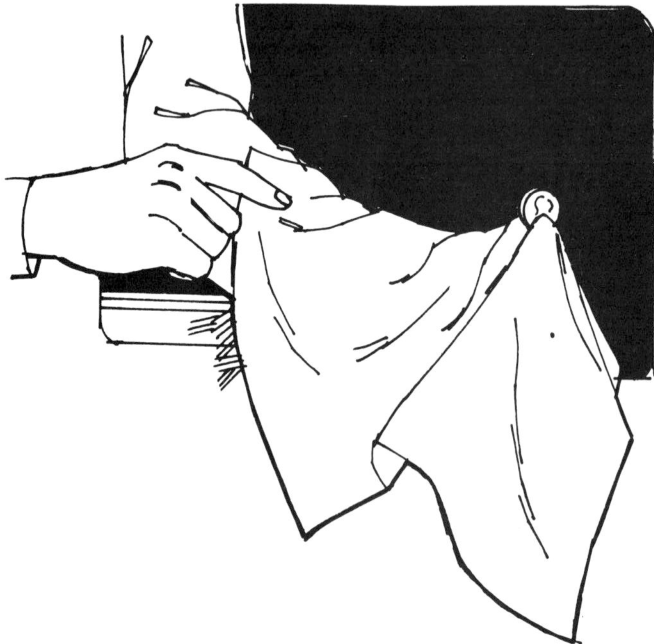

1. Spread the hankie's center over your left palm, with one corner draped over the forearm. Show the audience your coin and place it between your left thumb and first two fingers through the cloth.

2. With your right hand, flip the corner of the hankie from your forearm over the coin. Turn your left palm down, so the hankie drapes over the coin.

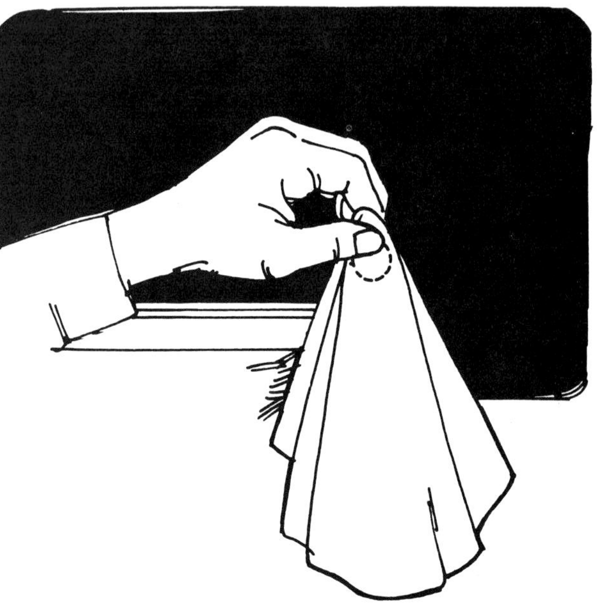

3. Now tell the audience you intend showing them that the coin is still under the cloth, and proceed to flip the corner of the hankie over the coin again, but this time, as you turn your palm downward, drop the coin into your cupped right hand; the left hand still holds the center of the handkerchief as if the coin were still there.

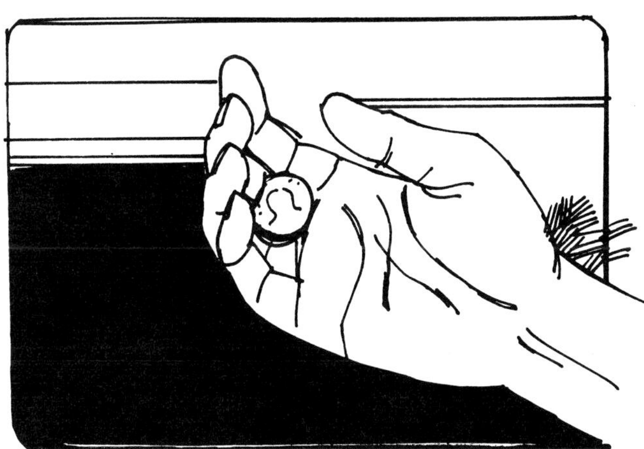

4. Finger palm the coin, holding it in your right hand as shown.

5. Hold up your right hand in this position and say, "Watch!" Your exposed palm will convince the audience the coin is not in your right hand.

With the coin still held in your fingers, pull up one corner of the hankie and release center from the left hand. The audience will expect the coin to drop as the hankie floats downward and hangs from your right hand.

Grasp an adjoining corner with your left hand and show your audience that the coin literally has vanished from the hankie. Show both sides to prove it.

ASTONISHING VANISHES

THIS MAY BE OVER YOUR HEAD

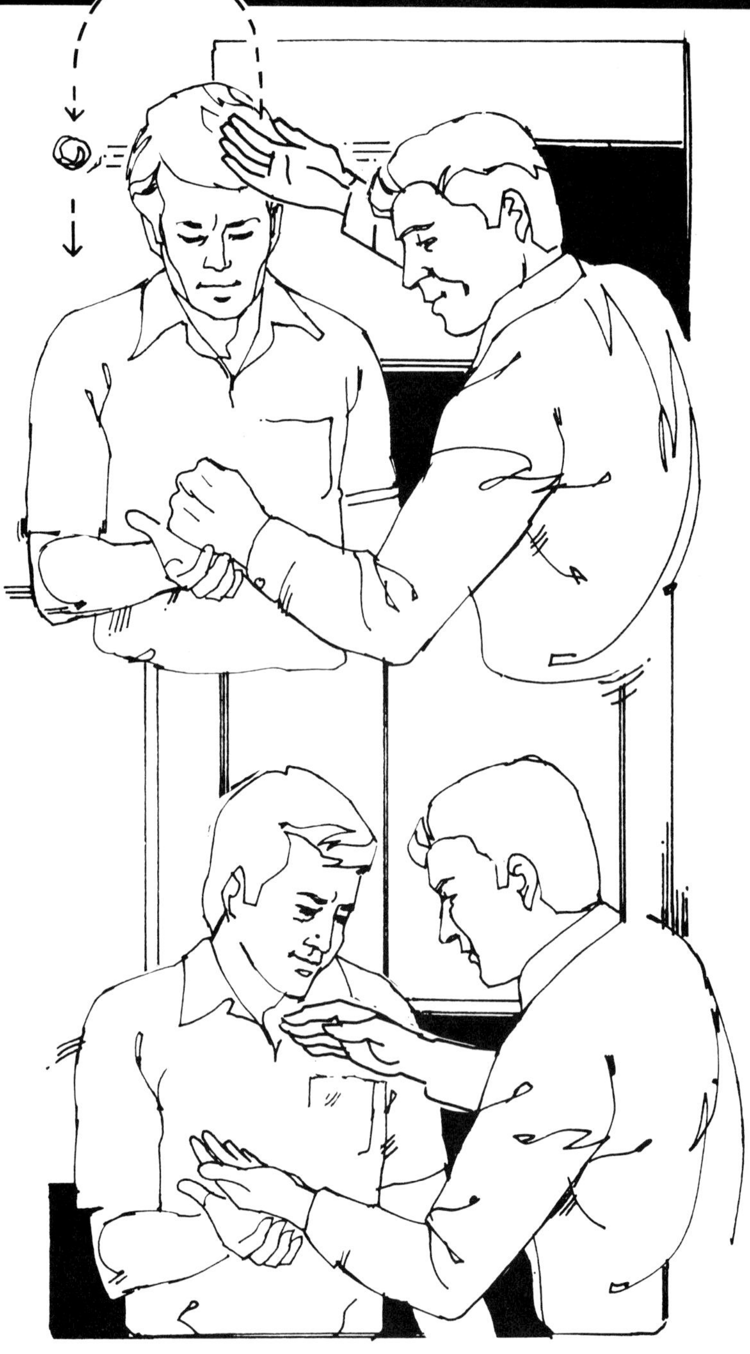

In this extremely popular handkerchief vanish, the entire audience, except for your chosen victim, sees your moves. They howl with laughter as they watch the victim fail to catch on, even after the trick is repeated several times.

Props:	a handkerchief or paper napkins
Advance Preparation:	This fairly difficult sleight with a very simple effect takes lots of practice. Be sure you can fool your victim before you try it in front of a stage audience.

Harry Blackstone, Sr., seems to have originated this as part of his "Nest of Boxes" routine. He would borrow a watch from someone and put the watch in a paper cone. The watch would vanish from the paper cone and Blackstone would ask the owner to keep his eye on the paper. He would toss the paper cone over the spectator's head to the waiting hands of brother Pete who took everything backstage and set up the completion of the routine, where the watch would be found inside the final box of a nest of six boxes.

George Johnstone used to work for Blackstone, and he took this fragment of tossing something over a spectator's head and got three minutes out of it by doing it several times with Kleenex, paper napkins and a towel.

Tony Slydini saw George do it and made a classic bit out of it to the point where most magicians think Slydini originated it. Sly does it with paper napkins, and when they can't see one vanish he does it with two, and three, and finally with a big ball of six paper napkins. Everybody except the one for whom it is being performed sees how it is done. Sometimes perspective makes it easier to see than really being up close.

Begin by asking someone to step forward and have him stand or sit facing the audience. Do not tell anyone what you intend doing.

When your victim is in position, hand him a stack of handkerchiefs or paper napkins. Pick up one handkerchief or paper napkin and crumple it into a ball. Pretend to pass it from your right hand to your left, but palm it in the right. (Close your left hand into a fist to suggest that the ball is inside.)

Quickly distract your victim by having him guess which hand holds the ball. Simultaneously raise your right hand above his eye level and toss the ball quickly from your right hand over his head. The victim will not notice you toss the ball over his head, but the audience will see the ball fly into the air and will love seeing your victim baffled.

To repeat the trick, you have only to crumple up another paper napkin. By the time the victim leaves the stage you can have as many as six crumpled paper balls on the floor behind him. You may have to caution your audience not to tell him how it is done. Thank him, and as he returns to his seat you can suggest, "I'm afraid that was over your head." Someone always tells him when he gets back to his seat.

THE DEPLETED DECK

This nifty card trick for the stage allows you to invite a spectator to come onstage as a witness.

Props: a deck of cards
a hat
a pencil
softened wax (There is a substance used to stick pictures on bulletin boards. The English call it Blue Tack. It's reusable. Use this instead of wax.)
a table

Advance Preparation: Put a bit of softened wax on the eraser of the pencil and lay the pencil on the table with the hat placed over it. Do not draw attention to the hat at the beginning of the trick—you might have several other objects on the table as well.

Sitting at the table with the spectator opposite you, have him pick a card from the deck and place it on top of the other cards on the table in front of you.

Pick up the hat at the crown, grabbing the pencil point through the hat, and place the hat over the deck of cards without lifting the hat very high off the table. Thus, audience and spectator will not spot the pencil.

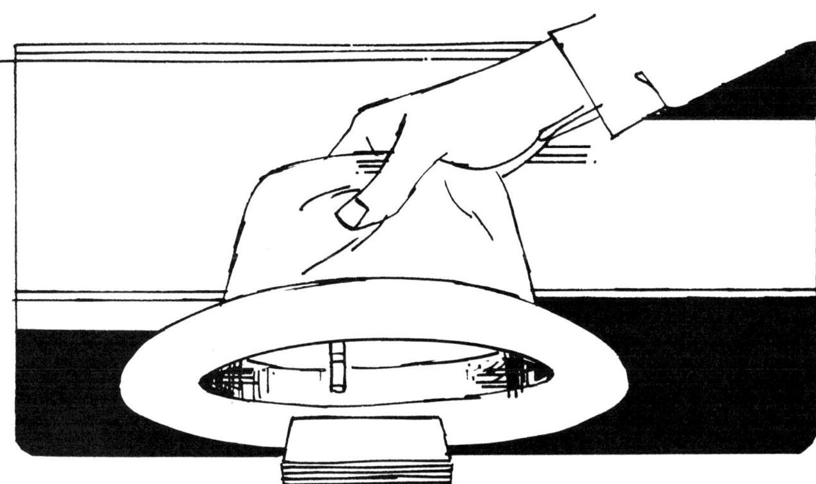

Speak mumbo jumbo over the hat to make the card disappear, making sure you press the wax from the eraser into the top of the deck. When certain the card is stuck, lift the hat, pencil, and top card off the table enough to clear the deck.

Casually draw the hat across the table toward you, making sure the brim is not tipped toward spectators. When the hat reaches the edge, release the pencil and card into your lap, disposing of them later.

Put the hat on your head and have the victim search the deck for his chosen card. Naturally, he will find it missing.

While he is looking for his card you can do almost anything with it. Retrieve it from your lap and put it under the table cloth in the action of straightening the table. You can palm the card into your pocket and pull it out of your wallet. I know a magician who always seems to find the lost cards in his shoe.

Besides vanishing objects and producing others, you can make various props move without apparent forces, hop from one spot to another, grow or shrink in size and remain impervious to destruction. Many of these tricks were designed specifically for stage performance, since the distance between magician and audience will obscure some props and preparations that must remain a secret between you and the spirit world.

MAGNETIC FINGERS

Another simple trick that is most convincing at a slight distance, this one takes practice and should be accompanied by an equally convincing story. Focus your patter either around the fact that you can magnetize your fingers to attract a handkerchief, or on a pantomime in which you draw an invisible thread through the handkerchief and pull on it to move the cloth.

Prop: a handkerchief or cloth napkin
Advance Preparation: Experiment with various types of cloth, but the fabric must be stiff enough to stand up when gathered to a point.

Announce the effect you intend to simulate, and pull the center of the handkerchief upwards through your left fist, smoothing the cloth upward with your other hand to make it stand up and sort of concealing the upright left thumb in the folds.

Pretend either to thread a needle and thread through the tip of the cloth, or to magnetize your other hand in some fashion.

Now pull your right hand off to the right and simultaneously move your left thumb in that direction. The tip of the cloth should appear to be pulled by the thread or magnetism in your right hand. Move things back and forth a couple of times before breaking the invisible thread.

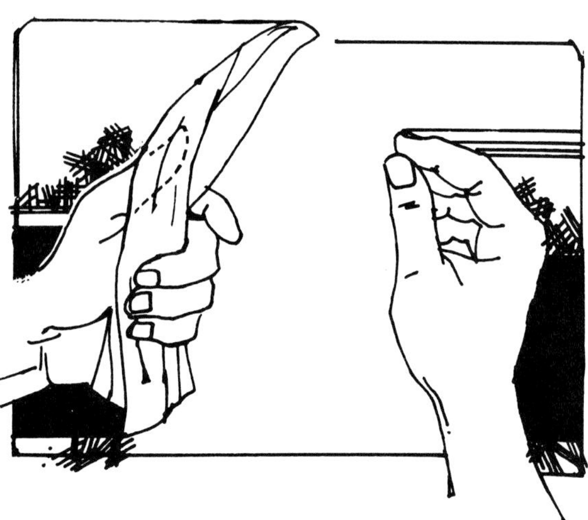

RIBBON OF STEEL

In this simple stage trick, a ribbon inserted through an envelope is uncut when the envelope is cut in half.

Props: a paper envelope
a length of ribbon (1 foot is plenty)
scissors
Advance Preparation: Cut a vertical, one-inch slit in the center of the back of the envelope.

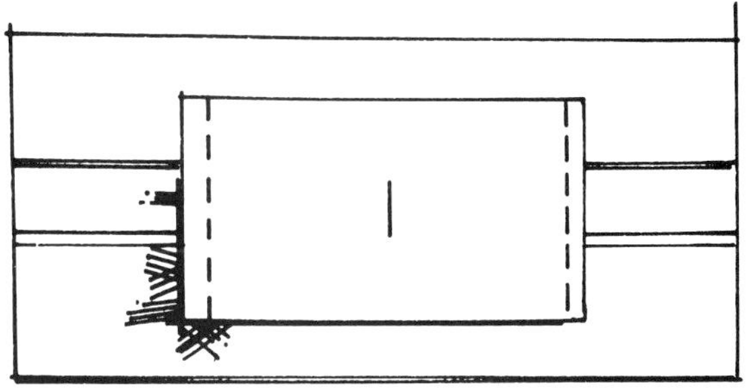

Announce the trick, then snip the ends of the envelope to pass the ribbon through, leaving the ribbon ends protruding from the envelope on both sides.

With the slit facing you and away from the audience, cut the envelope vertically in half along the same line as the slit cut earlier. To leave the ribbon intact, slip the scissors under it at the slit. Hold the cut parts of the envelope together as you pull the ribbon from one end to show it still in one piece.

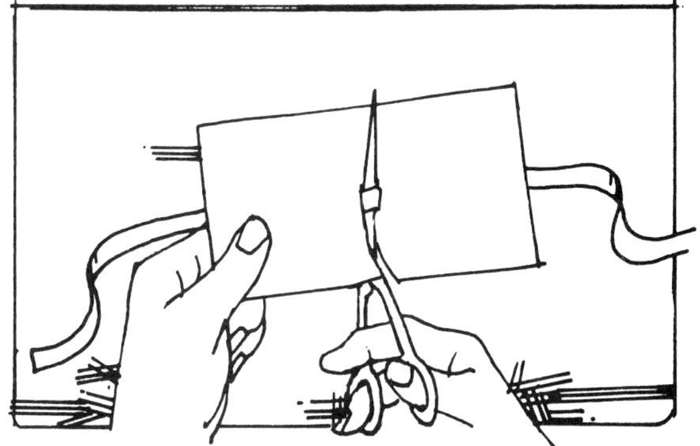

BEATING THE LAW OF GRAVITY

Attribute the effect of this trick to some supernatural power. You contradict the force of gravity by rolling a ball across a short piece of rope without letting it fall to the floor.

Props: 18 inches of rope at least one-quarter-inch thick
2 feet of black thread
a small ball (such as a ping pong ball)
Advance Preparation: Tie the thread to the rope about 2 inches from each end and trim the thread so no loose ends show.

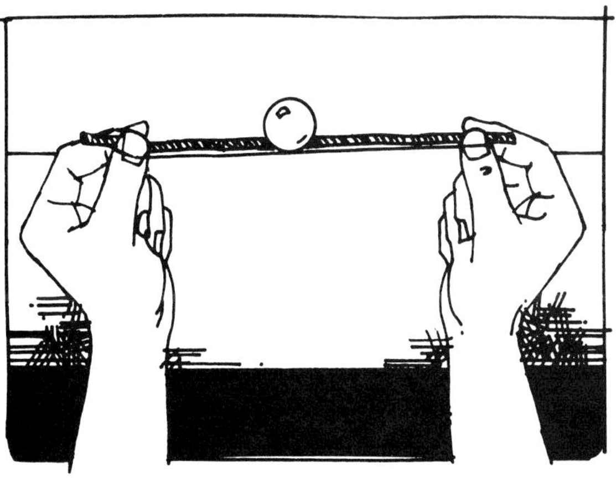

To start the trick, pick up the prepared rope and secretly insert your forefingers between rope and thread (with the thread facing you and away from the audience) as you lift the rope to hold it horizontally between your hands. Have an assistant place the ball on the rope near one hand, or lift the ball from a convenient spot without letting the audience notice the thread.

By lowering one hand a little, you can make the ball roll toward it on the rope, secretly balancing it between rope and thread.

SEANCE TABLE

This old effect used by phony mediums for ages is still an amusing gag to pull on friends, with a couple of secretly prepared spectators.

Props: a lightweight table (such as a card table)

Advance Preparation: Secretly prepare two of your guests or audience by explaining the following moves to them.

Pretend to choose your two assistants at random from a group and call them to the stage. Seated so you face the audience, seat the two assistants at either side. All of you place palms flat on the table edge.

Under the guise of your incantation, all pretend to push down on the table with the palms. On a prepared cue, the two assistants press their thumbs against the table edge to lift it slowly. They may have to put their thumbs under the edge of the table to get enough lift. I once assisted a magician who did this with a very heavy table and twelve volunteers, impromptu. He whispered, "When I say 'push' put your thumbs under the edge and lift." When he said loudly, "Push . . . push down on the table," the table rose almost four feet in the air.

This will be especially convincing if your assistants respond immediately on cue. You may wish to let the two assistants master the trick by trying it once or twice ahead of time.

May the force be with you.

Following are a few mind-reading tricks. For others, see chapter 3.

COIN IDENTIFICATION

This trick needs less-than-instant props and an assistant briefed in advance.

Props: 5 different-colored pencils or pens
5 coins of different denominations
a sheet of paper

Advance Preparation: Arrange with an assistant an assigned color of pencil or pen for each denomination of coin. Place each pencil or pen in a different pocket of your clothing.

Announce the trick, saying that your assistant has amazing vision and can see the impression left by a coin on a piece of paper.

Have a spectator come onstage as the assistant leaves the stage, or at least stands to one side with his back turned, so there is no doubt of his seeing the coin chosen by the spectator. Make it clear that the assistant does not see the coin.

Have the spectator place one of the five coins on the paper and leave it there for a second or two, alledgedly to make an impression.

Remove the coin and return it to its exact prior position so the audience will not think your placement of the coin is a signal.

Send the paper to your assistant with the proper color pencil to cue him about the coin. Have him write the coin's denomination on the paper, then bring it back to the spectator for the applause.

COMPASS PENCIL

This is not the most sophisticated of mind-reading tricks, but it might fool your audience anyway. You guess the direction a pencil is pointing when it is wrapped in paper.

Props: a pencil
a piece of paper of any type
Advance Preparation: none

To begin, call a spectator onstage and have him roll the pencil tightly in the paper while your back is turned. Have the ends taped shut, if you wish, so there is no way you can see into the paper tube.

Take the pencil in one hand from the spectator and pretend to read the vibrations around you to determine which end is which. At some point during this patter, hold the pencil between thumb and forefinger exactly in the center. As you loosen the pressure of your fingers, the eraser end, being heavier, will tip downward.

For a dramatic finish, after you have identified the tip end, rip off the paper fragment.

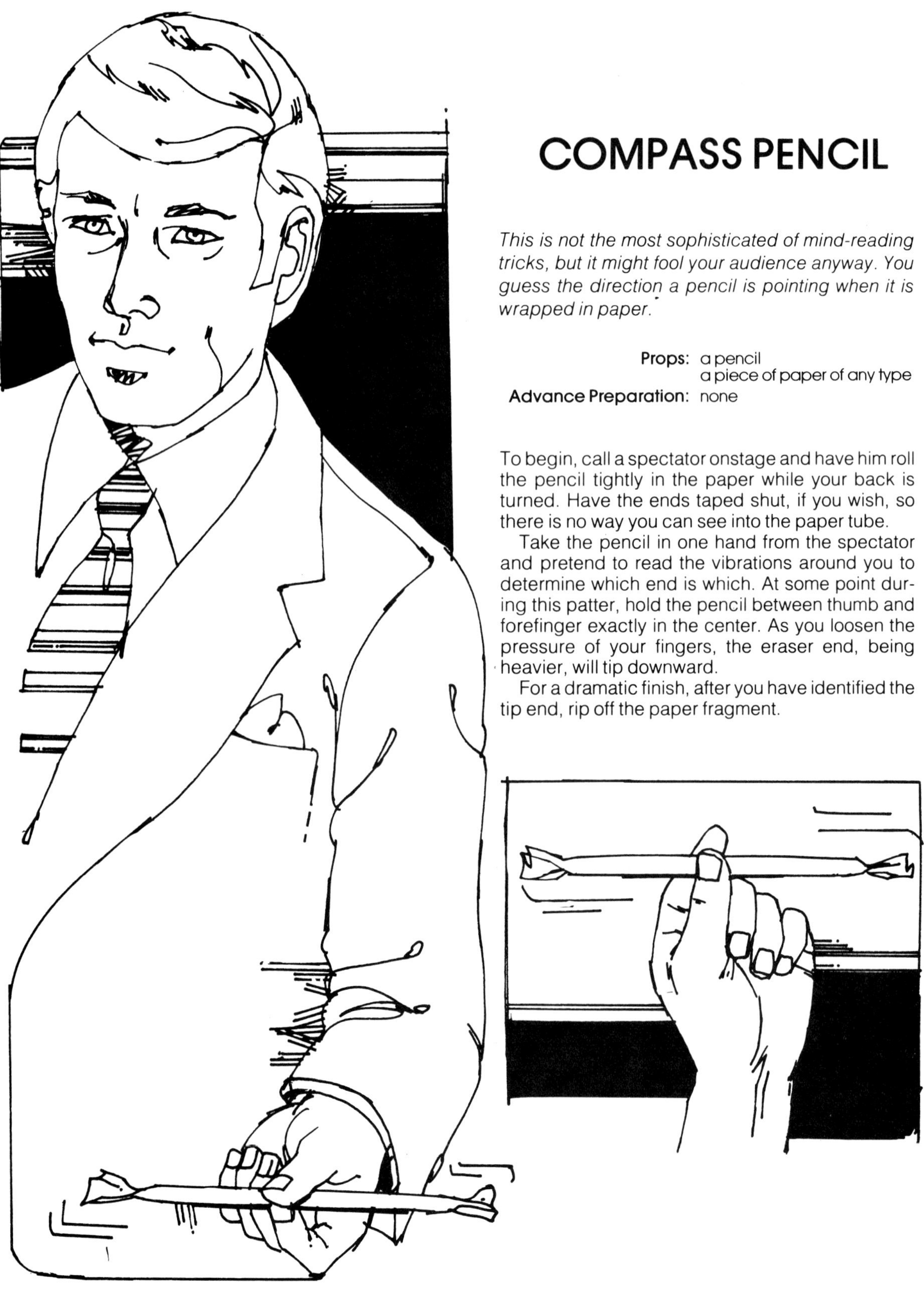

THE HIDDEN MIRROR

This simple procedure leads to surprising results when done correctly. Secretly checking the reflection in a mirror, you pretend to telepathically guess the color of a pen or pencil held behind your back.

Props: a selection of colored pens or pencils
a small mirror

Advance Preparation: Keep the mirror in a pocket where you can reach it easily with the right hand.

To start the trick, turn your back to the audience and have a spectator hand you one of the pencils, behind your back. The next move will be least noticeable if you begin the trick by leaving your right hand in front of you and extending only your left hand to receive the pencil.

Without moving your right elbow, remove the mirror from your pocket with the right hand and hold it at the proper angle in front of you and between your legs to get a reflection of the pencil. This must be done smoothly so no one sees you move.

The following tricks use a variety of techniques to achieve startling stage effects. Most are instant in preparation and performance and can be adapted to the living room.

SPEEDY SCISSORS

You can use this as a challenge to another member of the party or to a spectator. Say you can snip a piece of paper from a sheet thrown into the air. This is much more difficult than it sounds, so have several spectators try it after you. Do not let them try it before you do, though, unless you hand them another pair of scissors, because they will destroy your preparations.

Props: a sheet of paper
a tiny triangle cut from identical paper
scissors

Advance Preparation: Slip the tiny shread of paper between the scissors blades so that it cannot be seen.

Announce the trick, then toss the paper into the air and quickly snip the scissors into it as it falls. When the blades open, the hidden paper triangle will fall to the floor seemingly cut from the paper sheet. Once in a while you can get lucky and actually cut the paper as it falls.

THE UNFETTERED SCISSORS

This can appear to be a sophisticated maneuver but it is actually quite easy to perform. Claim that you can string a pair of scissors onto a previously formed knot without untying it.

Props: 2 or 3 feet of rope or cord
a pair of scissors
Advance Preparation: Learn the following sequence of moves so that you are successful every time.

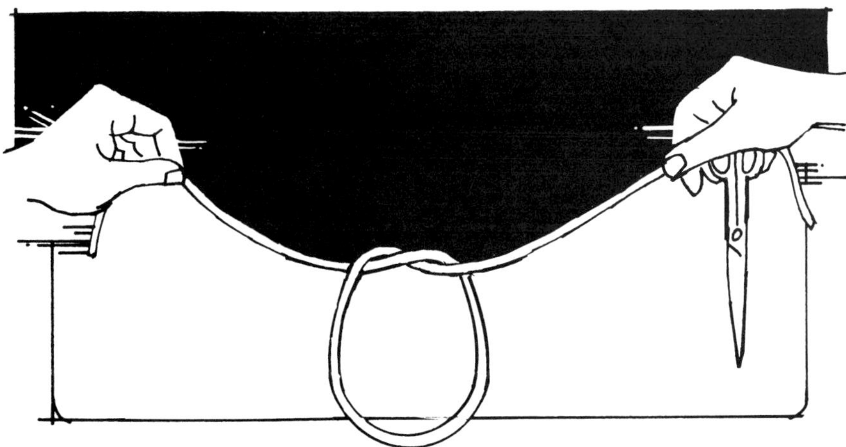

Announce the trick, then tie a simple knot in the rope and string the scissors onto the end of the rope as shown.

To string the scissors on the knot, toss them through the loop, tip end first.

After the scissors pass through the loop, pull both ends to show that the knot is tightening and the scissors are strung on it.

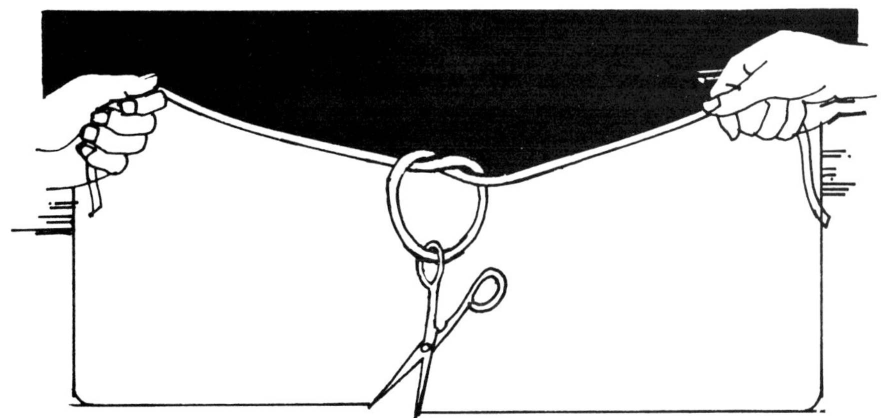

DAREDEVIL STUNTS, STRENGTH FEATS AND DEXTERITY DEMONSTRATIONS

A STATE OF UNDRESS

This old trick can be made very funny if you choose the right spectator from the audience as your subject. Do not tell him why you are calling him up, but begin by telling him that he will have to remove his vest, but not his jacket, for the trick. Then proceed to do so for him.

Prop: a spectator who is wearing a vest and a jacket

Advance Preparation: Memorize the following steps.

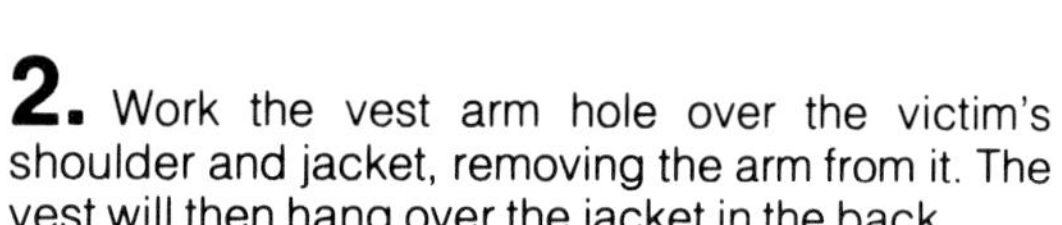

1. Call your spectator to your side. Unbutton his vest as you tell him he will not need it. Now tuck the left side of the jacket into the left arm hole of the vest.

2. Work the vest arm hole over the victim's shoulder and jacket, removing the arm from it. The vest will then hang over the jacket in the back.

3. Now work the vest over to the right shoulder and pull it down over the jacket sleeve and off the hand.

4. Grab the vest through the victim's right sleeve and pull it out.

Make sure the victim takes things out of his vest pockets before you start. If you offer to put the vest back on the way you took it off, the victim will refuse.

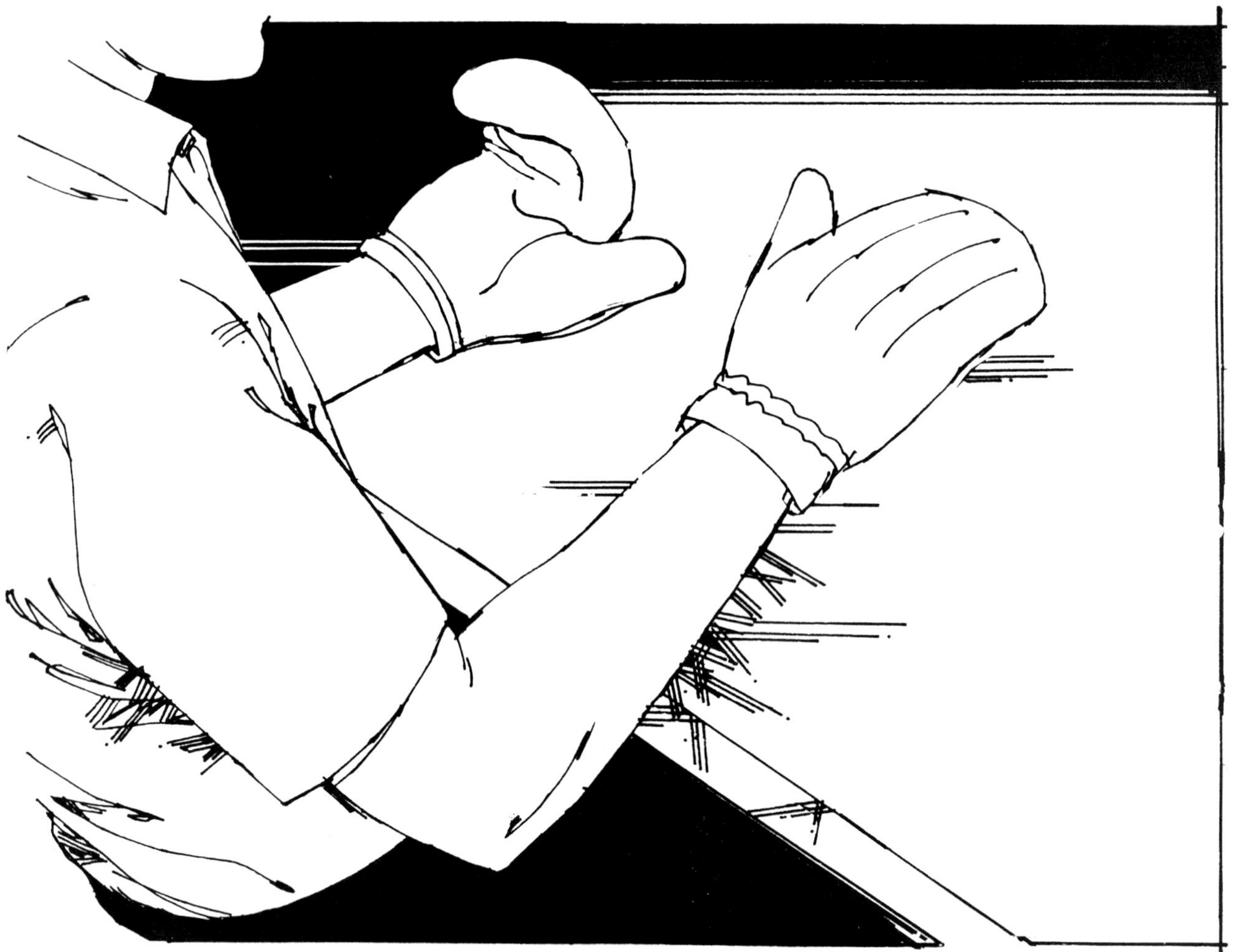

DOUBLE–JOINTED FINGERS

In this simple sight gag or strength stunt, you appear to bend your fingers backward to an unnatural angle.

Props: a pair of mittens or work gloves
Advance Preparation: Put the mittens or large gloves on beforehand or under cover of a table if you are seated. Put one hand backward into the work glove or mitten, leaving the thumb empty, of course.

Bring your hands into view so both palms appear to be laying downward on a table. For a sight gag, suddenly flip up the hand with the backward glove by curling your fingers toward the palm. The audience will gasp with surprise. Or, pretend to use your other hand to bend the fingers backward, interjecting grunts of strain and appropriate comments about the pain. Follow this by hitting the empty thumb with a glass.

The tricks that follow require no props; all focus on the hands, fingers and arms. As such, some may be done on an "instant" basis—in your living room, at a dull party, and so on. However, keep in mind that we have included these tricks here because they are most effective when performed at a slight distance from the audience. So be discriminating in adapting these tricks to the dinner table.

The tricks in this section range from simple to quite difficult. The most sophisticated are discussed in a general fashion, with only the foundational or most basic routines covered. For details on the more advanced states of these, readers may consult other sources, including their own imaginations.

The professional magician, or the amateur who enjoys putting together informal stage shows, will find these tricks, as well as those in chapter 1, extremely useful. The stretches and removals in chapter 1 and the various routines that follow serve as good fillers or bridges—or even introductions to other tricks in the show. For instance, as mentioned in chapter 1, many magicians use the finger and thumb stretches as preludes to finger and thumb removals. Or, while a trick is being set up the conjurer may wish to keep the audience entertained by throwing in a finger trick or two. Because most are simple and quick, they are perhaps most impressive when introduced casually or not at all. In other words, they will surprise and shock the spectators to a greater degree if no one expects a trick to be performed.

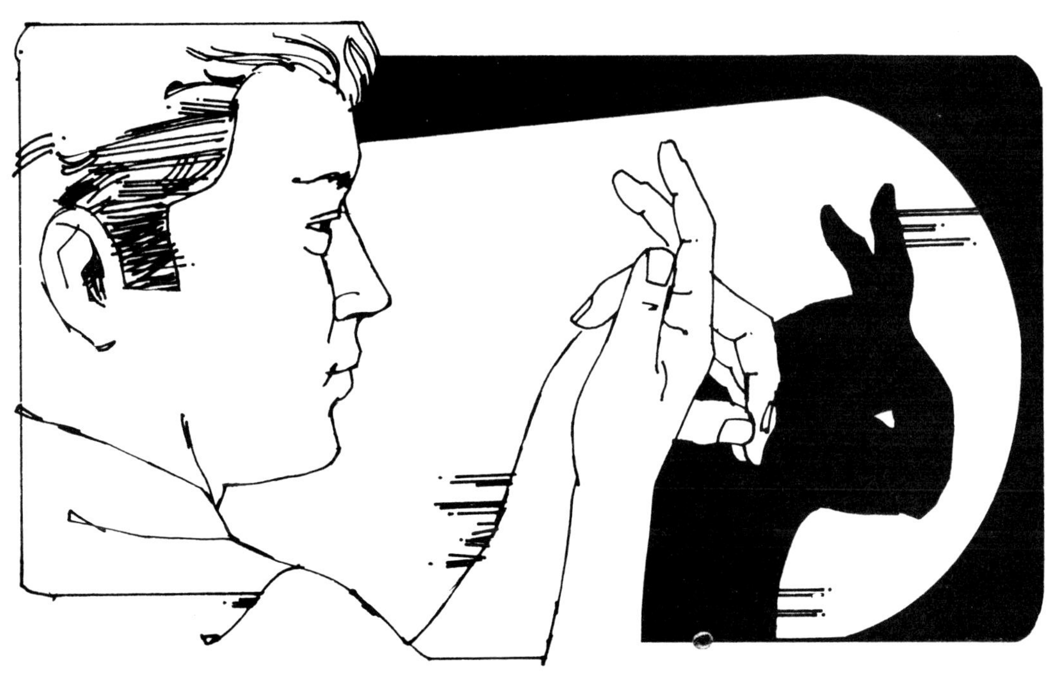

ARM STRETCH

This arm stretch can be done anywhere, but since you have to stand up as you do it, it is easily worked into an act done at some distance from your audience. Consider inserting the arm stretch between other tricks.

Props: none

Advance Preparation: To do this stretch, you must be wearing a loose-sleeved garment such as a jacket or coat.

Stand with your right side toward the audience and start by holding your left arm straight out from your body, the left sleeve motionless. Then use the right hand to pull the left arm out of the sleeve about 5 or 6 inches. (Moving your left shoulder forward does it.)

Make the most of this trick by pulling the arm out in a series of short tugs and comparing the length with the left arm; make if funny. Then push the arm back into your sleeve and show both arms are once again the same length. Accompany these actions with appropriate grunts and groans.

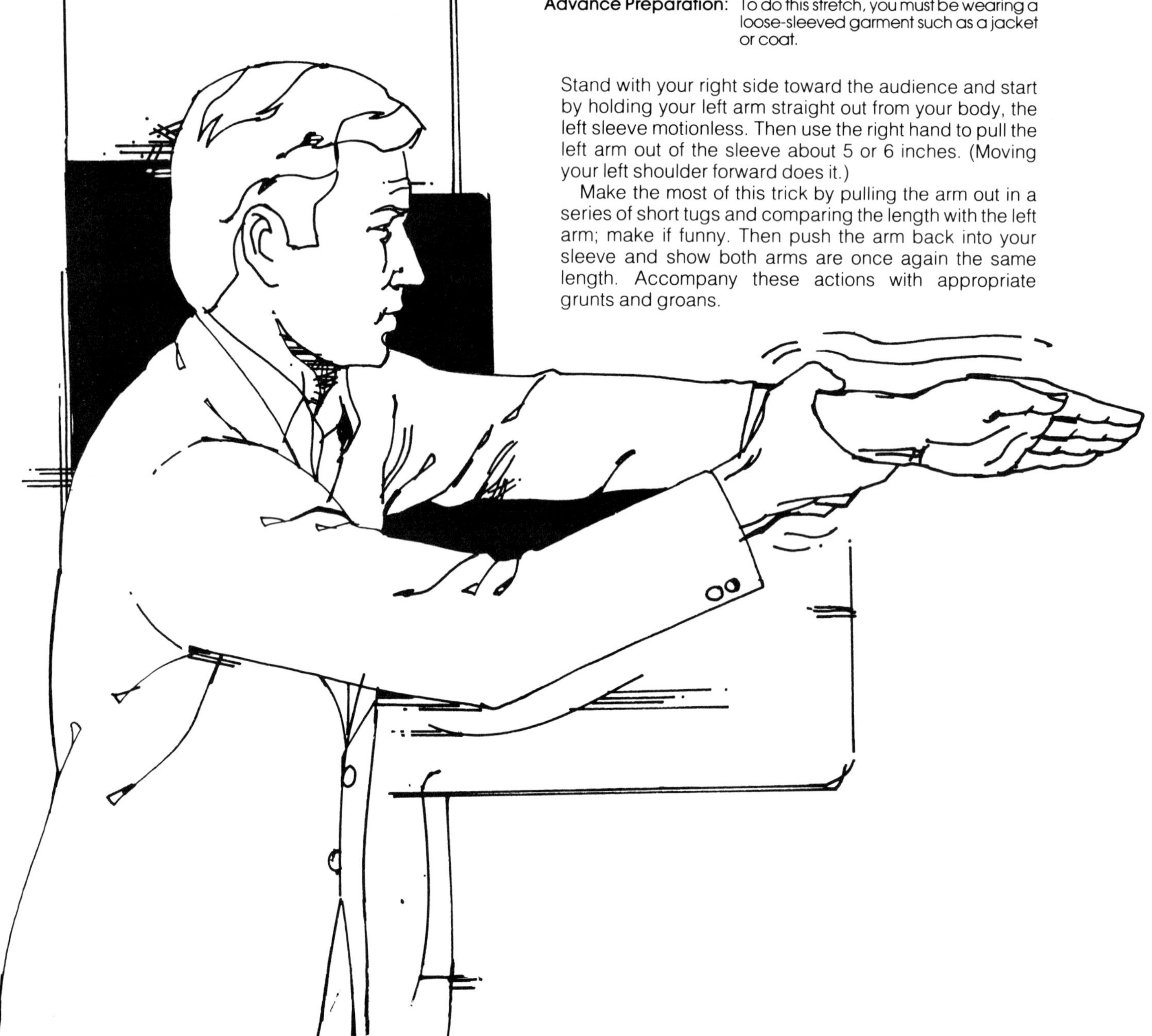

THE RUBBER HANDS

This very simple sleight makes a great introduction to a series of tricks done with the hands and fingers. The optical illusion of fingers bending at impossible angles is created. Note that a slight distance between magician and audience increases the effect.

Props: none
Advance Preparation: none

You might begin by suggesting that your fingers are a little stiff and that you hope the audience will excuse you while you warm them up. Now put your palms and thumbs together and point your fingers toward the audience.

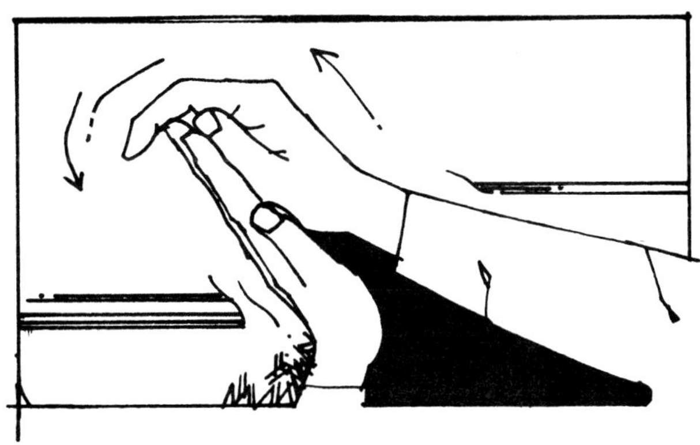

Next, simultaneously slide your right hand forward and turn both hands to the left, curling your right fingers over the left fingers.

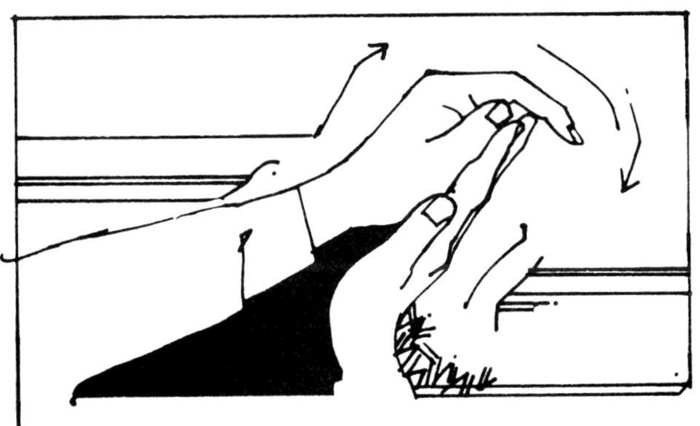

Now reverse the motion, simultaneously sliding your right hand back, your left hand forward, and curling your left fingers over the right fingers as you turn both hands to the right.

Continue to perform this motion back and forth from right to left. Spectators will be amazed as your hands appear to bend crazily, apparently made of rubber.

SHADOWGRAPHY

Like pantomime, this sophisticated art cannot be mastered by the beginner for instant display. However, with a little practice any amateur can learn to project a few shadowgraphs. Your best bet is to limit your shadowgraphy repertoire to few images because you must remember exactly how to perform them without referring to diagrams. As your confidence and skill increase, add new shadowgraphs to your bag of tricks.

Shadowgraphy is adaptable to impromptu performance at home if you have the necessary light and a wall on which to cast shadows. We include it in this chapter, however, because the magician who wishes to devote a healthy chunk of time to practice may use shadowgraphy as a substantial portion of a stage act.

Props: an illuminated wall (at home)
a lamp
a screen (onstage)

Advance Preparation: Practice to make sure you have memorized the proper hand positions.

The following illustrations give the hand position and corresponding result for some of the most common and simple shadowgraphs. Start with these and if you find yourself caught up by this art, consult books that deal exclusively with shadowgraphy for additional pictures. Dover has two. It should go without saying that in shadowgraphy, as with every category covered in this book, one should never hesitate to experiment with original versions of the tricks described.

A classic shadowgraphy bit is to make a rabbit with one hand and a dog or wolf with the other and have the dog eat off the rabbit's ears.

RABBIT I   RABBIT II

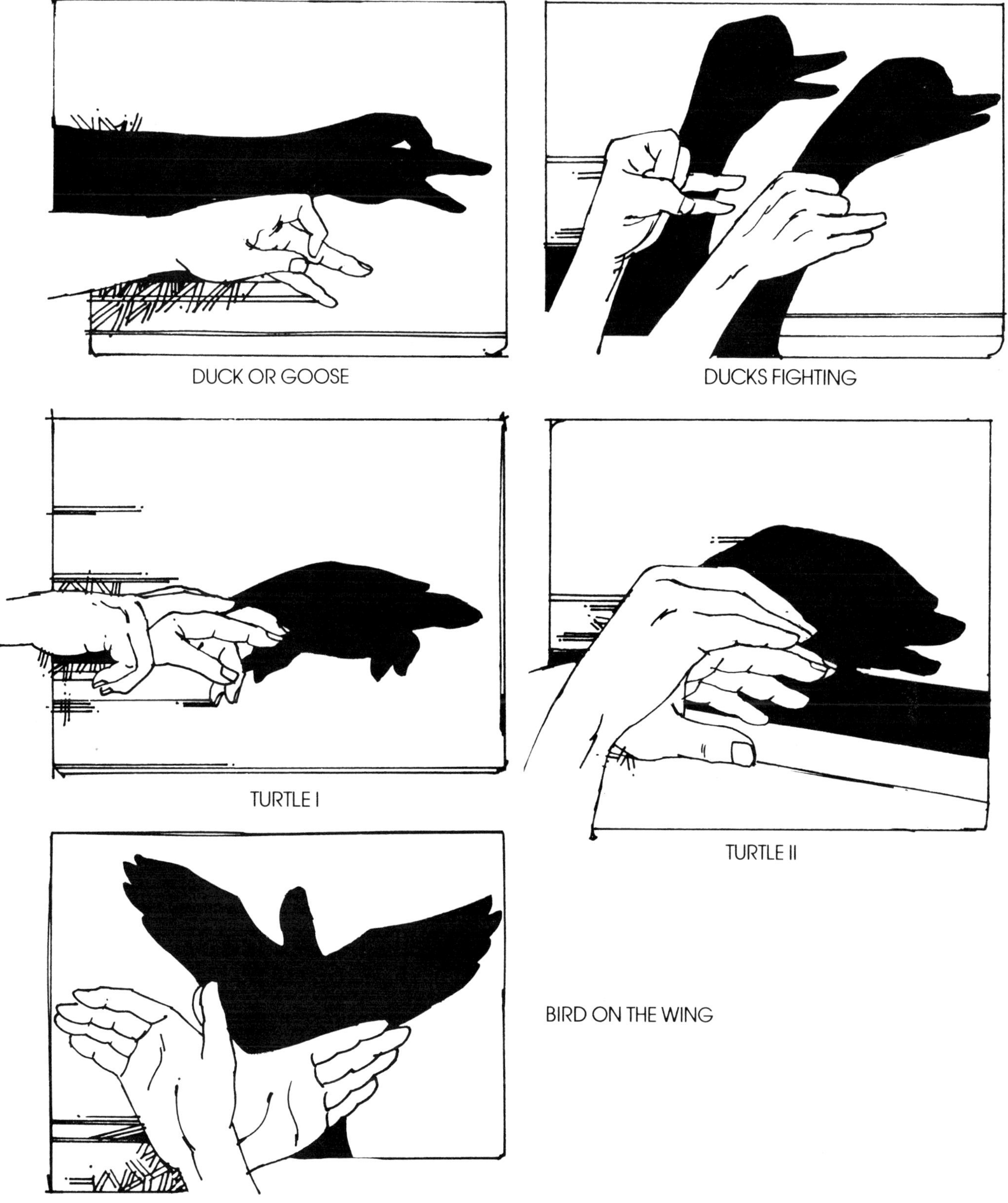

DUCK OR GOOSE

DUCKS FIGHTING

TURTLE I

TURTLE II

BIRD ON THE WING

MIDGET GIMMICK

This old gag, used often by Buster Keaton, offers a one-shot laugh and may be best used to begin a show.

Props: none
Advance Preparation: none

Since this is a sight gag, you might want to let the audience see the "midget" as the curtain opens at the beginning of your act. Simply remove your shoes and kneel on top of them. This image is most effective when you are wearing baggy pants so that you can bunch them at the knees to look like trouser cuffs draping over your shoes.

Another popular method for creating the midget is to place your shoes on a table top and insert your hands. This takes a bit more in the way of props and presentation, however. You must rig a pair of pants legs to fit over your arms, and an assistant must provide the midget's arms by standing behind you and thrusting his arms forward.

THE PSYCHIC SURGEON

This trick, a pantomime, may appeal to only a few amateur magicians. Obviously, pantomime is a highly developed art and the beginner cannot expect to become expert overnight. However, if magic of this type is attractive to you, you can work up your own simplified routine, avoiding the more complex moves.

A vast array of pantomime-type acts are available to the conjurer. Some famous entertainers, past and present, have created their own trademarks in mime tricks. Red Skelton's arm acts are well known universally, and while the beginner hardly can hope to top the original, adapting a similar routine to your own skills is certainly possible. Since these tricks are based on acting skills, each performer must use his powers of imagination to develop his own routines. In countless ways you can pretend that one hand or arm is immobile and controlled by the other. It's up to you to make it hilarious. The Psychic Surgeon is a classic example of this kind of trick.

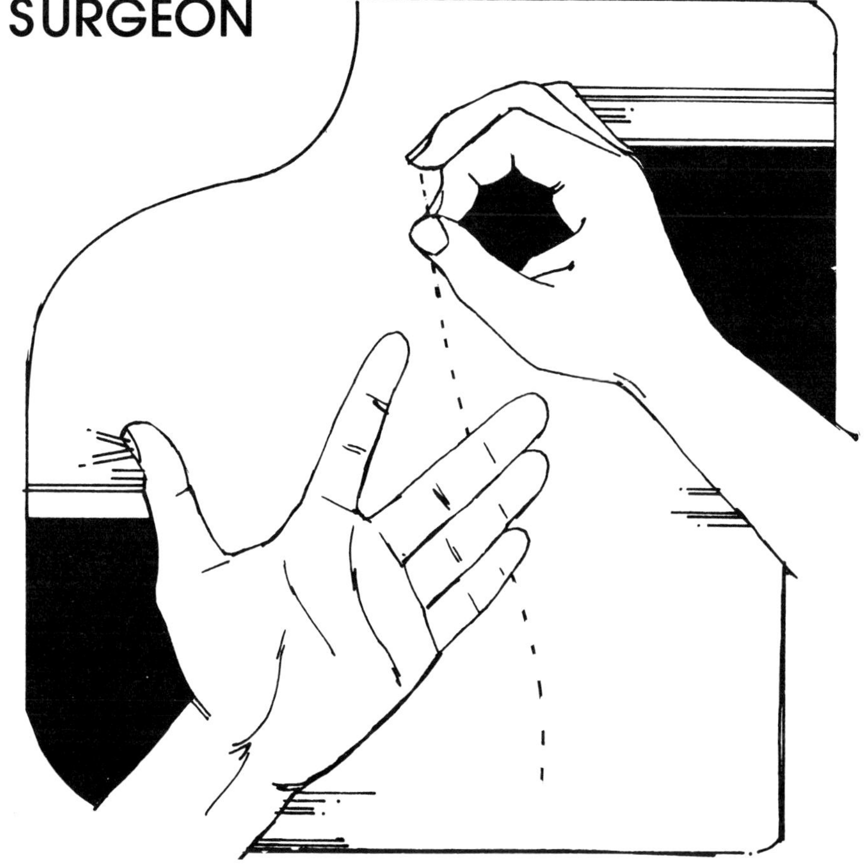

Props: none
Advance Preparation: This trick should be practiced in front of a mirror.

The idea is to pretend that you are sewing together various parts of your body so you can then pull on the threads and move individual parts like a puppet's. A few ways of doing this follow; use your imagination to come up with original routines.

In a classic trick, the psychic surgeon goes through the motions of sewing the fingers of one hand together, using the other hand to hold the imaginary needle and thread. Once the sewing is completed, you can pull the imaginary thread to lift or bend one finger, and so on.

In another version, sew hand or fingers and then push the needle through the top (or front) of your upper arm and out of the bottom (or back) of the arm. You then may pull on the thread from your arm, thus lifting your left hand. Elaborate on this. You can pull on the thread and thumb your nose.

In a third routine, push the needle and thread through one ear and out the other, then pull the thread back and forth through your head.

These are among the best known ways to use the imaginary-needle-and-thread routine. Obviously, you may apply the concept to any movable part of your body.

gags, mysteries of science & puzzles

The following tricks are used to shock, frighten, or amuse or fool your victims. These classic routines are just a few selected from thousands that many magicians consider traditional.

There are gags in which you seem to destroy a spectator's possession; stunts based on leverage rather than strength that fool the wariest watcher; tricks that employ slapstick gimmicks; puzzles based on scientific theories and principles.

After you have mastered these puzzles and optical illusions, you can invent hundreds of your own mathematical gimmicks and physical challenges, using common household items and game pieces. Several illusionary effects can be incorporated into more complex stage routines.

Remember, a certain amount of advance preparation and distracting patter guarantee success. But observe the fine line between too much prefatory chatter that might draw attention to your moves and a bit of sideline comment that directs your audience's attention elsewhere.

The following tricks are used at your own risk to shock, frighten, amuse or fool your victims. These are merely a few classic routines; other thousands are considered nearly traditional by some families.

A BROOM BET

This trick gives you the opportunity for a challenge of muscles. Claim that you, using only one hand, can prevent a challenger using two hands from pushing a broom to the floor.

Prop: a broom
Advance Preparation: none

Offer to bet that your strength will prove superior, then have the victim hold the broom as shown. Place your palm against the broom, and as the victim tries to push the broom toward the floor, press it horizontally. The challenger's energy will be expended in trying to keep the broom in place, leaving him none to guide it downward.

THE SILK ASHTRAY

This is a surefire way at a cocktail party to shock the owner of a fine silk scarf.

Props: a silver half dollar
a silk scarf
a burning cigarette

Advance Preparation: Palm the half dollar in your left palm. Borrow a scarf from a victim and flip it over your left hand without showing the coin.

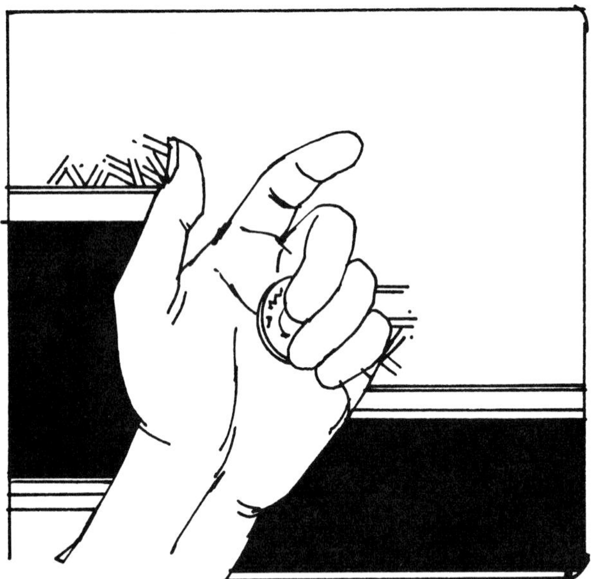

With the cigarette in your right hand, flick the ashes off to avoid soiling the scarf and quickly but firmly jab the coin into your palm through the scarf a few times to put out the cigarette. If you use a silk tie, make sure the lining does not get in the way. The heat from the cigarette butt will be conducted through the cloth to the coin without damaging the scarf.

Confidently whip the scarf off your palm, reclosing your fist quickly to hide the half dollar, and show the unchanged scarf to the owner.

If the scarf has burned, RUN!

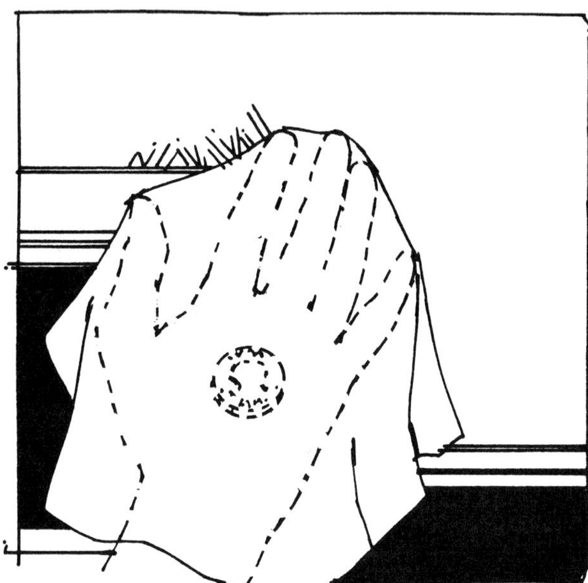

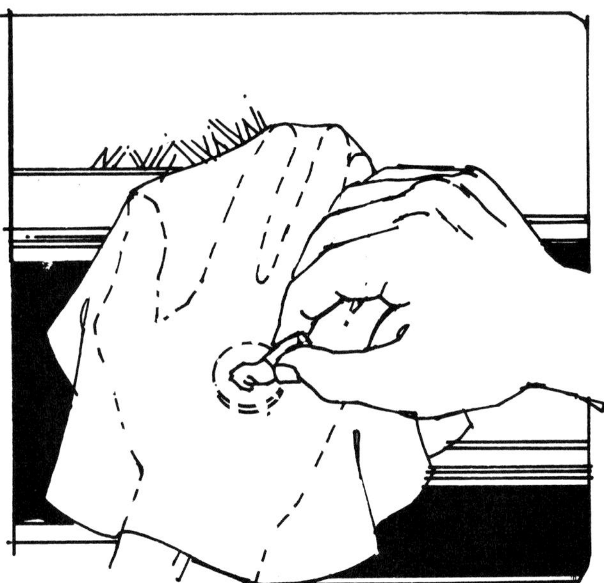

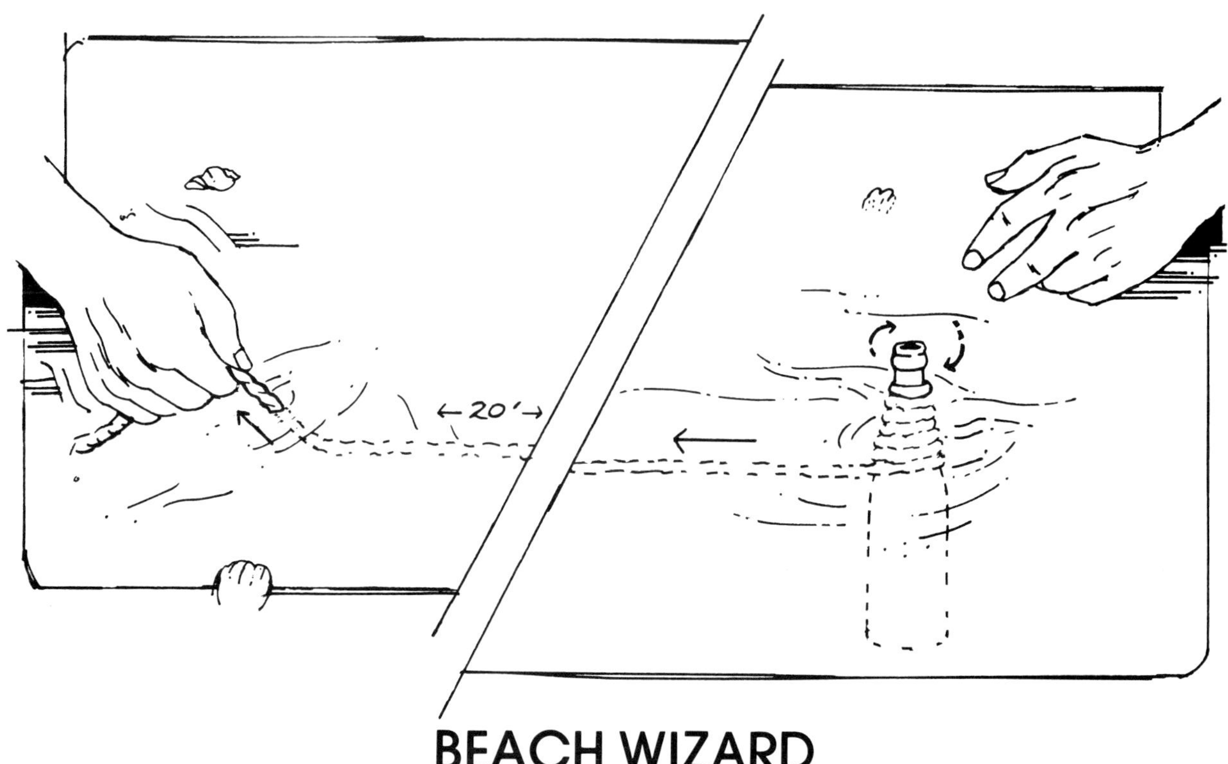

BEACH WIZARD

If you have the patience for the preparations, this is an amusing stunt to perform on the beach. You need an assistant to make a bottle in the sand move on command.

Props: an empty bottle
about 30 feet of cord or rope

Advance Preparation: The most difficult of the necessary preparations for this trick is hiding your moves from the spectators who will become your audience. Do the best you can. Dig a shallow gutter about 20 feet long in the sand; lay the cord on it, leaving a few inches protruding at one end. At the other end, tie the rope around the bottle's neck, then loop it around at least six times more. Bury about two thirds of the bottle in the sand at the end of the trench, letting only the single loop of cord show. Have your assistant sit at the other end of the trench, secretly holding the rope in one hand.

Announce that you can use your supernatural powers to rotate the bottle in the sand without touching it. On most occasions, if you speak loudly, your commands to the bottle will be heard by your assistant, who can then pull on the rope to make the bottle at the other end twirl.

To end the trick, secretly slip the cord off the bottle as you pull it out of the sand; your assistant then can pull the rope through the trench, leaving no trace of the props.

THE WATCH STOPS

In this cute little gag you pretend to destroy a victim's possession. Some sleight of hand is involved, but with practice beginners can handle the trick.

Props: a bunch of keys on a ring
a watch (borrowed from the victim)
a table
a handkerchief or other cloth

Advance Preparation: Have the key ring sleeved in your right arm and borrow a watch from a member of your audience, taking it in your right hand.

Do not announce the trick. As soon as you have the borrowed watch in your right hand, put that arm at your side to let the keys drop into your hand secretly.

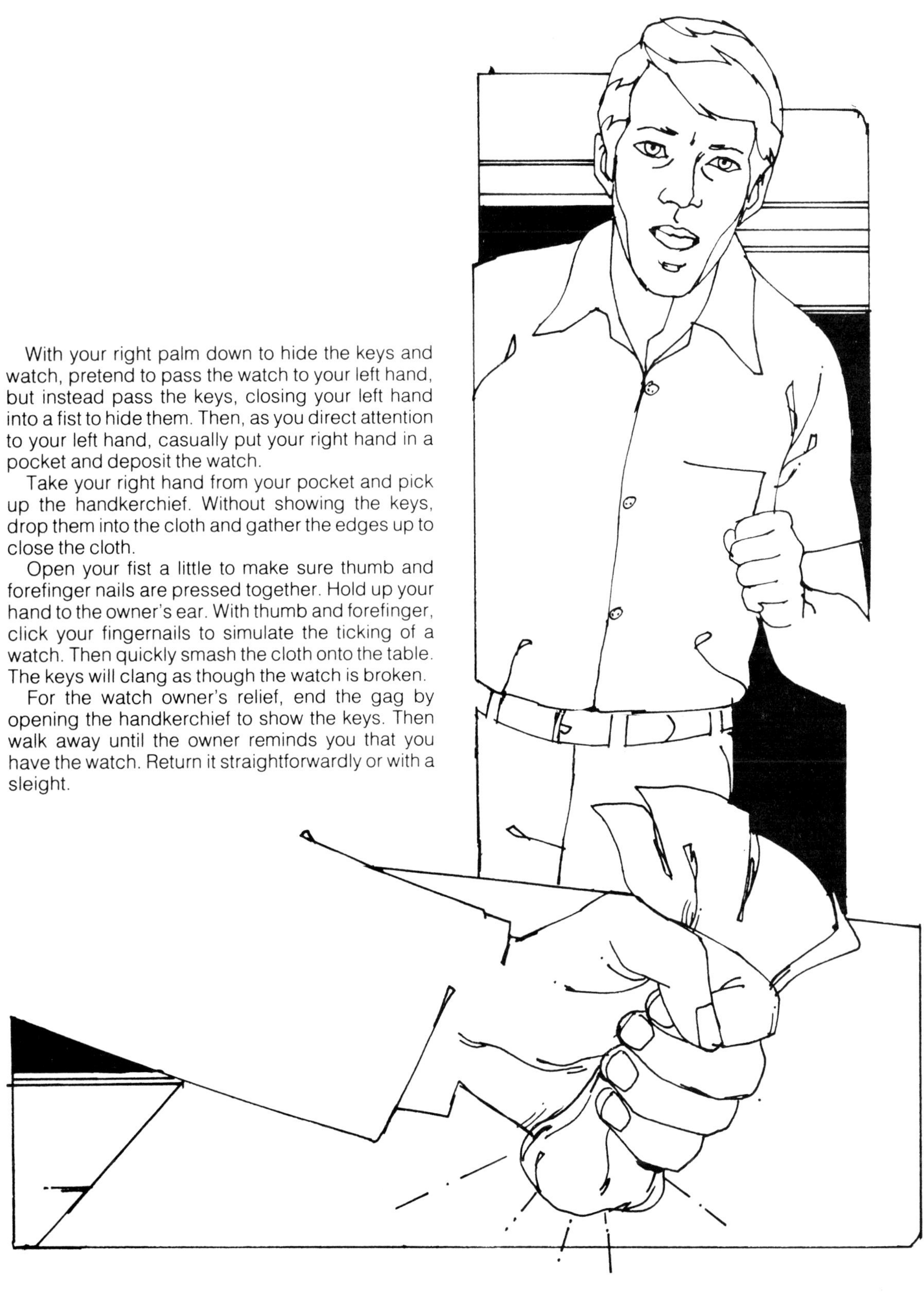

With your right palm down to hide the keys and watch, pretend to pass the watch to your left hand, but instead pass the keys, closing your left hand into a fist to hide them. Then, as you direct attention to your left hand, casually put your right hand in a pocket and deposit the watch.

Take your right hand from your pocket and pick up the handkerchief. Without showing the keys, drop them into the cloth and gather the edges up to close the cloth.

Open your fist a little to make sure thumb and forefinger nails are pressed together. Hold up your hand to the owner's ear. With thumb and forefinger, click your fingernails to simulate the ticking of a watch. Then quickly smash the cloth onto the table. The keys will clang as though the watch is broken.

For the watch owner's relief, end the gag by opening the handkerchief to show the keys. Then walk away until the owner reminds you that you have the watch. Return it straightforwardly or with a sleight.

HAND PUPPETS

I certainly cannot knock a simple puppet, because I devised one that has taken me around the English-speaking world. You see, I had been a professional magician and ventriloquist before I was drafted for World War II back in 1944. I found I couldn't carry a ventriloquist's dummy in a barracks bag and I had a funny routine that was going to waste on the GI shows. About that time an English book, The ABC of Ventriloquism, *by Douglas Craggs, came out and I was sent a copy. From this book I picked up the idea of the talking mitten, and I put some of my old gags into a format that was new to me.*

By the time I got out of the army in 1946 I had a pretty tight routine. Instead of adding to it I have done nothing but cut it down since. Now I do one chorus of "If I Had My Way" in G and it takes six minutes to do what used to take twelve minutes. But it has taken me to the Palace Theatre in New York and the Palladium in London and a lot of theatres and nightclubs along the way.

If you look in the old books, you can find "The Talking Hand" in the Art of Amusing, *by Frank Bellew, as far back as 1866 and Hogarth shows it in the "Election" and since Hogarth died in 1764, the talking hand is not really a new bit.*

Senor Wences paints his hand and talks to Johnny. He carries a body and a wig and he's also famous for the head in the box. All right? "All right."

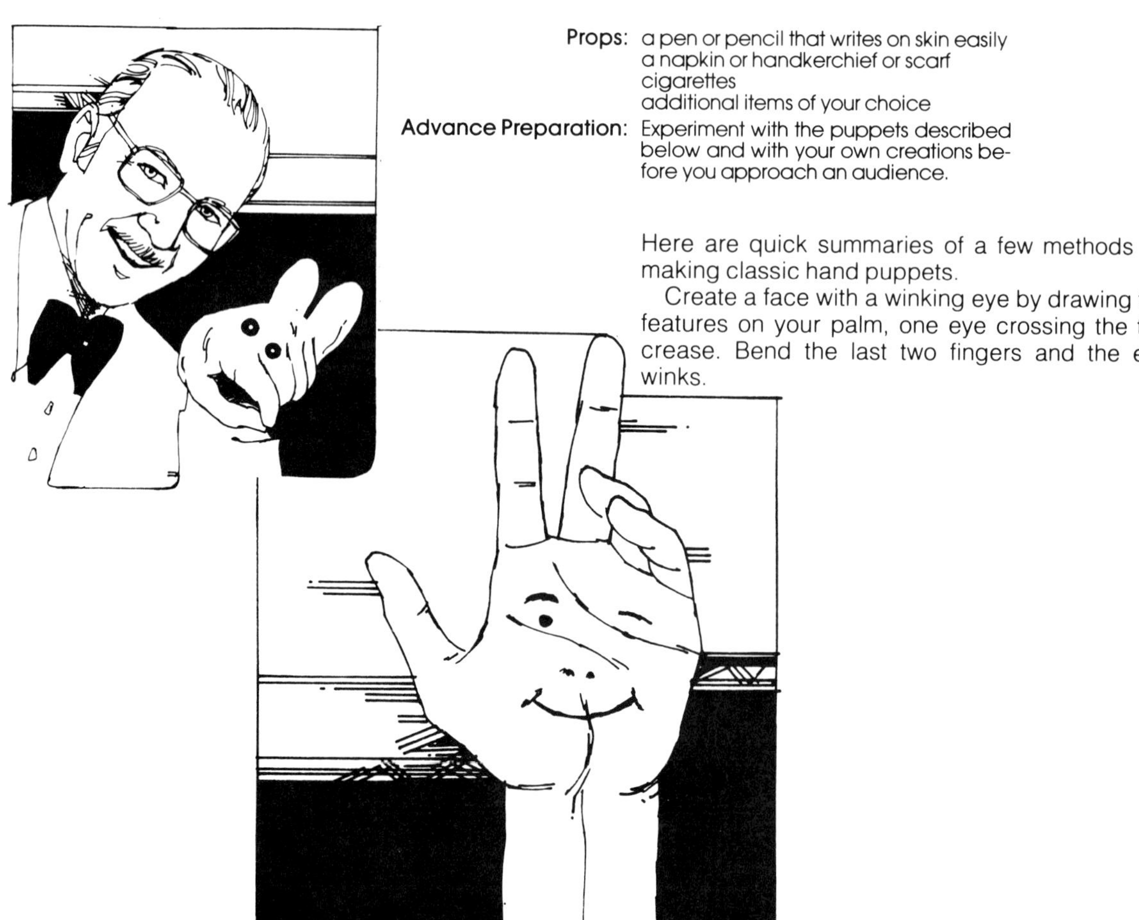

Props: a pen or pencil that writes on skin easily
a napkin or handkerchief or scarf
cigarettes
additional items of your choice

Advance Preparation: Experiment with the puppets described below and with your own creations before you approach an audience.

Here are quick summaries of a few methods for making classic hand puppets.

Create a face with a winking eye by drawing the features on your palm, one eye crossing the top crease. Bend the last two fingers and the eye winks.

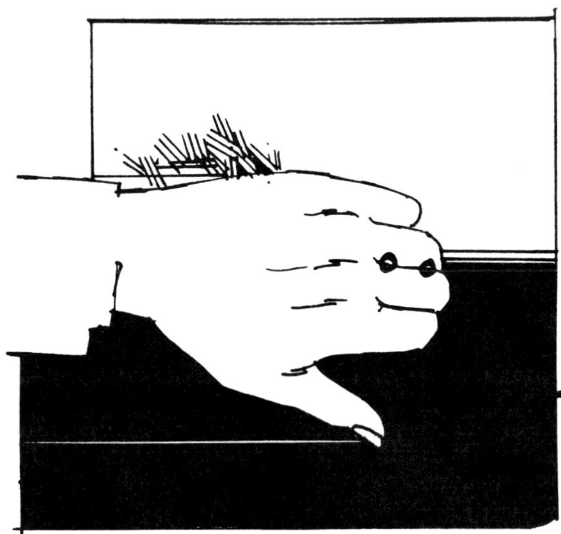

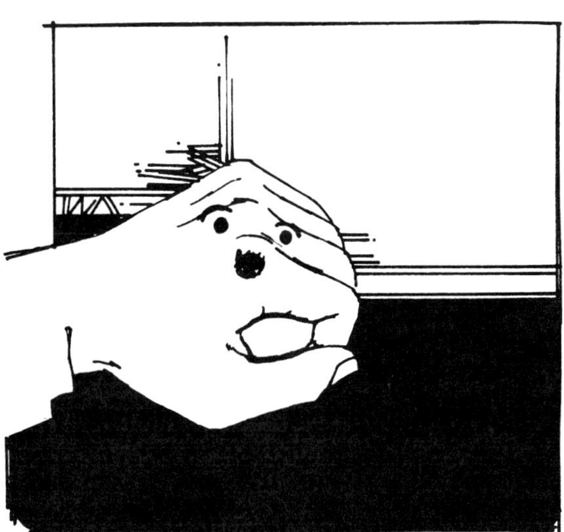

Create a talking puppet by drawing the face on the back of your fingers, with the eyes drawn between second and third fingers and the mouth between first and second fingers. Moving the forefinger away from the middle finger makes the puppet talk.

Finally, try drawing the face to form the puppet's mouth by the gap between thumb and forefinger. Draw the nose on the large knuckle of the forefinger. Since you have much flexibility in changing the shape of the "mouth," you can make the puppet talk with expression, and even yawn.

A popular puppet is the old crone formed by holding tips of cigarettes between the second and third fingers of one hand. The line between the first and second fingers becomes the puppet's mouth. Wrap a handkerchief, napkin or scarf around the hand and hold it in place with the free hand. If it is slippery, clip it in place on top of the puppet's "head" between two of your fingers. To make the crone talk, move your forefinger up and down, showing toothless "gums." A thumb inserted between the forefinger and middle finger can be the crone's tongue.

Again, when you find yourself at a loss for something to do, why not pick up a pen, lipstick, grease pencil or chalk and experiment with new forms of hand puppets?

FINGERS OF IRON

Following are classical strength stunts requiring no props but the hands. All are based on balance and leverage rather than strength, but they can make for some amusing challenges.

Props: none
Advance Preparation: none

Many people will know at least one or two of these tricks, so you might include several versions in your repertoire as spares.

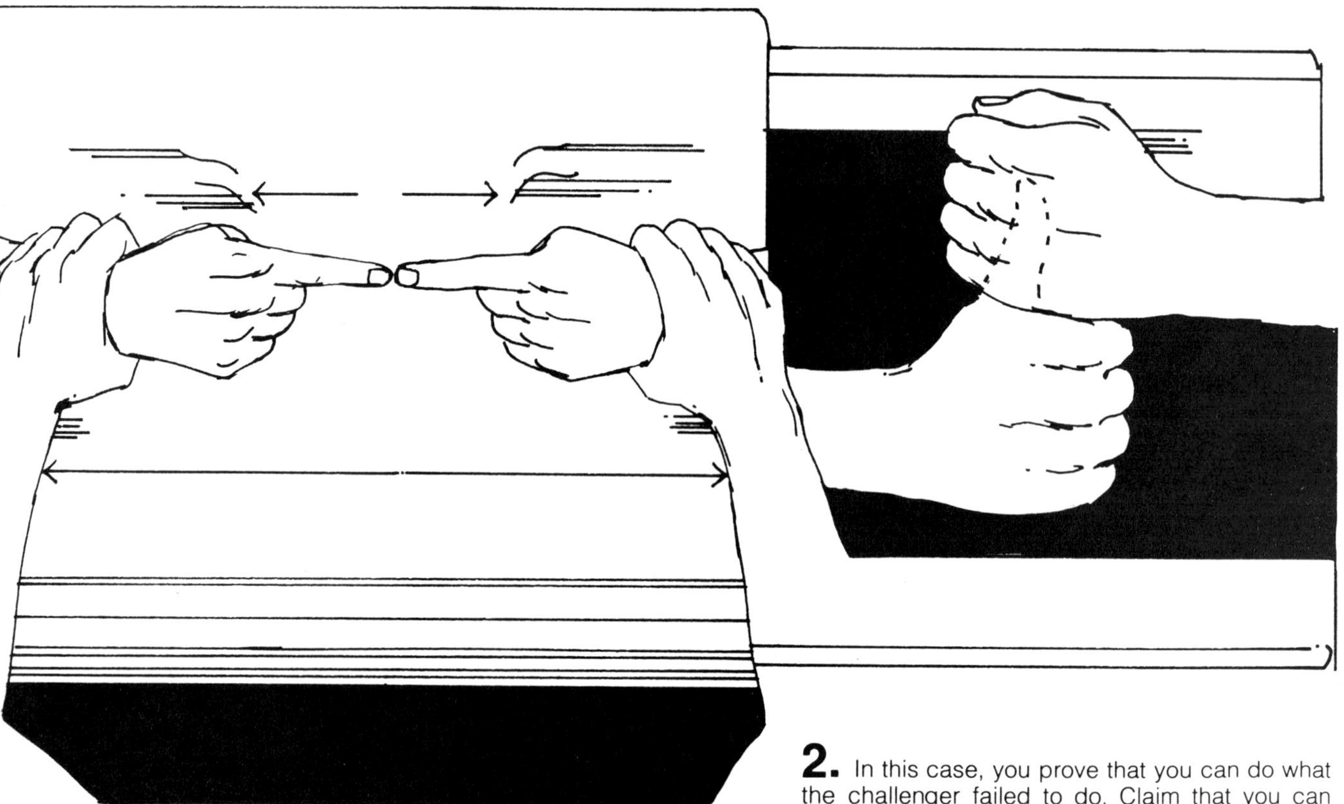

1. Bet that someone cannot stand directly in front of you and pull your forefingers apart. Put the fingertips together in front of you, elbows out to the sides, and have the challenger pull on your wrists to separate your fingers. Only if you make sure the victim is standing centered in front of you will this work.

2. In this case, you prove that you can do what the challenger failed to do. Claim that you can knock his fists apart with your forefingers only, but that he will be unable to do the same to you.

Have the victim put one fist on top of the other in front of him. Put one of your forefingers on the side of each fist and knock them in opposite directions. This will work every time. For the trick's second part, secretly insert your bottom thumb inside the top fist before letting the challenger strike with his forefingers. Naturally, he will be unable to separate your fists.

INSTANT SCOOTER

This low-brow sight gag is meant to humiliate your victim.

Props: 1 or 2 paper matches
Advance Preparation: If using one match, split the end of it about one-third of the way toward the head.

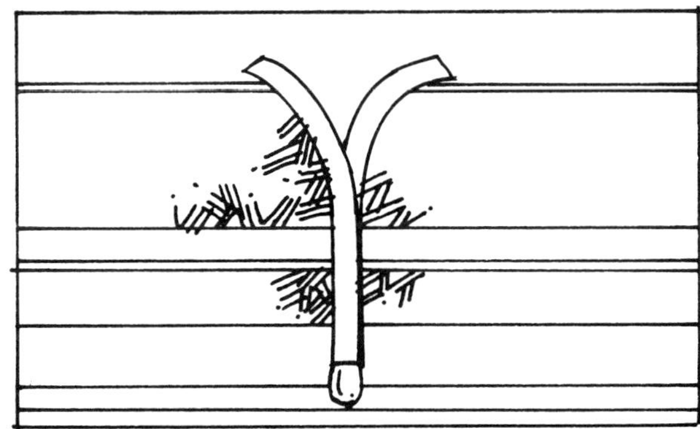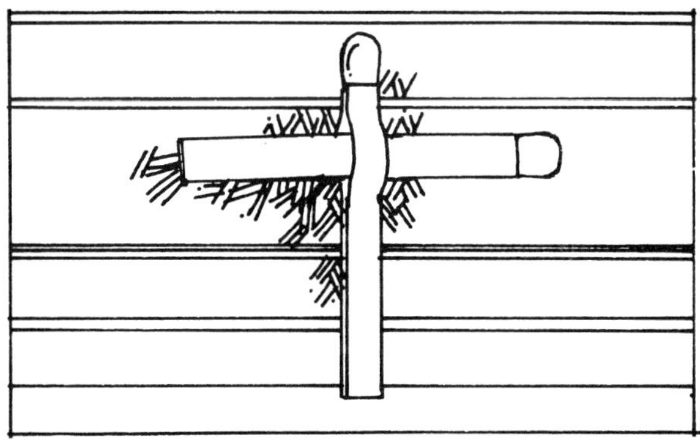

Hand the match or matches to the chosen victim, instructing him to hold in either hand the prongs of the split end or the horizontal ends of the crossed matches. Inventing an imaginative excuse for your request, ask the victim to scuff one foot on the carpet. You may be so bold as to ask him to hum in a monotone under his breath.

When he is performing the motions above, make some deprecating remark within earshot of nearby crowds, to the effect that he seems a bit mature to be riding a scooter.

THE ONE-STEP KNOT

This is an ancient stunt, but you might enjoy fooling children with it at the dinner table or in the living room. Ask if anyone in the room can tie a knot in your napkin or handkerchief holding the diagonal corners, one in each hand and never letting go of the ends.

Props: a cloth napkin or handkerchief (or any other cloth)

Advance Preparation: It is a good idea to cross your arms smugly as you make your challenge. This puts your arms in the proper position for the trick. Have the cloth lying horizontally on the table in front of you.

With your arms still crossed, bend toward the table and simply pick up one end of the cloth with each hand.

Now uncross your arms without letting go of the handkerchief ends. The handkerchief will tie itself in a knot.

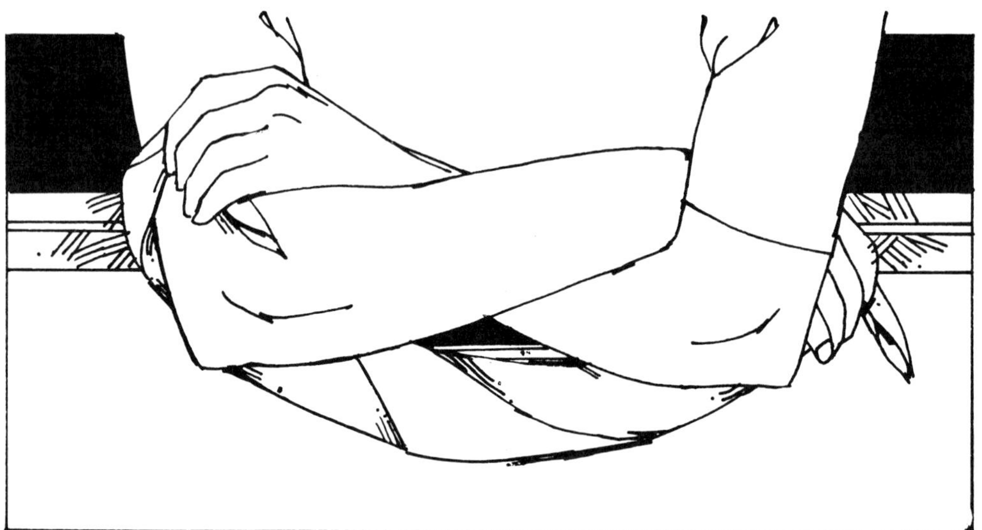

THE ARMORED ARM

This is a slightly grisly trick, but if you go for the horror-movie effect, this is your kind of magic. Do not announce the trick; just demonstrate.

Prop: a pin
Advance Preparation: none

Place the pin across the inside of your elbow, lengthwise on your arm. Make sure that your audience sees where it is.

Quickly close your arm (bending it at the elbow) and open it to show that the pin has not pierced your skin at all.

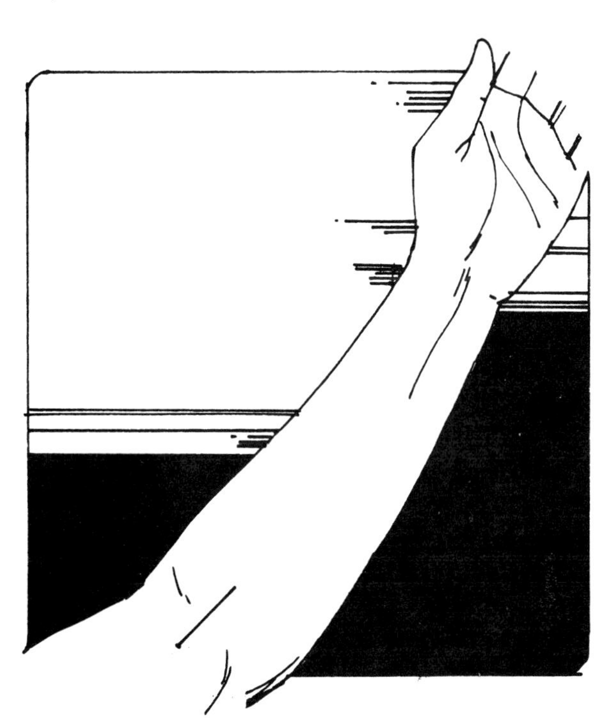

NOTHING AT ALL

This simple, ridiculous gag to humiliate a friend is such basic slapstick that everyone might not think it is amusing. Judge your timing well.

Prop: a full dinner plate
Advance Preparation: Wait until a fellow diner or someone in the living room is in a heated harangue about some subject or another, then somberly hand the person your full dinner plate, or an ashtray full of burning cigarettes (or some other silly object).

Success for this trick is based entirely on using your best deadpan to stare the victim straight in the eyes while he holds your plate. Most people will not ask questions for at least a few minutes, especially if you are in a position to get up and move out of arm's reach of the victim. Eventually, he will wonder why he is holding the plate, and we hope others in the room will laugh.

These puzzles, challenges and gags are based on some property of science, be it physics, chemistry, biology or mathematics. Included in this group are classic illusions, great impromptu challenges and several effects to be incorporated into more complex stage routines.

NO-HANDS BANANA PEELING

This simple effect is based on creating a vacuum in a glass bottle and peeling a banana over it.

Props:	a banana a glass bottle (some juice bottles are O.K.) a match a piece of paper
Advance Preparation:	Peel the banana a few inches. Light the paper with the match and drop the burning piece into the glass bottle. The mouth of the bottle must be filled by the banana.

Casually turn the partially peeled banana into the top of the glass bottle. As the flame consumes the oxygen, the banana will peel itself. Of course, you wind up with ashes on your banana, but you proved you could do it.

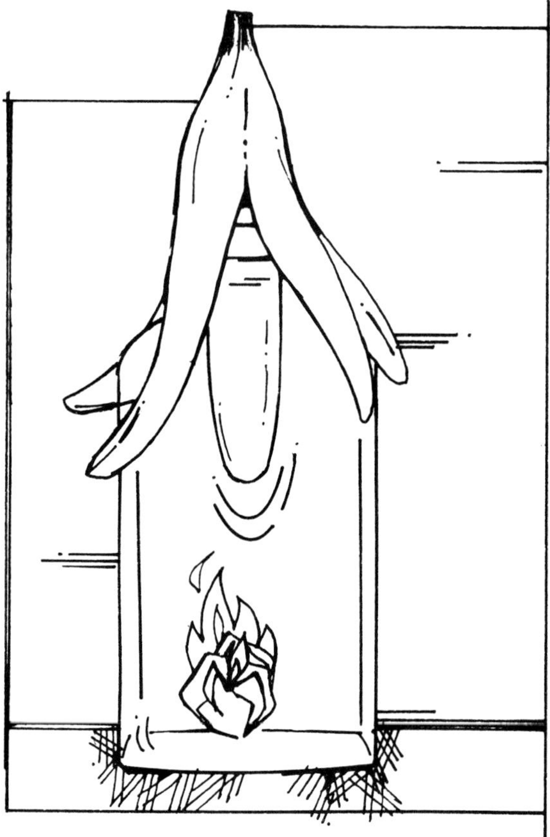

GRAVITY PARADOX

The basis for this little feat is centrifugal force. A bottle inverted on a table over a marble or other spherical object is moved without dropping the ball.

Props: a wide-mouthed bottle or carafe
a marble, ball bearing or other small sphere
a table

Advance Preparation: Place the sphere on the table with the bottle inverted over it.

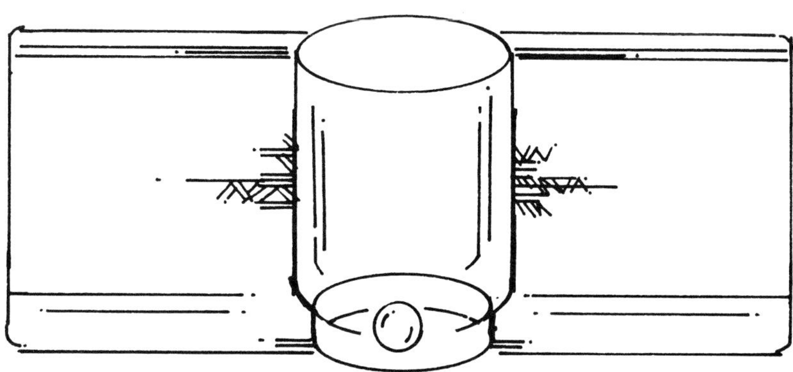

Start by challenging other diners to move the bottle a certain distance without dropping the ball.

If no one guesses how it is done, grab the bottle with one hand and rotate the bottle neck so the sphere rolls around the neck preventing the ball from falling as you move the bottle horizontally and lift it from the table.

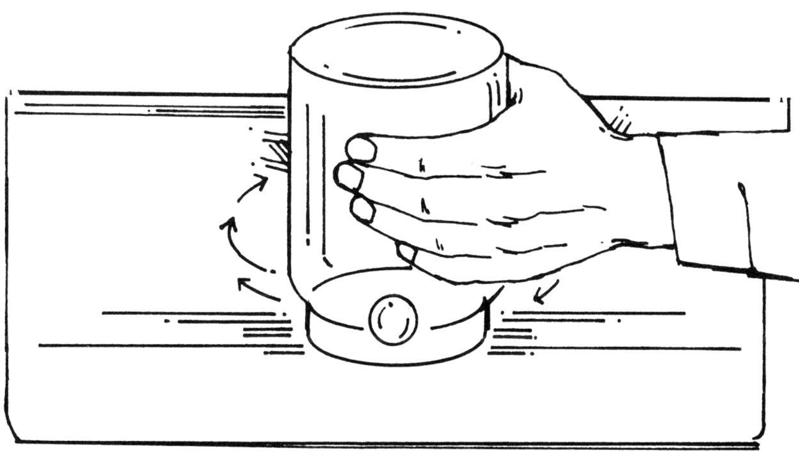

RISING SALT

This fairly obvious gimmick might not fool anyone but can be good for filling conversation gaps. It must be done at the table.

Props: a glass of beer
a salt shaker
Advance Preparation: none

Announce the trick and pour a small pile of salt on the table. Put the glass of beer over it, say magic words, then tap the salt shaker on the edge of the glass. Bubbles rising in the beer glass will simulate salt penetrating the glass and rising through the beer.

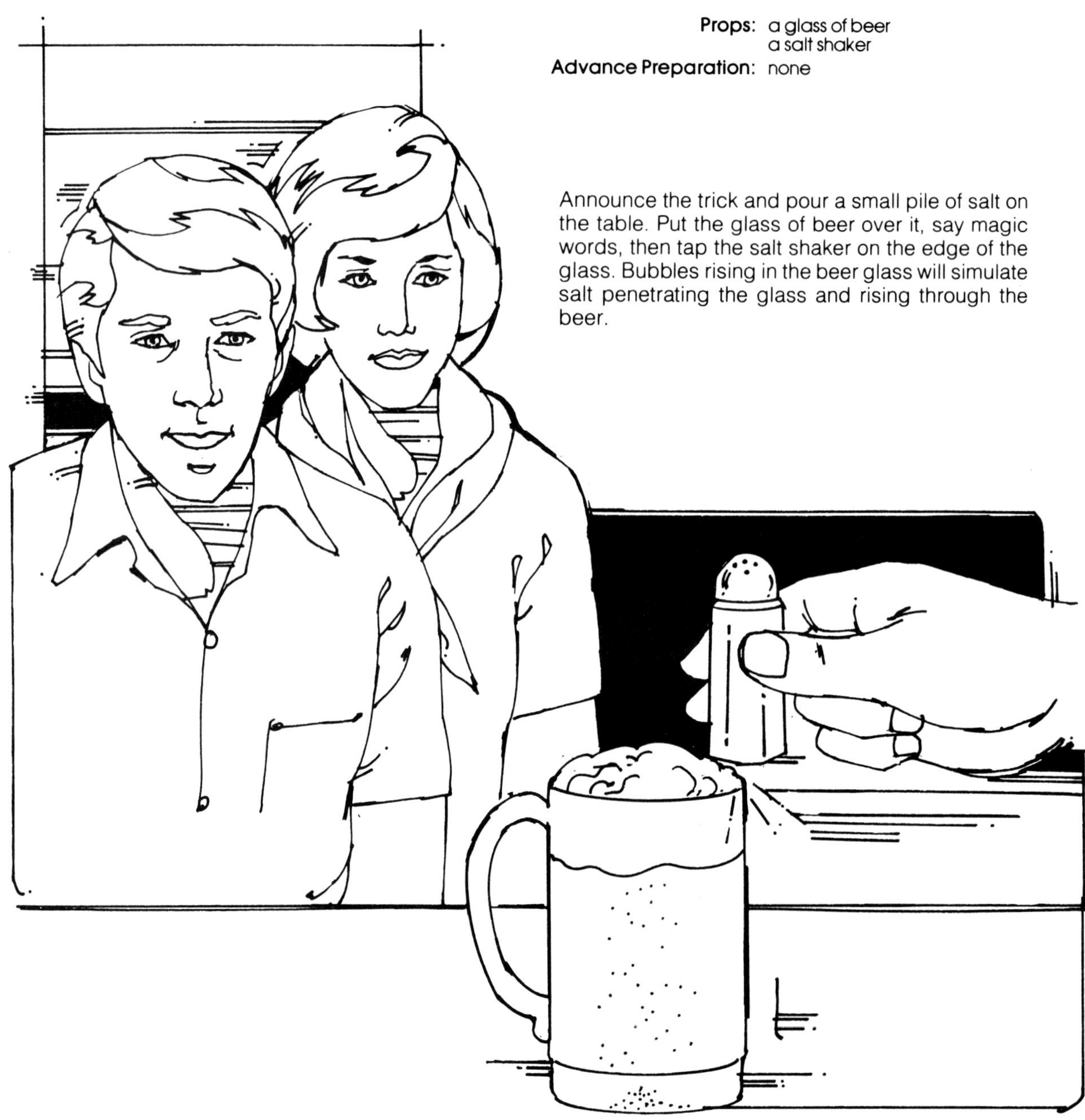

ELUSIVE PEPPER

Good old static electricity comes to fore in this trick, which is perfect for the dinner table.

Props: a salt shaker
a pepper mill
a comb

Advance Preparation: Charge the comb with static electricity. For instance, leave the table and comb your hair thoroughly to get a strong charge.

Claim to make the pepper disappear from a pile of salt. Shake salt into a small pile on the table and top it with a bit of pepper.

Dramatically whisk the comb from your pocket and pass it over the salt and pepper. The pepper will adhere to the comb. For extra effect, palm the comb as you pass it over the salt and pepper, so no one suspects static electricity.

LEVITATING AN ICE CUBE

This is a simple challenge at the dinner table. Using a piece of string or other handy, lightweight object such as a toothpick, the diners are challenged to lift an ice cube from a glass of water.

Props: a glass of ice water
a short piece of string or a toothpick
a salt shaker

Advance Preparation: none

Make your challenge, warning that your audience may not touch the ice cube or tie the string (if used) to the cube.

When no one succeeds, place the string or toothpick on top of the floating cube, then grab the salt shaker and pour a liberal amount over both. Wait a few seconds, then nonchalantly lift the end of the pick or string and pull out the cube, which has been melted by the salt and has adhered to the string.

CIGARETTE STRETCH

This trick is based on a familiar optical illusion, but since your audience will be unaware of your advance preparations, the result will be convincing.

Props: a half-full pack of king-size cigarettes
a 100 ml cigarette
a table

Advance Preparation: Put the long cigarette into the half-full pack diagonally.

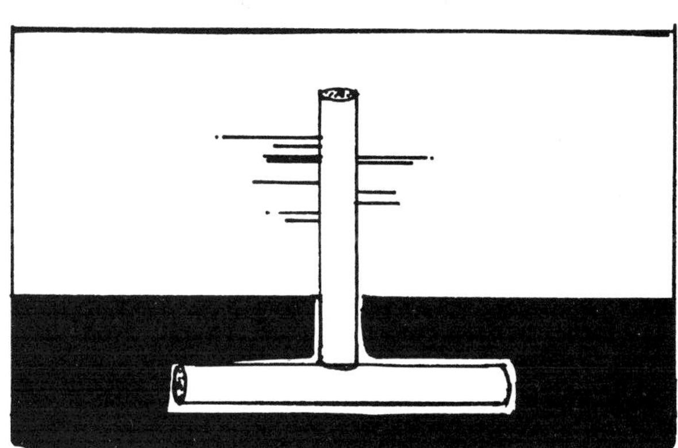

1. To start the trick, plant the suggestion that both cigarettes are the same length by taking one king-size cigarette from the pack together with the long one, and placing them in a "T" position, with the long cigarette horizontal.

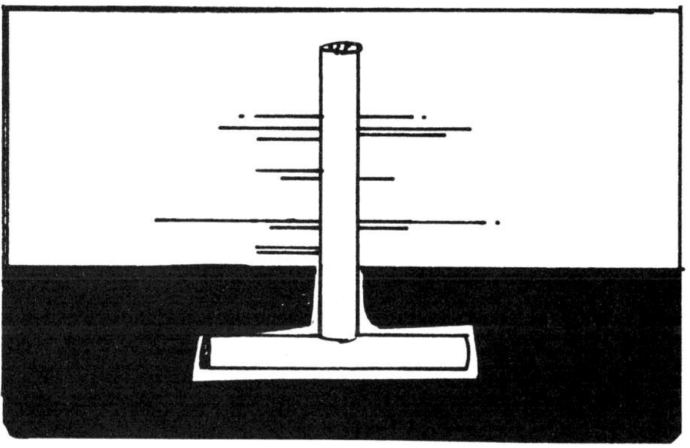

2. To your audience, the two cigarettes will appear equal in length. Smoothly pick up the long cigarette with one hand and attract attention to it while subtly moving the short one to the horizontal position. Then pull on the ends of the long cigarette, exaggerating your efforts, and put it down to complete the "T," in its stretched state.

INVISIBLE WRITING

There are many versions of this old-time gimmick, and a few can be done with items available in the household. Use invisible writing to amuse children at a party or to add to a stage routine. For instance, for an improved ending to a mind-reading trick, guess the answer and then pull from a pocket one of several prepared pieces of paper with the answer in invisible writing.

Prop: paper
Advance Preparation: a narrow eye dropper (or any other pointed object that could be used as a pen)
the juice of an orange, lemon or lime (or milk)

Whenever you wish to reveal the invisible writing, recite an appropriate spell over the paper while you hold it above a light bulb or a match or candle flame, being careful not to set the paper on fire. Gradually the words will appear in brown on the paper.

THE GOOSE THAT LAID THE SILVER EGG

Use this trick to tell children at the dinner table the familiar fairy tale, substituting the silver egg for the golden egg or use it for an interesting illusion. It is based on the mysterious results of light refraction.

Props: an egg
a candle flame
a glass of water
Advance Preparation: none

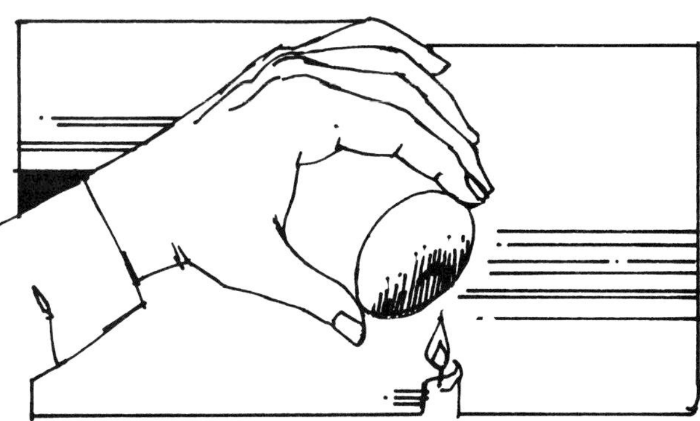

Announce the trick as you hold the egg over the candle flame to cover it with soot.

After the egg is coated with soot, drop it into the glass of water, timing this properly if you are telling a fairy tale along with it. The egg will appear to turn silver in the glass.

Perform another light refraction trick with a half dollar. Place the coin under a glass of water, lay a plate on top of the glass, and the coin appears to disappear.

RUBBER BAND BREAK-OUT

Crack a joke at the beginning of this challenge trick by calling this one of Houdini's earlier efforts. Place the rubber band around a victim's hand and ask him to remove it without using the other hand.

Prop: a rubber band
Advance Preparation: none

Challenge your friends to remove the rubber band as you place it around the hand of one of them. Very few will succeed. You will not have the answer either; but it is good for a laugh.

Following are challenges to pose for your friends or dinner companions. While a few actually are based on scientific principles, most are merely confounding solutions to specific tasks and they require the performer to memorize several steps.

BALANCING GLASSES
AND CURRENCY

This is a perfect example of a puzzle you can lay out for your dinner or drinking companions. Challenge your fellows to balance a bill on top of two glasses, then balance a third glass on top of the bill.

Props: 3 empty glasses
a bill of any denomination
Advance Preparation: none

After the other diners fail miserably, show them how to do the trick. Pleat the bill accordion style and lay it between two of the glasses. Then merely place the third glass in the center of the folded bill.

COIN, CURRENCY AND GLASS BALANCE

Similar to the previous routine, this trick involves moving a bill from under a glass without dislodging a coin balanced on the glass's rim.

Props: a glass
any coin
any bill

Advance Preparation: Casually place one end of the bill underneath a glass on the table. Then balance the coin on the edge of the glass.

Challenge onlookers to remove the bill without toppling the coin from the glass.

When all else fails, take over and merely begin to roll the bill from the end away from the glass. When the roll reaches the glass, keep the motion going; this will pull the edge of the bill from under the glass.

You can roll the bill up on a pencil.

Sometimes you can give a very quick tug on the bill and the bill will come out cleanly and the coin will remain on the edge of the glass. Someone told me this was inertia and my wife complains I have plenty of that.

TIGHT SQUEEZE

In this puzzle, the challenger is instructed to remove one soda bottle from between two others without also removing a match balanced between the two bottles.

Props: 3 Coke-type soda bottles
a match
Advance Preparation: none

To start, lay one bottle between two upright bottles. Balance a match between the bottles' bulges.

Make your challenge, then watch your fellow diners fail time after time. Sent up the props again, and show them how it is done.

With another match, light the head of the one between the bottles, immediately blowing out the flame. The match will hang by its head, now adhering to one bottle, allowing you to shift the other upright bottle and remove the horizontal bottle.

ADVANCED SILVERWARE BALANCE

This trick takes practice to perfect, but it offers a simple and amusing challenge for bored diners.

Props: a spoon
a butter knife
a fork

Advance Preparation: Put in some practice, especially to experiment with different types of silverware so that you are not embarrassed when confronted with utensils of unusual weight or shape.

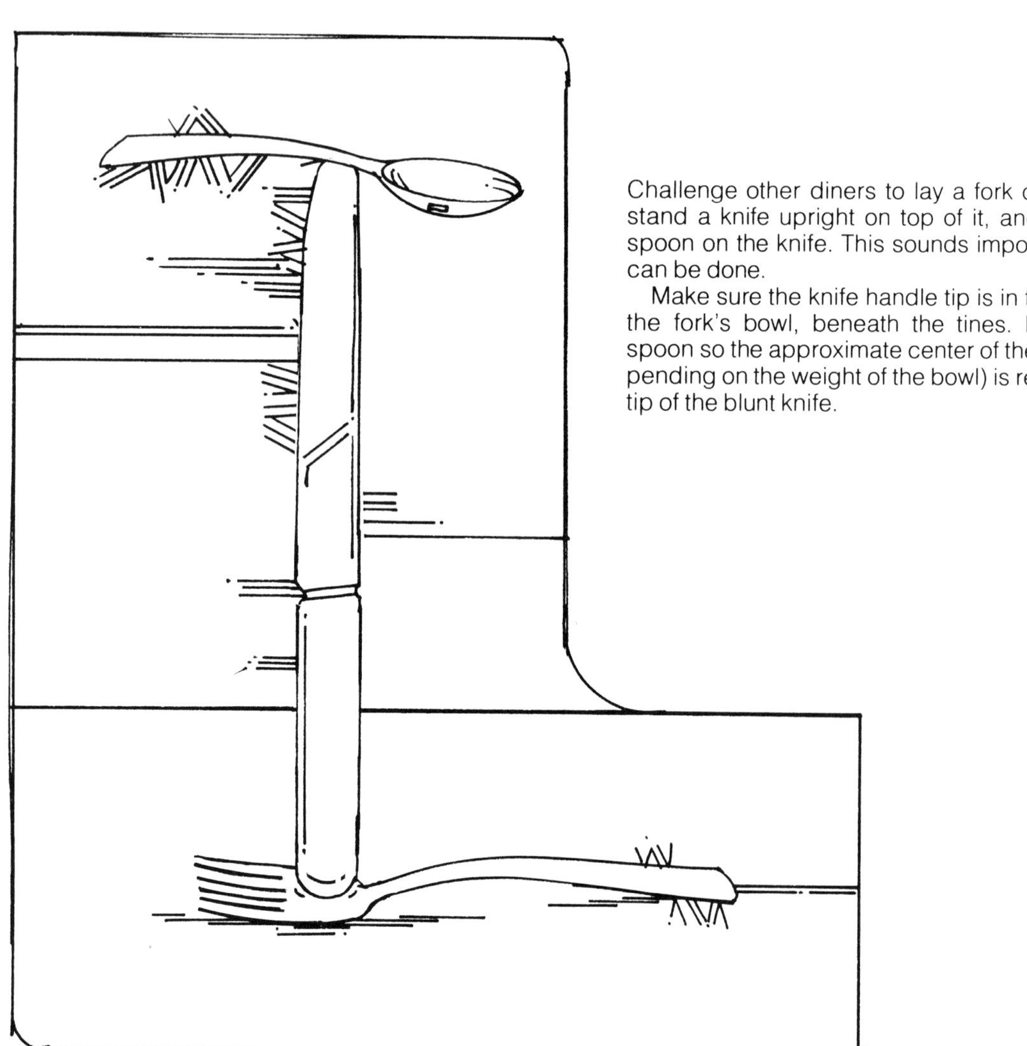

Challenge other diners to lay a fork on the table, stand a knife upright on top of it, and balance a spoon on the knife. This sounds impossible, but it can be done.

Make sure the knife handle tip is in the center of the fork's bowl, beneath the tines. Balance the spoon so the approximate center of the spoon (depending on the weight of the bowl) is resting on the tip of the blunt knife.

PENNY PINCH

Another good trick for bar or restaurant, this seems to require great agility, but once you know the gimmick, it is a snap.

Props: 2 pennies
a glass
Advance Preparation: Balance a penny on either side of the glass's rim.

Challenge someone seated next to you to remove the coins, ending with the pennies pinched between thumb and forefinger. Warn your victim that each finger must touch only one coin.

Most people will try drawing the coins together by sliding them around the rim toward each other. This does not work, and the only thing that does is this procedure: with thumb on one penny and forefinger on the other, slide the pennies down the sides, with pressure against the glass. At the bottom, slide them around the circumference toward you, pulling them off the glass as the two coins meet. Pinch them together and hold them to a cheering audience.

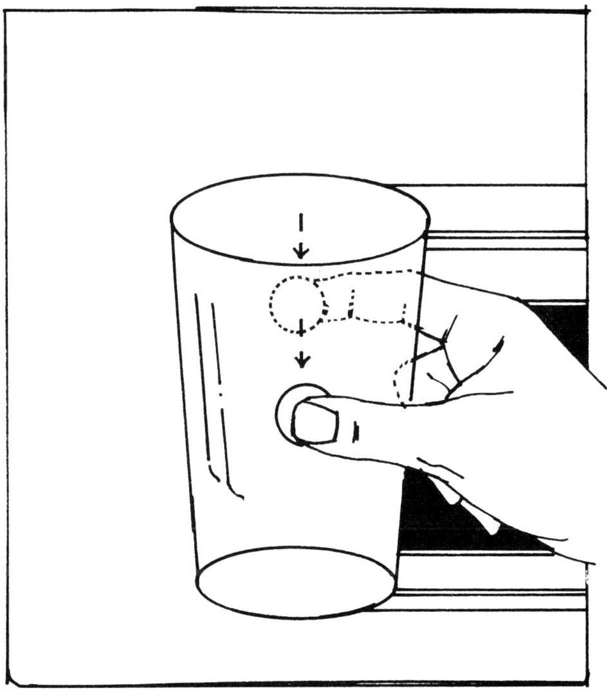

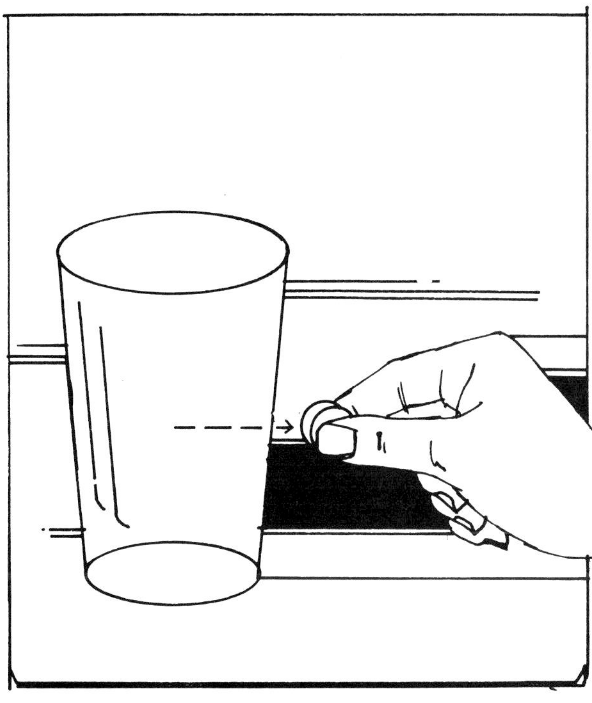

SOBRIETY TEST

If anyone at a bar questions your capacity for liquor, have the following puzzle—and its solution—on hand to vouch for your sobriety.

Props: 3 empty glasses
3 identical glasses filled with liquid
Advance Preparation: No tinkering with props, but memorize the correct sequence of moves.

State the challenge: Move the glasses in pairs and in three moves have them alternately full and empty.

To begin, line the glasses along the bar, with three full glasses to the left and three empty glasses to the right.

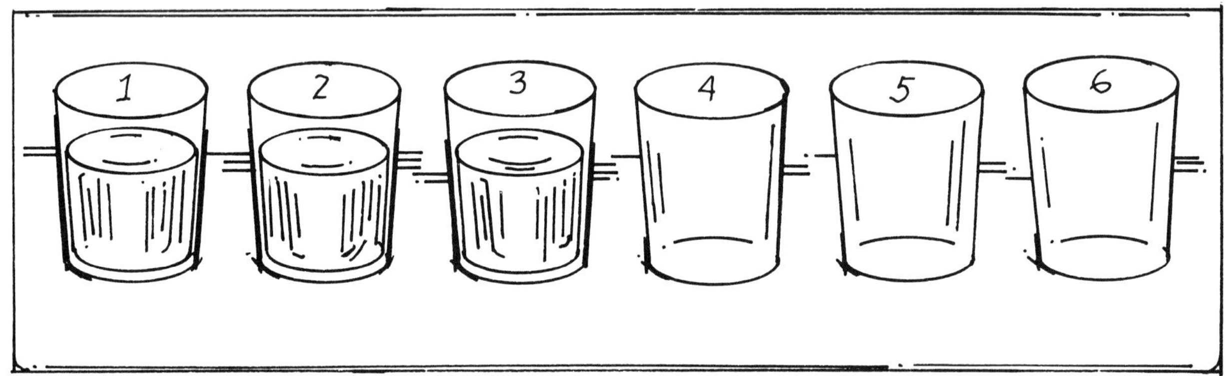

After a few of your fellow barflies fail to come up with three moves of pairs in which to alternate filled and empty glasses, show them the following steps.

First, move glasses 1 and 2 to the right of the line.

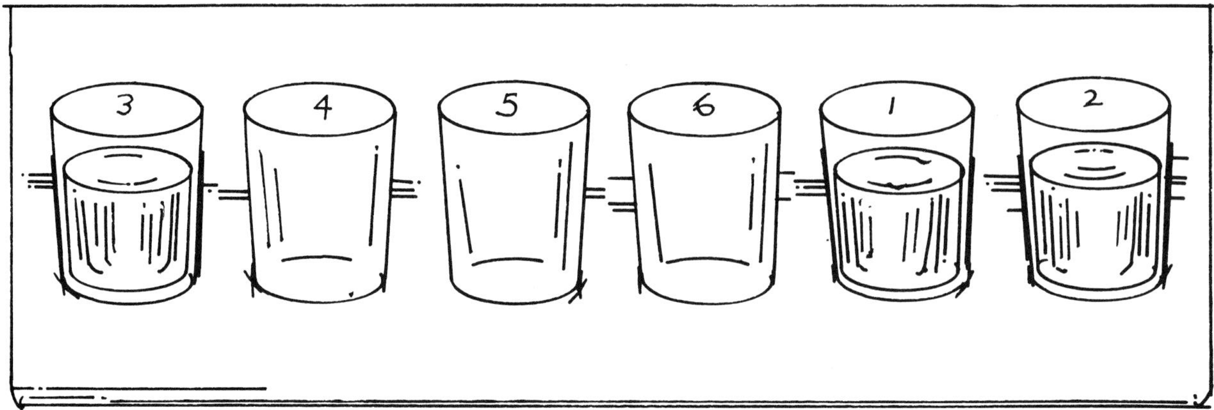

Now move glasses 6 and 1 to the right.

Finally, put glasses 3 and 4 into the gap left by moving the others.
If someone says, "That's alternately empty and full," you can either walk
around the table or count from right to left.

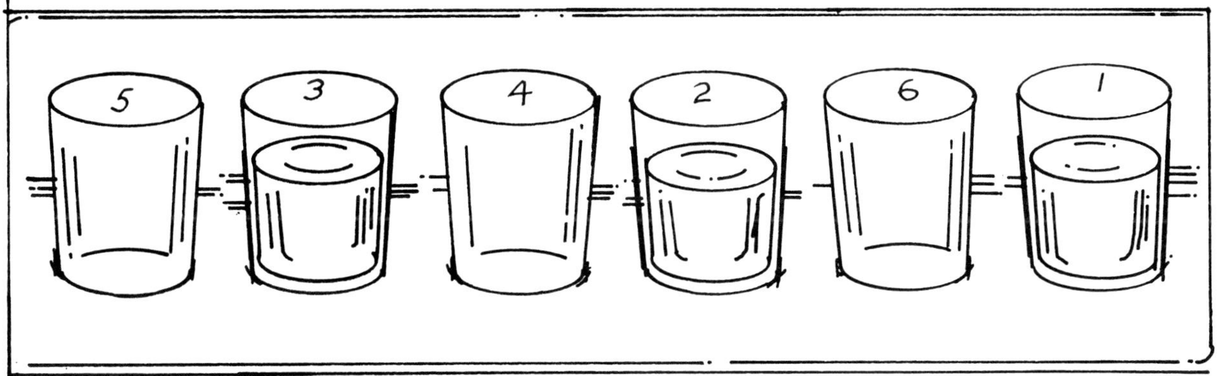

There are literally thousands of other puzzles you can do with common
household items and game pieces. Try inventing your own mathematical
gimmicks and physical challenges using dice and cards, coins and dominoes,
paper and pencil, matchsticks and other objects.

AVERTING A DISASTER

Though not exactly a puzzle, this is a nifty way to use leverage to give your fellow drinkers or diners a momentary scare.

Props: 2 wine or other stemmed glasses

Advance Preparation: Before trying this feat, be sure your intended victim's glass is filled only partially with liquid.

Under cover of proposing a toast or reaching across the table with your glass in your hand, pretend to accidentally knock your glass into another. As it begins to tip and people jump from their chairs to avoid getting wet, quickly press the base of your glass carefully on the base of the other. This motion will tip the glass toward you to rest intact on the table.

LIST OF MAGIC DEALERS AND SUPPLIERS

Martin Breese
31 Richmond Way
Hammersmith
London, W.4

Camtryx (Magic) Ltd.
187 Gilbert Road
Cambridge, CB4 3PA

L. Davenport & Co.
51, Gt. Russell Street
London, WC1

Goodliffe the Magician
Arden Forest Industrial Estate
Alcester, Warwickshire

Barry Gordon
125 Whitecrest
Great Barr
Birmingham, B43 6EX

Hamilton, Kay & Co.
160 Stubley Lane
Dronfield Woodhouse
Sheffield, S18 5YP

Jack Hughes
2, Evelyn Avenue
Colindale
London, NW9 0TH

International Magic Studio
(R. MacMillan)
89 Clerkenwell Road
Holburn
London, EC1

Luna Magic
(Bob Lunn)
Southend House
The Southend, Ledbury
Hertfordshire

Magic Books by Post
29 Hill Avenue
Bedminster
Bristol, BS3 4SN

Magictrix
(E. Burke)
26 Hope Street
Hanley
Stoke-on-Trent, ST1 5PS

Mayes & Warren Enterprises
(Stevenage) Ltd.
22 The Hyde
Stevenage, Hertfordshire

Miss Terry Magic Studio
35, Cavendish Road
Colliers Wood
London, SW19

Murray's Magic Mart
27, Cookson Street
Blackpool, Lancashire

R & R Magic
(R. Roth)
82, Pennard Drive
Swansea, Glam., South Wales

Paul Scott Magic
32 Ipswich Crescent
Great Barr
Birmingham, B42 1LY

Silray Magic Co.
(Ray Silver)
53, Chesterfield Avenue
Thundersley
Benfleet, Essex

Supreme Magic Co. Ltd.
64 High Street
Bideford, Devon.

Terry & Norma
(T. & N. Burgess)
2 Hill Crescent
Harrow, Middlesex

LIST OF MAGIC DEALERS AND SUPPLIERS

A & B Novelty & Magic
(Gibbs-De Armona)
4005 S. Dixie Hwy.
West Palm Beach, FL 33405

Abbot's Magic
Colon, MI 49040

Aladdin Enterprises
(Bill Pitts)
06 N. 2nd St.
Fort Smith, AK 72901

Aldini
(Alex Weiner)
11712 Fredrick Dr.
Garden Grove, CA 92640

Al's Magic Shop
(Al Cohen)
1012 Vermont Ave. NW
Washington, DC 20005

Archie's Fun & Nov. Dist.
(James A. Taylor)
909 S. Shaver St.
Pasadena, TX 77502

B. C. Magic Mfg. Co.
(Dr. A. Brodeur-Bob Chaney)
5747 Helen Ave.
St. Louis, MO 63136

Top Banana
1902 Penn Mar
South Elmonte, CA 91733

Barry's Magic Shop
11234 Georgia Ave.
Wheaton, MD 20902

Bill's Magicorner
(Charles W. Pryor)
4810 Cooper Rd.
Cincinnati, OH 45242

Bravo
5 West Steele St.
Orlando, FL 32804

Syd Brockman
7330-18th N.E.
Seattle, WA 98115

Marshal Brodien Catalog
(Marshall Brodien)
2127B Hammond Dr.
Shaumburg, IL 60195

Brucini
P.O. Box 1556
Rockville, MD 20859

Callin Novelties
(C. Weber-Manager)
412 S.W. 4th Ave.
Portland, OR 97204

Cards by Martin
509 West Ave.
Lancaster, CA 93534

Cards by Martin
24261 San Fernando Rd.
Newhall, CA 91321

The Comedy Center
700 Orange St.
Wilmington, DE 18901

Dave's Magic & Fun
(David S. Evans)
38 7th Ave.
Carbondale, PA 18407

Donn Davison
Dept. H
P.O. Box 49483
Atlanta, GA 30359

Delben Co., Inc.
(Ben D. Stone-Del Stone)
Box 3535-GSS
Springfield, MO 65804

Devoe Magic Den
(Gene Devoe)
704 Chestnut
St. Louis, MO 63101

Walt Disney World
(Walt Disney Productions)
P.O. Box 40
Lake Buena Vista, FL 32801

Ed. O. Drane & Co.
(W. L. Robinson, Pres.)
410 N. Ashland
Chicago, IL 60622

Bert Easley's Fun Shop
(Bert Easley)
509 W. McDowell Rd.
Phoenix, AZ 85003

Fabjance Studio, Inc.
P.O. Box 123
Bethalto, IL 61462

Fantasio Magic Prod.
(Fantasio-Fassini)
1002 Country Club Prado
C. Gables (Miami), FL 33134

Fantastic Magic Co.
(Gary Frank)
P.O. Box 33156
Granada Hills, CA 91344

Fedko Magic Co.
(John Fedko)
13111 Flint Dr.
Santa Ana, CA 92705

Flosso-Hornmann Magic
304 W. 34th St.
New York, NY 10001

Franco-American Nov., Co.
(Robert Oumano)
1209 Broadway
New York, NY 10001

Frank's Magic (Clador Investments)
(Howard M. Symons)
107 906 8 Ave. S.W.
Calgarry, Alberta T2P 1H9

Funny Farm Clowns, Inc.
(James P. Russell)
Route #2 Box 170
Butler, GA 31006

Gambler's Book Club
(John Luckman)
630 S. 11th St. Box 4115
Las Vegas, NV 89106

The Ghastly Gallimaufry
(Billie & Reece Jensen)
P.O. Box 971
Los Gatos, CA 95030

Gibson Magic
7 Amherst St.
Nashua, NH 03060

Gill's Nov. & Magic
(Robert & Betty Gill)
1530 S. Seneca St.
Wichita, KS 67213

Guaranteed Magic
(Bob Little)
27 Bright Rd.
Hatboro, PA 19040

Micky Hades
Box 476
Calgary, Alberta
Canada T2P 2J1

Haines House of Cards, Inc.
(Betty R. Winzig, Pres.)
P.O. Box 12527-2514 Leslie Ave.
Norwood, OH 45212

Hocus Pocus Magic Shop
(Ron Ehrmantraut)
618 El Camino Real
San Carlos, CA 94070

Hollywood Magic, Inc.
(Louis St. Pierre, Jr.)
6614 Hollywood Blvd.
Hollywood, CA 90028

House of Magic
(Marvin M. Burger)
2025 Chestnut St.
San Francisco, CA 94123

Ickle Pickle Products, Inc.
(Steven Bender)
883 Somerton Ridge Dr.
St. Louis, MO 63141

Illusion House
(Keith Allen-Craig Denny's)
2617 Herr St.
Harrisburg, PA 17103

Izzy Rizzy's Tricks
(Michael Rzeminski)
6034 So. Pulaski St.
Chicago, IL 60629

Lee Jacobs Prod.
(Lee Jacob)
P.O. Box 362
Pomeroy, OH 45769

Jan's Magical Mfg.
1071 E. 28th St.
Hialeah, FL 33013

Ken's Magic Shop
28-01 Broadway
Fairlawn, NJ 07410

Bob Kline
1122 Washington St.
Indiana, PA 15701

Kogel's Magic
(Gottlieb Kogel)
6751 Colbert St.
New Orleans, LA 70124

Krugger's Magic
929 Kruger Ave.
Erie, PA 16509

La Wain House of Magic
(LaWain)
P.O. Box 160
Monmouth, IL 61462

Hank Lee's Magic Factory
(Harry Levy)
24 Lincoln St.
Boston, MA 02111

Magic Emporium
Metcalf-J. Maney)
61 Jonesboro Rd.
Forest Park, GA 30050

Magic, Inc.
(Jay & Fran Marshall)
5082 N. Lincoln Ave.
Chicago, IL 60625

Magic Center
739 8th Ave.
New York, NY 10036

Magic City
(Chuck Kirchner)
369 Junipero
Long Beach, CA 90814

The Magic Corner
(Hughie Olmstead)
3913 Western Blvd.
Raleigh, NC 27606

Magic Emporium
19554 Ventura Blvd.
Tarzano, CA 91356

Magic Limited
4064 39 Ave.
Oakland, CA 94619

The Magic Room
(Bruce Kalver)
1153 N. Main St.
Providence, RI 02914

The Magic Shop
(Carroll Taylor)
P.O. Box 5215
Cresaptown, MD 21502

Magic Towne House
1026 Third Ave.
New York, NY 10021

Magic Toy Box
(Stephen Sutherland)
1317 W. Valley Blvd.
Colton, CA 92423

Magic Unlimited
619 Somerset St. W
Ottawa, Ont. K1 R 5K3

Magicians World
(Chuck Martinez)
3811 30th St.
San Diego, CA 92104

Magico Magazine
47-36 41 St.
Long Island City, NY 11104

Mandini's
(Manny Sperling)
4269 Bayard Rd.
S. Euclid, OH 44121

Martinelz Magic Mart
(Martin C. Elz)
141 Third St. No.
St. Petersburg, FL 33701

Mecca Magic Inc.
9 So. Harrison St.
E. Orange, NJ 07018

Mickey Hades Enterprises
(Mickey Hades)
Box #476
Calgary 2, Alberta, Canada

Jack Miller Enterprises
P.O. Box 439
Waterloo, NY 13165

Milson/Worth Industries
(C. Lynn Johnson)
8255 San Fernando Rd.
Sun Valley, CA 91352

Mingus Magic Shop
(Wayne Shifflett)
115 N. 9th St.
Reading, PA 19601

Moore's Magic Inc.
Box 1405
Plymouth, MI 48170

Moorehouse Magic
(Hank Moorehouse)
954 W. Cross
Ypsilanti, MI 48197

Morris Costumes
3108 Monroe Rd.
Charlotte, NC 28205

Morrissey Magic Ltd.
(Herb Morrissey)
927 St. Croix Blvd.
Ville St. Laurent
Quebec, Canada H4L-3Y9

Mystery Castle
349 E. Cooke Rd.
Columbus, OH 43214

Mr. Mystic's Magic Corner
(John A. Lewis)
464 Court St., N.E.
Salem, OR 97301

Murray's Magic Mart
(Murray E. Sobel)
32067 Sedgefield Oval
Solon, OH 44139

Mystofire Magic Co.
Box 906
Bellaire, TX 77401

Novel Inc.
(Armando Rengifo)
356 Fortaleza St.
San Juan, PR 00901

**Novelty Village Magic &
Costume Shop**
(Dobronski & Gilman)
505 E. University St.
Champaign, IL 61820

Pandora's Box
(Joe Lefler)
Rm. 1080 Richmond Mall
691 Richmond Rd.
Richmond Heights, OH 44143

Paul's Magic & Fun Shop
(Paul Diamond)
903 N. Federal Hwy.
Ft. Lauderdale, FL 33304

Perfect Magic Reg'd
(Philip Matlin)
4781 Van Horne, Suite 206
Montreal, Que.
Canada H3W 1J1

Premier 75 Magic Studio
75 Chruch St.
New Brunswick, NJ 08901

Pressley Guitar Creations
P.O. Box 20485
Dallas, TX 75220

Prynce E. Wheeler
P.O. Box 349
Great Falls, MT 59401

**James Rainho Products
Simplex Magic**
(James & Alice Rainho)
14 Windsor Rd.
Medford, MA 02155

Ramsey Magic & Nov. Co.
(Paul Maffia)
72 E. Main St.
Ramsey, NJ 07446

The Real Magic Co.
(Marvin & Hazel Taylor)
10843 N.E. 8th #110 St.
Bellevue, WA 98004

Riley's Trick & Novelty
6442 West 111th St.
Worth, IL 60482

D. Robbins & Co., Inc.
(Paul Freid, Pres.)
70 Washington St. 9th Floor
Brooklyn, NY 11201

Romig Magic & Book Co.
(C. A. & R. S. Romig)
195 W. 9 Mile Rd. Room 208
Ferndale, MI 48220

Ron's Trick Shop
(Ron Meadows)
311 W. Prince
Beckley, WV 25801

Ronjo Magic
Arcade Shopping Plaza
1080 Route 112
Port Jefferson Sta., NY 11776

Jack Rosa's Magic Shop
6601 Bay Parkway
Brooklyn, NY 11204

Betty Jo Standridge
700 Hickory Tree Rd.
Mesquite, TX 75149

Sterling Magic Creations
(Palmer Tilden, Pres.)
P.O. Box 251-945 Easton Ave.
San Bruno, CA 94066

Stevens Magic Emporium
(Joe Stevens)
3238 E. Douglas
Wichita, KS 67208

Stoner's Magic Shop
(Al & Dick Stoner)
712 S. Harrison St.
Fort Wayne, IN 46802

Suds
(Ted Sudbrack)
3203 W. Ball Rd.
Anaheim, CA 92804

Tannen's Magic, inc.
(Tony Spina-Jack Ferror)
1540 Broadway
New York, NY 10036

Viking-Haenchen Magic Mfg.
(Geo. Robinson, Jr.)
P.O. Box 674
McAllen, TX 78501

Warner's Magic Factory
Box 455
Hinsdale, IL 60521

Webb Magic Co.
(Walter A. Webb)
5915 Olentangy Blvd.
Worthington, OH 43085

**Wilcox Magicrafters
Magic Manor**
Altus, AK 72821

The Wizard's Den
(Dale & Carol Claiborne)
1610 W. Gore Blvd.
Lawton, OK 73501

The Wizard's Hideout
1104 State Rd.
Webster, NY 14580

World of Magic
(Bill Adams)
707 N. Milpas
Santa Barbara, CA 93103

Yogi Magic Mart
(Phil & Ann Thomas)
217 N. Charles St.
Baltimore, MD 21201

SELECTED PERIODICALS

Abracadabra C. Goodliffe Neale, Ltd. c/o Goodliffe the Magician, ed. Arden Forest Industrial Estate, Alcester, Warwickshire, England.

Genii Wm. Larsen, ed. and pub., P.O. Box 36068, Los Angeles, CA 90036.

Hocus Pocus 1026 Third Avenue, New York, NY 10021

Linking Ring International Brotherhood of Magicians, Kenton, OH 43326.

MUM (Magic, Unity, Might). Society of American Magicians, c/o Herbert B. Donns, National Secretary, 66 Marked Tree Road, Needham, MA 02192.

Magic Cauldron F. William Kuethe, Jr., ed. and pub., 700 Glenview Avenue SW, Glen Burnie, MD 21061.

Velki (English magazine). Joy Dev Ray, 123-2 Acharya Prafulla Chandra Road, Calcutta 6, India.

INDEX